Land of Bear and Eagle

A Home in the Kodiak Wilderness

LAND OF BEAR AND EAGLE

A HOME IN THE KODIAK WILDERNESS

Tanyo Ravicz

hancock
house

Copyright © 2022 Tanyo Ravicz

Cataloguing data available from Library and Archives Canada
978-0-88839-722-5 [paperback]
978-0-88839-703-4 [epub]

Printed in the USA

FRONT COVER ARTWORK: Mark E. Anderson

PRODUCTION & DESIGN: J. Rade, M. Lamont

EDITOR: D. MARTENS

We acknowledge the support of the Government of Canada through the Canada Book Fund and the Canada Council for the Arts, and of the Province of British Columbia through the British Columbia Arts Council and the Book Publishing Tax Credit.

Canada

BRITISH COLUMBIA   BRITISH COLUMBIA ARTS COUNCIL

Hancock House gratefully acknowledges the Halkomelem Speaking Peoples whose unceded, shared and asserted traditional territories our offices reside upon.

Published simultaneously in Canada and the United States by

HANCOCK HOUSE PUBLISHERS LTD.
19313 Zero Avenue, Surrey, B.C. Canada V3Z 9R9
#104-4550 Birch Bay-Lynden Rd, Blaine, WA, U.S.A. 98230-9436
(800) 938-1114   Fax (800) 983-2262
www.hancockhouse.com   info@hancockhouse.com

CONTENTS

A BEGINNING

I had seldom admitted it to anyone, but the idea of homesteading in Alaska was simmering in me when I first set foot in the place. The word itself—*homesteading*—was magical to me, a passport to freedom and adventure. The frontier hadn't closed yet, not for me, though knowledgeable people had declared it closed. Almost any way you turn in Alaska, nothing stands between you and the wild, and the frontier was always half inside us anyway, a state of mind and approach to life. In June of 1986, homesteading, that old dream of the West, the ultimate symbol of freedom, was still alive in Alaska, where the state and federal homesteading laws remained in effect, the federal program an extension of the very Homestead Act that Abraham Lincoln inaugurated in the 1860s. You could claim a piece of government land, live on it, prove up on it and make it yours.

Life has a way of separating us from our dreams. We lose our heading, fortune diverts us, and before long a gulf of circumstance separates us from the desired destination. It wasn't for another nine years that I recovered the old homesteading dream. My father had died and the shock of grief had caused me to reexamine my life. With my wife's blessing I had decided to return to school to get a master's degree. We had a young daughter, and the degree offered a possible route to a more consistent income. I entered a respectable graduate program in California, and three months later I left it. Maybe my years in Alaska had changed me more than I realized, but I was dumbfounded by how wrong I had been in my expectations of the university. It was rather like seeing the truth about a person I had previously idealized.

ADVENTURE ROAD, FAIRBANKS, ALASKA, 1997

I returned to Alaska in a funk, unsure which way to turn next. Thirty-three years old, I was lost in an exploration whose end was obscured by clouds of marijuana. I lived with my wife and daughter on five acres on Adventure Road outside of Fairbanks, and it pained and perplexed me that I loved them so much but couldn't rest content. After my California interlude, my return to fighting wildfires was a letdown. For a firefighter, the summer of 1995 proved unprofitably dreary. Wildland firefighters *love* fire, and we weren't getting enough love that summer. There wasn't much I could do about it, short of start a blaze or pray for lightning.

I often hung around headquarters at State Forestry, and one day I saw, posted in the window at the Department of Natural Resources, a notice of an upcoming land offering that included fifty-five homestead parcels. I stood there a while, face to face with my longstanding dream of homesteading. *You have no excuse now,* I told myself. *You want it. You're ready for it. Why not you? Why not now?*

The truth is, when I arrived in Alaska I was too green and squishy—green from inexperience and squishy from college—and too ignorant to head into the Alaskan bush and fend for myself. I could never have homesteaded in Alaska without the confidence and skills I had acquired in nearly a decade of living and working in Alaska, of operating equipment and getting to know the land. But I was ready now. I had made a years-long exploration of freedom and selfhood, of what it means to be an individual in this world, and although I had come far, to my mind it was not far enough. But I was ready.

I was conscious of another motive, too. I had a gut sense that we were coming to the end of something, all of us, even in Alaska, not just the end of a century but of a defining period in our history, a period in which individualism was a living creed, a creed so vital to our identity that our government actually blessed the proprietary claims of determined, hardworking men and women by ceding to them, on their fulfilling certain obligations, a portion of its vast hoard of territory. In the years since I had moved to Alaska, the federal homesteading program had shut down. The last homestead on federal land in Alaska was granted in 1988, and Abraham Lincoln's Homestead Act was no more. Worse, Alaska's homesteading program appeared to be in jeopardy too, bogged down in litigation and budget shortfalls. This newly announced land offering was the first since 1991. It was well publicized, and as the dream of homesteading revived in Alaskans, homestead fever spread across the state.

If it's land you want, state's got it
State opens huge land offering

These were among the thrilling headlines I saw in the pages of the *Fairbanks Daily News-Miner.* The application deadline was approaching. I handed over $8 for a copy of *Land for Alaskans: 1995 State Land Offering.* And as I write these words, it is twenty years to the day since I filed, on October

4, 1995, eleven homestead applications with the Northern Regional Office of Alaska's Department of Natural Resources.

The $275 in application fees was, for me and Martina back then, a lot of dough. Unfortunately I wasn't the only dreamer to throw my hat in the ring. I was one of 4,300 applicants competing for fifty-odd homestead parcels in a stampede more bureaucratic than horse-and-saddle. A lottery drawing was held in Anchorage on October 26, 1995. My name wasn't drawn. Twelve of the awardees failed to meet their obligations under the homestead rules and my name went back into the lottery drum. Another drawing was held on September 17, 1996. I followed the proceedings from the Department of Natural Resources office in Fairbanks. Applicants' names were drawn and called aloud. As the homestead parcels were claimed, I struck lines through the wish list in front of me. My heart thumping, I focused on Parcel 1009 on Kodiak Island, focused with such intensity that the letters and numbers seemed to come alive on the page. Had I ever wanted anything with more decisive a yearning?

In the next instant, my name was called. I went and signed some papers. This was the day after my daughter Miranda's fourth birthday, and she still remembers my happy enthusiasm when I picked her up at the Lighthouse preschool that day. I must have flown her through the air a few times.

And now I knew what the task ahead for me was. A cabin rises in the mind's eye before a single nail is driven. A journey begins in the heart before the first step is taken. I saw a pathway where there was no path yet because I hadn't trodden it yet. Destiny without the predestination.

My life had been building to a crisis, but whatever its dissatisfactions, I couldn't blame them on the latest fire season. 1996 was an excellent year for wildfire, busy and productive from a moneymaking point of view, though I felt sorry for the Alaskans and Washingtonians who lost their homes in the flames. The firefighting was good that summer, but I was morally in decline. I had been in two scuffles; I was temperamental; I was smoking too much dope. I was the wounded bear and I was the hunter who had wounded the bear and not forgiven himself for not finding it. But I had learned something important by now, too. Society, as it's called, is a soulless abstraction, and if it's your soul that's ailing, society doesn't and never will offer the salve you need. The crowding of your inner and outer space by urban megalomania, by every kind of pollution, and by the assaults of media and digital technology—this crowding eclipses the soul. And as for societal fellowship, that old dream of the poets has utterly been forsaken, sacrificed for the self-serving advantage of grasping tribes.

But enough of this. Social criticism is de rigueur for us graduates of the liberal arts colleges. I could snipe and gripe ad nauseam and be one of those whose best idea is to replace other people's corruption with their own, or I could heed the counsel of the great religions and do something that would make a difference in the world: tend to my soul.

The commitment worked changes on me immediately. I quit smoking dope, for one thing. I had a sixty-day staking authorization to travel to Kodiak Island, to identify and clear the boundaries of the tract I proposed to homestead—the land was accessible only by boat or seaplane—to complete a sketch plat of it, to fill out a Homestead Entry Permit Application, to pay a survey deposit, and to file all of this with the Department of Natural Resources by November 18, 1996.

It was done in October. I received my Homestead Entry Permit and began to take possession of the land.

This was not an open-ended privilege. Homesteading is governed by statute and regulation. There's an irony here. I was clawing back government land on the government's terms. Within three years I was required to build a dwelling that satisfied the Homestead Habitable Dwelling Requirements. I had to submit proof. Within five years I had to live on the land for at least twenty-five months. I was required to submit witness affidavits. In the end I needed to submit a Homestead Request for Patent and pay the state any survey costs I owed. If I failed on any count, my entry permit would expire.

And so it began. In youth, all the powers of life are allied with us, and for me the promise of homesteading took on the proportions of a prophetic calling. My Homestead Entry Permit was the only library card I needed now. I was setting out to read the Book of Nature, the predecessor and superseder of all the Libraries of Alexandria and Congress combined. I would build a life from the ground up, free of prejudice and false constraint. I would live independent of the material infrastructure and social superstructure of established society, confident that, with the removal of the filler and falsehood that sap and distract the soul, I would learn truths about myself and about nature that had been hidden from me. I would not be a statistician's or demographer's version of myself; far better to be a version of my dreams. And I would know and test my full capacities as a man, so that I would not go to my grave beset by any of the doubts and miseries of regret.

There was the matter of my wife getting pregnant around this time. I have made much use of the first-person singular—the I—but Martina was always my partner and inspiration in the homesteading. Best friends since college, she from Hawaii and I from California, we had headed north to Alaska a couple of cheechakos. Without Martina's daring and her trust in me, the homesteading might not have ended well. That winter in Fairbanks, while I drew up the homesteading plans, she practiced law and carried our second child. I won't pretend it was always easy for us. We had our disagreements. Early in life, Martina had known fraught years as an immigrant from South Korea, and for her the idea of giving up the security and prosperity of town life for the uncertainties and rigors of the bush made little sense.

The arrival of our second child, a son whom we named Kodiak, complicated the homesteading plans by highlighting the costs. To live on the homestead for twenty-five months in five years meant that I must leave the family for at least one calendar year plus four full summers. My expenses for the recent staking trip had been modest but not negligible ($346 Fairbanks-Kodiak roundtrip air ticket, $182 roundtrip seaplane charter, $25 staking application fee, $15 staking packet, $10 survey tape, $15 machete), and going forward the costs would rise. I owned a chainsaw, a drawknife, a cant hook and a log-building scribe, and I had expected to build in log but had discovered, during the staking trip, that our Kodiak land, a low-lying parcel, though blessed with a rare grove of cottonwood trees and plentiful water, was short of spruce trees for building, with the consequence that my lumber outlays would increase. As for our house in Fairbanks, we owed a monthly mortgage of $700, but Martina, having at last paid off her student loans, assured me that she could cover the mortgage.

On July 4, 1997, I drove a loaded pickup truck from Fairbanks to the harbor town of Seward, and from Seward I ferried to Kodiak Island, where I stayed the summer and put into effect the plan that Martina and I had arrived at. I would live on the homestead for two successive summers, and when the cabin was ready at the end of the second summer, she and the children would join me there. We would live on the homestead for twelve months, a full year. I would return alone for eight or more months. Our prove-up requirements then having been met, Cottonwood, as the homestead came to be known, would be ours.

My first summer at Cottonwood was spent cutting trail, digging postholes and standing foundation posts. Where to locate a cabin in more than fifteen acres of wildland? I considered the sun and wind, drainage, proximity to fresh water, the access and overall feel of a spot, and I broke ground in an elevated meadow in the southwest corner of the homestead. The factor least well served by my decision was the access. My chosen meadow was a fifth of a mile uphill from the ocean. It was hard enough to hump a stack of two-by-fours up the sea cliffs. I had tons of material en route, lumber from Kodiak town and insulated panels and support beams from Seattle, and I didn't understand how impossibly heavy those eighteen-foot beams were until I saw them. I hired Captain Dick Ross to transport my supplies to Cottonwood in the *Schatzie Girl*, and I hired two men to assist me for ten days in moving my lumber uphill to the cabin site and in hoisting the beams—three foundation beams and a roof beam—into place in their brackets. We worked fast to raise the load-bearing walls.

Casey Westbrook, I am sorry to say, has passed on, and Tim O'Connor, a self-styled drifter, might be anywhere in this world or in the next. I often think of them. You don't live ten days in the bush, share the yoke of labor, share meals under the stars and the unforgettable experience of being charged by a Kodiak brown bear and easily forget your companions. They were good company and good hands—hired men, yes, but they brought to my project an enthusiasm they weren't paid for. And this was something they had in common with other sympathetic souls whom I had met over the months and who wished me success in my endeavor. The warehouseman at the lumberyard, the floor clerks at the hardware store and builder's supply, the receptionist at the borough office—these ready spirits looked beyond the bearded, long-haired stranger who addressed them and saw a piece of open land and the vision of a life lived apart from the sometimes stifling grind of everyday existence. Shopkeepers and tradespeople, when they learned of my homesteading, grew friendlier, shared their know-how, went out of their way to find me the three-eighths instead of the half-inch—or threw in an extra yard of chain or rope or a handful of shims or nails and told me "not to worry" about it, in these little ways investing in my fledgling mission so that over time I came to feel that I was homesteading for them, too.

In August 1998, toward the end of my second summer at Cottonwood, I filed with the Department of Natural Resources a Homestead Entryperson's Affidavit of Dwelling Completion. The cabin was done. The last roof panel was fastened down. I had painted the siding, caulked the windows, installed heating and cooking stoves, built an outhouse and raised a radio antenna. The cabin was snug, eighteen feet by twelve feet in size, an area economical to maintain and to heat but definitely snug for a family of four, and I expanded the usable space by adding a half loft. I ran twelve-volt cable through the cabin for electric lights. I installed a twelve-volt pump to deliver water to us from a food-grade plastic barrel. Lastly I built a ramp from the beach to the blufftop so that we could winch up our incoming supplies.

Martina had found a tenant for our house on Adventure Road, and we purchased an old shipping container in which we stored whatever possessions we hadn't sold to raise cash. And so we said goodbye to Fairbanks, a town we were fond of, the birthplace of our children. We ferried to Kodiak Island, and from Kodiak town we chartered a boat to the island's north coast, the four of us with many hundreds of pounds of equipment and provisions. And for the next year we lived at Cottonwood as people live their lives anywhere, from one day to the next, with joys, fears, doubts and aspirations, laboring and resting, but with this difference: that our nearest human neighbor lived a mile away, that we did without roads, cars, telephones, internet or services of any kind, and that truly we lived in the land of bear and eagle.

This book is an account of our lives at Cottonwood, of the plants and animals we shared it with, and of the people we met. In it, I draw on the observations of more than twenty years, but at the heart of the book is our first year of homesteading at Cottonwood. We schooled our children, supplied our drinking water, generated our electricity, explored our habitat, cut our firewood, baked our bread, hunted our meat, and sometimes fended off aggressive brown bears. The book comprises a series of chapters, each of which opens as a window on Cottonwood and the surrounding country. The arrangement of the windows is less important than the views they afford, and I encourage the visitor to move among them according to whim or natural preference. Taken together they offer, I hope, a rounded view, a total ecology of the place.

ALASKA HIGHWAY

I got to talking with the handyman at the Northern Rockies Lodge in Muncho Lake, British Columbia. It was summer's end and Martina and the kids and I were driving south on the Alaska Highway after leaving our Kodiak Island homestead. I had been at Cottonwood for sixteen continuous months, the longest single stretch of time I had spent on the homestead, and it felt good now to be on the road and off the island. I was eager to talk to people and to hear what they had to say.

Not a lot of people live around Muncho Lake, a historic outpost with a beautiful mountain backdrop, but the handyman, a younger man than I, felt that the place was getting crowded, and after I had answered his questions—Where were we from? Where were we going?—and given him a brief account of our homesteading in Alaska, he confided to me that his desire was to homestead in Yukon Territory.

The lodge's European owners catered to European tourists, he complained, "and to them we're just plain people, they treat us second class." Something else that rankled the handyman: he had been forced to cut his hair before he was hired. "I used to have long hair like you and a beard out to here," he gestured. "Looked like ZZ Top," he added.

He was soft-spoken, but he bristled with dissatisfaction, and as we talked, we gravitated around to the north, toward Yukon, which for me was in the rear-view mirror, but for this handyman lay somewhere ahead, in the future. "I hope it works out for you," I told him.

"Oh, it will," he said. "I'll make it work."

And with his handyman skills and his will-do attitude, I believed he would. He may have been using the word "homesteading" loosely, as people use the word to signify an up-from-the-ground, off-the-grid lifestyle, something more pioneering than just rustic living, but clearly he was talking about a better life that he imagined existed over the horizon, a life within his control, more fulfilling, more worthy of him.

I had met the friendly Swiss named Urs who owned the lodge, and for all I knew, he and his wife had come to Canada and the New World looking for the same things the handyman missed and wanted: personal freedom, respect, self-determination. For the handyman the lack of these things wasn't redeemed by Muncho Lake's open spaces and natural beauties. For one thing, open space isn't always as open as it appears: government and private ownership see to that. At a deeper level, nature disquiets us by whispering to us of human equality and natural freedom and causing us to compare our current straits with our potential.

I always get a kick out of meeting Alaskans who think Alaska has gotten too crowded. A thousand miles earlier, while pumping gas in Fairbanks, our road trip's first layover after we had returned to the Alaska mainland from Kodiak Island, I met an old-timer who groused that Fairbanks—Fairbanks!—had outgrown itself. He had known Fairbanks half a century earlier, when he worked on construction of the Canol Pipeline during World War II, and since then he felt the quality of life in interior Alaska had deteriorated, and indeed he was thinking of moving out—at his age!—moving into the bush to live a life that better resembled the life he thought a man, regardless of his age, should live.

Six hundred miles south of Muncho Lake, in Prince George, I met a thirty-year-old from Juneau who was driving north from Idaho with the pickup truck and freezer his late father had left him. Six months after the old man's death, the son had the need-to-talk manner of an anxious survivor, his busy mouth at odds with the narrow black beard that encircled it. With a hundred-ton skipper's license to his name, the fellow had enough paying work to keep him busy in Juneau, and his wife had a well-paying job as an accountant, but they were both tired, he said, of feeling isolated in Juneau, and they were fixing to leave Alaska and to start somewhere new, if not this year then the next.

Another day, another six hundred miles. At a Days Inn in Seattle I met an independent trucker, a Minnesotan who had just found nightly contract work driving the US mail between Eugene and Portland. The hours were difficult, the shift was a graveyard shift, but he saw it as a temporary gig while he found his footing after his divorce.

On we drove, southward, the hours passing and the miles passing with them. The multilane freeways, the sprawling cities, the countless people and vehicles—I saw it all with wondering eyes. After my months at Cottonwood Homestead, I was hungry for contact and conversation, and I talked with people in parking lots and coffee shops, at trailheads and visitor centers, and to me their stories were as fascinating as our story of homesteading on Kodiak Island was to them.

In Redding I met a family of six who were staying for the coupon rate in a ground-floor room at the Econo Lodge. Out of work and out of money, a middle-aged couple with four children, they were living on the road. In the sweltering heat the man could barely contain his desperation. I felt awful for him. The tailgate of our Sierra was down and he kept looking in the truck bed at my family's belongings. His wife, a large woman, observed us from her doorway. Martina and I had no income and scant savings, but we had our educations to fall back on, and we had two kids to feed, not four, and we had our dream of Cottonwood to sustain us, too. We didn't own the land yet, not on paper, but after our time at the homestead we brimmed with enthusiasm and with the confidence that we could make a place for ourselves anywhere.

There were wildfires burning, big ones, and I pointed north at the stained yellow sky over Weed in Siskiyou County and told my friend he should drive up there and get a job on one of the fires. I didn't know what else to suggest to him. It wasn't a bad idea. And he wasn't the first person to leave me wishing I could do something more for him. I didn't see myself as the best person to be offering advice to anyone. In Grants Pass I had met a seventeen-year-old cashier named Cassie, a brunette who wanted to get to Alaska so bad that she offered to give me her resume. I guess she thought I could help. I asked her if she had finished high school. "If I were you I'd go back to school," I told her, "but if you feel like getting a little messy next summer, you could head north and get a job in one of the salmon canneries."

What had I seen during my days on the road? Everybody was on the move. Wherever we had traveled, people were restless and searching and wanting, looking ahead and wanting more, always looking looking looking.

Well, not always. Not everybody. In Portland I had met a middle-aged night auditor who lived upstairs in the hotel that employed him. This impeccably dressed gentleman ate breakfast in the hotel restaurant at night. After his meal he pressed his napkin to the corners of his mouth, read the newspaper, looked at his wristwatch, surveyed his fellow diners, drank his tea or coffee and consulted his watch again, and eventually he rose and walked down the hall to take his place in one of the back offices, never to be appreciated by the myriad guests who called at the front desk. And if he was satisfied with this life for the next ten or twenty years, excellent! We can't be a nation of tumbleweeds. The uprooted and persecuted millions who live in the world's red zones would look on such a safe clockwork existence as the highest blessing.

Still, with the exception of the night auditor, my impression was a strong one. Traveling the West Coast from north to south, from Alaska to California, I saw a cross section of a people on the move. And I liked what I saw. I liked the dynamism and the hope in it, but the underlying restlessness was regrettable. People hankered for a change. Into the Big Wide Open they drove, they rode, they biked, they hiked, they hitched—it didn't matter how they made it as long as they were at it, if not outwardly then inwardly in motion, yearning and dreaming and wanting and planning and hurtling on.

I thought of my friend Doc back in Kodiak: Doc, the maintenance man, who saw his life as a journey of self-discovery through world-discovery, a native Mainer who went by the motto "Born in Maine, living in exile," an army vet of decades, a chemistry major in his youth, trained at Bethesda Naval Hospital, a field doctor who'd patched up fighting men in Korea and Vietnam, or tried and failed to patch them up and afterwards carried the memories as he traveled the world working in the energy field, staying curious and staying generous, the anti-Ugly American, never inflating himself by throwing dollars around in Third World countries: Doc, who finally came to see the world as one big beautiful port city, bustling with people, and nobody caring where anybody else came from. And this was the thing that Doc wanted people to know and to take away with them, an old man's life lesson: that by exploring the world we eventually come home to our best selves.

From Fairbanks to San Diego, from tundra and boreal forest through cropland and hayfield and orchard, over the mountains and through the valleys and cities of the Northwest and the Bay Area and on down into the Western deserts and over the passes to the sea we drove, through Alaska, Yukon Territory, British Columbia, Washington, Oregon and California, meeting a panorama of people and ecologies and industries. And whenever the homesteading came up in conversation, the look in people's eyes and the questions they asked me and the reminiscences sparked in them told me what the word *homesteading* meant to them. And what it stood for in people's minds was freedom and self-determination, not *my* freedom and self-determination, not freedom and self-determination in the abstract, but *their* freedom and self-determination, their own.

Everybody's a dreamer, and what people wanted, many, if only meta-phorically, was to homestead too, to start over on new terrain. People long to be in a place where they can be themselves, not be *by* themselves but just be themselves without falseness or fear or apology. A lot of people feel trapped, beset, poor, disrespected, unsatisfied; they've been told they're free to take risks and to better their lives, but they're tied down in various ways. They weary of complaining. Weariness begets futility. And in truth it's not as easy in reality as in story to make a stink about things-as-they-are and to go rogue in the temple of conventions and start overturning stuff, your own life to start with. And this helped me to understand a feeling I'd had since I started homesteading three years earlier, a feeling that people were on my side in the homesteading. Not everybody, not the top-down folks, but most of the people I had crossed paths with, they liked the idea that it could be done and that someone was doing it, and they were rooting for me the way you root for somebody who has had enough and is running for the fences. And so I got to feeling that I was homesteading for them, too, taking the opportunity to do what they might have done as well. And this feeling that I was doing something that mattered to more than just me and mine, it made me even more stubborn than I already am, and in the coming years it helped to carry me through trials and setbacks as I proved up on the land at Cottonwood and saw the homestead to completion.

ANIMALS

One summer day after a storm had cleared, the animals emerged to stretch their legs and to look for something to eat. I, also stretching my legs, encountered no other humans, but I met brown bear, deer, fox and hare, and saw otters and whales in the strait and bald eagles in the sky. I was distinctly in the minority at Cottonwood.

I have come to expect the prevalence of other species at Cottonwood, but every so often the wonderful strangeness of it breaks into my awareness. That humans dominate the planet, that cities swell while wilderness dwindles, this heightens the unusualness of finding myself surrounded by wild creatures. But in the deep experience of the race, going back millennia, it's not a novelty to see ourselves as part of an organic life web, one in which the other species outnumber us. This is our original condition.

When I return to Cottonwood after an absence, I have an impression that the animals are coming by to greet me—fox, hare, deer, bear. Not to greet me personally, of course (though I like to think so), but to investigate the newcomer's arrival. A feeling of harmony, of belonging, underlies this sensation. Just outside of the cabin, just outside of its insulated walls and double-paned windows, the animals go on living in the old way, mating and hunting and grazing and birthing and dying. The animals live close by as they cannot do in a city of millions, where, lapdogs aside, animals survive in the shadows as nuisances or in the captivity of zoos and the negative symbols of the pigeon prongs and the animal control trucks.

A CURIOUS HARBOR SEAL, KUPREANOF STRAIT

At Cottonwood the animals may inconvenience me, by defecating under the cabin or gnawing the plywood, and in the case of brown bears they may frighten me, but the animals are never an afterthought here, where almost every activity brings me into relationship with them.

Animal neighborhood is a fact of life at Cottonwood. The species generally mind their own business, but our trails and routines intersect. A rangy fox the color of an orange creamsicle leaps back in surprise when I open the cabin door. I nearly drop my fishing pole in the water when a couple of barnacled minke whales surface by my raft instead of the codfish I expected. I have many times skipped a heartbeat over the rustle of a songbird or a tundra vole in the shrubbery and laughed at my being so easily rattled. The birds, attracted by the seeds and worms that my shovel has turned up, will scatter in a flash if I stride near. A heavy crackling in the trailside thicket tells me that I have caught a brown bear off guard. If I don't put the bear at a disadvantage, though—and this goes for the deer and fox as well—if I let them hear my voice by greeting them from a respectful distance, they will, instead of bolting in alarm, peer around in bland curiosity and go about their affairs.

"Each animal is nothing but a parcel of joy," André Gide writes, and I know I am in wilderness, I know I am alive and free, when this joyful vitality courses through me. My animal neighbors are relatively guileless, and their unconscious antics endear them to me. A short-tailed weasel, normally a shy creature, challenges me to a game of hide-and-seek around the woodpile. I am in a spruce tree when a flock of chickadees surrounds me and loudly queries me, chirping and hopping among the branches. A red squirrel, miffed by the disturbance, takes a flying leap at the chickadees and ends up empty-handed, or empty-pawed, on the ground. I laugh aloud at this carefree disorder. It's refreshing to remember we aren't the only troublemakers in the animal kingdom.

On the beach at Cottonwood, seagulls have gathered around the remains of a halibut. The bald eagles watch from the blufftop spruce trees. While the seagulls squabble over the halibut's remains, the bald eagles give up their pretense of indifference and fly back and forth eyeing the carcass. In the middle of the commotion, a red fox slips in, seizes the halibut carcass in its mouth, gallops up the beach with it and disappears. Now the seagulls, realizing what has happened, turn on one another with renewed bitterness while the bald eagles, lamenting the loss, fly about in futile circles.

A variety of land and sea mammals, of fish and birds and intertidal creatures, make their homes in the Kodiak Archipelago, and not all of them are native here. The brown bear and bald eagle are native—this is truly the land of bear and eagle—but some of our animal friends, the beaver and deer among them, were introduced fairly recently by man. Do the deer and beaver count for less? But I can't imagine this island ecosystem without the Sitka black-tailed deer. D.H. Lawrence felt that to really know the animals you have to go where they are and to observe them in their natural haunts. So is my experience of the Kodiak wilderness less natural, less genuine, because humans in their meddlesomeness brought the deer and beaver here?

Wilderness is never static. Every living thing is a kind of hitchhiker. It was only a matter of time before a pregnant beaver stepped off a floating log and made landfall here. The thick, sour smell of the beaver lingers in the trampled rush grass as if the beaver had always inhabited this lakeshore. I watch the beavers at swim practice, two parents and two little ones, they paddle back and forth and touch noses—it's an idyllic family outing. The young beavers, curious, stray toward me, and their mother, warning all parties, wallops the water with her tail. Her stout back legs turn up and she submerges in a tizzy and dismisses them. School's out!

The animals are generous with me. What do the animals give me? Awe, kinship, amusement, humility, community, memory, even moral instruction. I don't believe that a prelapsarian tranquility ever reigned on earth, but I believe that it reigns in our hearts all the time and we're ashamed by the knowledge of how good it could be if the good in us were uppermost. From the animals I get every kind of self-knowledge. They vitalize me. They feed me.

These are the things the wild animals give me. They uplift me, and I want to save what uplifts me, because what uplifts me saves me. Two-thirds of Kodiak Island, wild habitat of mammals, birds and fish, and several satellite islands and abundant offshore waters fall within the sanctuary of the Kodiak National Wildlife Refuge and the Alaska Maritime National Wildlife Refuge, and for this I am grateful to the far-seeing conservationists of the past. We are materially so far ahead of the other species that generosity, evolutionary noblesse oblige and self-serving science insist that we consider their welfare and embrace the measures that help them to flourish. We love our fellow creatures and reverence our heritage. In conserving the wilderness, our own animal spirits are at stake. Without them we die.

BIRD & BIRDSONG

Abird of the spruce wood that reminds me of the city is the woodpecker. *Brrratatatatat.* This isn't a call or a song but the jackhammer percussion of the woodpecker's sharp bill as it bores into a tree to dig out a bug or to hollow its nest hole. When I lived in the city I often woke in the morning to the sound of jackhammers below in the street. That's what the woodpecker reminds me of.

I sometimes hear woodpeckers working in different quarters of the forest. One woodpecker stops hammering and a second woodpecker picks it up. They seem to be playing alternate parts in a score or debating like birds in a medieval allegory. The sound carries far and echoes among the spruce trees, an acoustic phenomenon that gives an inflated sense of the woodpecker's numbers. They aren't common here.

A pair of three-toed woodpeckers used to explore the driftwood posts outside the cabin window. They climbed up and down the decaying logs and hunted out the wood borers. From my elevated angle I could see the yellow head feathers of the male woodpecker. He wore what looked like a yellow bowler, not the armored helmet I might have expected of a bird who repeatedly bangs his head against a tree.

It saddens me to think of the post-birdsong future of our megacities. Urban apologists like to describe the city's noise as a kind of jazz, but if jazz, it's a cold, unnatural, inorganic jazz. Surely to live in harmony with nature means that the voices of the songbirds count for something. In the city I may go for days without noticing the songbirds, their small voices crowded out by noise and distraction. What can't be heard is neglected, and neglect of the songbirds hastens their decline.

WILSON'S WARBLER NESTLINGS

When I return to the wild I hear the songbirds again. They contribute to the endless hum of energy that's the backdrop of a summer's day here. Some days so many birds flit and flutter about, the air positively glitters with song. It's an incessant traffic, a constant patter in the branches, a weaving of color and motion, a daylong cheeping and twittering—not an electronic twittering but a twitter of flesh-and-blood birds. With the avian chorus there's never a final performance, just a perpetual rehearsal. Sometimes the birds are singing and shrilling and whistling and hammering all at once, without my being alive to it—thrush, chickadee, sparrow, seagull, eagle, magpie, widgeon, woodpecker—solo, duet, family glee—and suddenly I become conscious of the chorus as a boisterous riot. I had thought it was a quiet day!

A yellow-breasted bird, something like a small canary, caught my eye as soon as I arrived on the Kupreanof Peninsula. It flitted from spruce bough to cow parsnip head to elder switch, never staying still for long. This is the Wilson's warbler, a migratory songbird, and they're a cheerful warbler to have around, flashing yellow in the sunshine or dashing brightly against the gloom of an overcast sky.

Nothing draws me out of my cloistered solitude like one of these yellow songsters darting into view. During my nineteenth summer on the peninsula, I finally saw a clutch of the warbler's eggs. The nest was underfoot in a recess in the moss, camouflaged by the grass and forbs. I admired the nest's compact construction, but I would have advised its builder to locate her nest in a place less (if there is such a place in the wild) vulnerable to predators. The nest contained six creamy speckled eggs that hatched at the end of June. From day to day, the nestlings matured in size, color and feathering, and on the tenth day they were gone. I feared the worst, but the activity of their parents in the adjoining alder grove and their lively chipping when I approached assured me that the fledglings were safe.

"The only birds I can identify are the dead ones—they stay still for me," my neighbor Laurel Peterson lamented, surrendering to the despair that birders at one time or another will feel. A red-breasted bird about which Laurel and I disagreed was, if not a male pine grosbeak, perhaps a robin or other thrush, though Laurel denied that we have true robins on the peninsula. She must have had in mind the varied thrush. An April returnee, ruddy and large-statured, the varied thrush is an outspoken bird whose long, shrill note reminds me of the low-voltage alarm on my homestead inverter. The song is unmistakable. It's not a lovely song, but because it's one of the earliest of the season, it projects the joyful inspiration of a trumpet flourish, waking us to the good news of the spring.

Bird watching is easy in May before the leaves shroud the thickets and while the earth around the cabin is exposed. Thrushes, sparrows and warblers arrive. Heads raised, beaks vibrating, the songbirds trill and announce themselves. I know spring is here when I hear a light scratching of bird feet on the cabin siding. They kick up the soil and pick out a seed or draw out a worm. Where I have raked aside the needles in the spruce grove, the birds peck at the earth and crack the seeds in their bills. Meanwhile they busily gather the moss, straw, deer hair, twigs and other materials for nest-building.

July is a loud and stressful month as the fledglings leave their nests and learn to fly. Along shore, the enchanting melody of the song sparrow can still be heard. But by early August the birds have mellowed. They chuck and chirp with restraint. There's not the musical fever of spring and early summer. The song of the golden-crowned sparrow is but a seductive memory. The migrants, long journeys ahead of them, eat with appetite. A torn salmonberry hangs from the lower mandible of a fat fox sparrow. The red-berried elder is mobbed by sparrows and thrushes. Hurrah! Hurrah! On a sunny August morning after rain, the birds enjoy their hour afield, feasting, primping, fluttering from tree to shrub to earth, full of the same vital energy that makes men and women rejoice.

Here the raven insists on getting a word in edgewise. I seem to see him mugging at me from the wings. The raven's is the only voice that sometimes irks me, but it's a mistake to let a raven know he irritates me—that's music to his ears. The raven being a year-round resident, I am wise to make peace with him, but his racket, his cacophonous crowing, is hard to forgive. The hermit thrush distracts me too, but with an altogether different lure, a song of irresistible beauty that nothing stops me from attending to. With the raven I stop my ears.

In March I hear, rising from the marsh beyond the spruce wood, the call of the snipe. It's an atmospheric call, especially plaintive at night when the country otherwise slumbers. In the muskegs of interior Alaska the snipe used to zigzag truculently over our heads when we firefighters tramped too close to their nests. These plump, long-billed shorebirds are capable of dizzying turns of flight. At Cottonwood I have seen them in their wheeling, high-speed courtship flight. All day long the lovers sprung and dove near and far in the air around the cabin, and even after their shapes had dissolved in the darkness I heard them, the wind ripping through their feathers as they beat on into the night.

A relative of the snipe, the sandpiper, frequents the shoreline, and the comical oystercatcher, black with a long red bill, an eater of shellfish, patrols the rocks and tidepools. The gull, the black cormorant, the murre and some of the sea ducks are all-season birds here. The horned puffins and tufted puffins, big-billed and parti-colored, remind me of Toucan Sam on the Froot Loops box. The puffins flock offshore and dabble at their ease, but without a boat it's a challenge to get near them. It's not that the puffin is nimble when approached. A puffin flies as short a distance as necessary at the lowest possible altitude to put some space between itself and you. One chunky puffin wouldn't move aside or climb into the air no matter how much time we allowed him. His belly and webbed feet splashing, he slowed or accelerated or tacked as we did in our raft, only speeding up to stay in front of us, pointing the way with his bright orange forebill, ardently flapping his wings and paddling his orange feet but never getting airborne until we made a hard turn and left the odd seabird behind.

The scintillating colors of the harlequin duck in spring plumage, the finely crested head of the merganser ... I understand why so many master painters have been drawn to the challenge of depicting these waterfowl. Art honors nature without hope of rivaling its magnificent subtlety and providential totality. On the last morning of April, I walk the low tide with my infant son on my back, a flock of snow buntings before us, optically dazzling me as they fly arabesques over the beach and out over the water, white and black and abruptly white and black again, swerving and switching in flight, warm feathered bodies in motion, their many wings beating as one. In a flash they separate and again as suddenly they draw together, a single shining mercurial body. Swift, deft, turning sharply, holding together and pulling apart, their center always shifting, they dip and soar and spin and—whoosh!—glide out over the water, and all the while warbling the loveliest song.

BOATS

odiak is a major fishing port and home to the largest Coast Guard base in the country. Boats here are a matter of livelihood and sometimes of life and death. Kodiak Islanders rely on boats when they travel, ship cargo, and fish for subsistence and recreation. For those who live in remote villages, as many Alutiiq families do, boats are essential to their way of life.

At Cottonwood we have a rough sense of the fishing calendar by watching the boats come and go in Kupreanof Strait. When the commercial fishing has closed, a flotilla of vessels passes east to the Port of Kodiak where an earlier flotilla passed west to the fishing grounds. Purse seiners, crabbers, longliners, trawlers, fish tenders, each with its peculiar gear, its nets, pots, booms, winches, power skiffs, bright flags and buoys—these fishing boats ply the strait. But more than fishing boats, a cavalcade of watercraft passes before us: ferries and trampers and tugs with barges, charter boats, a landing craft, a sailboat or luxury yacht—not all at once, of course, and there are days, fair or stormy, when we see no boats at all, but eventually from our fixed point on the land we see them all, from the lone kayaker to the Coast Guard cutter, and in this way over time we view life's passing parade in all of its pluck and variety.

Before I came to Kodiak Island, I wasn't much of a boatman. On Kodiak I learned the difference between an inboard and outboard motor and I learned to say "twenty-five-horse kicker" instead of "twenty-five-horsepower outboard engine." I learned to tie a few knots, but mostly I encouraged my children to learn them so that I wouldn't need to. As homesteaders we depended on our inflatable boat for fishing and for traveling to the local salmon cannery to get our mail. We towed driftlogs by boat and we explored the Kodiak coastline. I was never much of a boatman, but when I close my eyes I'll always hear the keel song *slappity-slap* of a skiff going by in stormy seas.

There is heroism in the life of a mariner, and sometimes it's a forlorn heroism. In the hushed heart of a winter's night, when our children slept, we looked out the window at the faint glow of a boat on the water, and we were grateful for what we had on the land, for the warmth of our homestead cabin, for the roof overhead and the solid floor beneath. At three o'clock in the morning I might hear the muffled hum of an engine, something rare enough that I would sit up and look out at the twinkling red or yellow light of a fishing boat at sea. Did the crew notice a glimmer in our cabin window? Maybe it warmed their hearts as much as the light on their boat warmed mine.

The mercurial weather and extreme tides here, the exposed beaches and lack of an anchorage make it a challenge to keep a boat in the water. We chose an inflatable boat for the convenience of its portability and stowability. But the convenience comes at a cost. A fourteen-foot raft, even one with a rigid floor, isn't a vessel to launch in rough seas, and an inflatable boat is vulnerable, pitifully, to puncture by rocks and by the teeth and claws of Kodiak's brown bears.

Inevitably I learned to patch the holes in the boat and to stop the air leaks. A friend who drilled me in boat and motor care was Shaw Patterson of the US Coast Guard, a true oceangoing man who spent most of his career as a search and rescue coxswain. I think Shaw saw in me a drowning waiting to happen and took a sympathetic interest. Stern, thorough, marginally obsessive-compulsive, Shaw required me to soap my boat vinyl, to flush the salt from the motor, to burn the fuel out of the lines, to grease the fittings and propeller shaft, and even to varnish the chipped transom and floorboards, so that when I had prepared my boat and motor for long-term storage and presented them to Shaw for inspection, it was like preparing my body and soul for the afterlife and going before the judge.

Shaw showed me around the bridge of the cutter *Storis* one day when he went to check the track lines on the charts prior to getting under way at the start of a patrol. The fight against smuggling and illegal fishing is a never-ending one, and the *Storis* traveled more than 20,000 miles a year in its patrols of territorial waters. I met the navigators and toured the engine room, the quarters and galley, and I considered this a tremendous privilege not only because the *Storis*, which had seen active duty in World War II, was a legendary vessel, the oldest continuously operated cutter in the Coast Guard, but also because I so admired the Coast Guard for the lifesaving searches and rescues they conduct by boat and helicopter in Alaska's waters.

> **Vessel sinks, man missing**
> **Searchers look for overdue skiff with four**
>   **people aboard**
> **Dark Star sinks; crew safe**
> **Four fishermen lost in rollover**
> **Attempts to retrieve lost skipper's body suspended**

Such headlines are all too common in the *Kodiak Daily Mirror*. Each year brings new maydays and new fatalities, new heartaches and new names to be remembered at the Fishermen's Memorial Service. We followed with dread, with a can't-bear-to-look melancholy, the stories of boats like the *Evanick* and the *Sea Wolf* that had broken up or sunk at sea. Boats founder, roll over, capsize, ice up, are struck by a wave, or they simply vanish. Crew members fall overboard or they go missing and are presumed lost. Rough weather is often to blame, but sometimes the investigators don't know why a boat flooded or why its weight shifted or what bad luck overrode good seamanship. Yesterday's lessons never seem to prevent tomorrow's catastrophes. We came on a visible reminder of this truth one day near the sea lion haul-out where Whale Passage runs into Kizhuyak Bay. The fishing vessel *Miss Linda* teetered in the foreground while an old wreck, the *Selief*, was visible on the rocks behind her. The *Miss Linda*, a fifty-odd-footer with a blue hull, listed sharply to starboard, and rescuers had tied a line to a spruce tree on shore to keep her from going all the way over. The *Lucky Lady* and another boat stood by, waiting for high water before they pulled her off the rocks. The seas were mild and the mishap wasn't disastrous, but in the shadow of that earlier wreck we wondered if the *Miss Linda* had lost power and drifted aground or if instead the skipper had been listening to the popular old ballad "Asleep at the Wheel."

I won't conclude on a gloomy note. Boats offer a livelihood and a way of life that many Kodiakans love. At Port Wakefield we meet a family preparing to go to sea in their purse seiner *All Saints*. Commercial fishing reopens tomorrow noon, and they are heading around the island for it. "Cook Inlet red salmon are moving in," the son tells us, optimistic. "Fishermen have been catching nothing but pollock, but that's about to change."

We step onto the dock and share in the family's bantering excitement. They have fueled their boat and are reviewing their supplies. The son, plump and cheerful, raises his sunglasses to his forehead and instructs the deckhand, "Be sure and let the hose run so we don't taste the rubber in the water." His father leans out of the cabin and asks if anyone remembered to bring coffee. The son joshes his old man, telling us, "Nobody drinks coffee on board except for him. He makes it straight from the grounds. Tastes like creosote, his coffee, but it's always on and always warm."

The father peers out of the cabin at us and laughs. The son's wife lounges in an aluminum skiff behind the *All Saints*, smoking a cigarette and never saying a word. It's a warm July day, a gorgeous day, and the pilings, driven deep into the seabed, glisten with tar.

The boat's window frames are dry and peeling, and when the season is over, the son plans to sand the dry wood and to oil it with linseed oil. He doesn't want us to confuse him with the deckhand, and he issues needless commands to keep the young deckhand busy. The deckhand, spraying water at the cabin windows, is splashed by the water, and the son laughs at him and tells him to lower the hose so he doesn't squirt himself.

The woman in the skiff smiles at these exchanges and drags on her cigarette. Around her the pilings rise at angles from the saltwater, the water lapping gently at the pilings and at the boats. Nearby, the shake siding of the old dock house is green and heavy with moss. Port Wakefield, once a cannery, is today the dock and ferry terminal for the village of Port Lions.

Now the mother and daughter arrive from the village with bag lunches for the family. They eat their lunches while they finish making ready. The *All Saints*, a forty-foot boat, needs a good scrubbing, and after the season they will lay it over on the beach and copper-paint the hull from the keel to the waterline. "Helps keep off the barnacles and slime," the son tells us. He bites into his sandwich. "Fiberglass hull," he adds, rapping the boat with his knuckles.

SALMON SEINER, KUPREANOF STRAIT

"Why not drive her up on the ways instead of beach her?" we ask.

"It gets slippery on the ways. People spill paint and stuff on it and there's never enough room up there. Someone always falls off or gets pinched. We lay the boat over on the beach and everyone comes down and helps."

His mother smiles at these words, and she nods her head in approval. They're a mixed-heritage family, white and Alutiiq. The incoming tide has caused our boat to bind up against the ladder we tied it to, so we take our leave now and descend the short ladder from the dock. The family, those who are staying and those who are going, hug one another and shout back and forth in farewell. "Goodbye!" "Good fishing!" "Forget anything?" "Love you!" "Love you!"

It's a cheery sight, the *All Saints* putting to sea in the sunshine, the family waving their hands and singing out their love. The fishing boat rides high and proud, towing its silver skiff and making its way out of port and into the bay.

BROWN BEAR

I was with Casey Westbrook and Tim O'Connor, men I had hired as day laborers, and we were a mile east of the homestead when a mother brown bear charged us in defense of her cubs. We had unintentionally surprised her in the spruce forest in the twilight, and she reacted instinctively and charged to within ten feet of us. We responded by climbing onto the roof of a derelict cabin and staying there. Maybe later we'd be able to say what we meant to do with the rusty axes we took with us. I could spin an ax through the air and sink it into the side of a spruce tree twenty feet away, a trick I had learned from some Athabaskan firefighters, but I wasn't about to try my axmanship against an angry brown bear.

The bear woofed at us in warning and bawled at her cubs to climb down from the spruce tree into which they had fled. This "woofing" of a brown bear is a violent exhalation of air from its lungs, repeated and interspersed with growls. The bear stood on her back feet and raked her claws through the tree bark, looking up at her cubs, and they eventually descended and went away with her.

Bears woof and huff and gnash their teeth when agitated, and I was fine with waiting on the cabin roof for as long as this bear needed to get her woof out. I remembered a case in interior Alaska of a black bear that pursued a woman onto a cabin roof and killed her. We don't have black bears on Kodiak Island, but forgive me for not putting all of my trust in the notion that adult brown bears won't climb. It reminds me of my Canadian friend who, when I had moved to Alaska, mischievously advised me, "Just remember, bears can't run downhill."

Sooner or later, every resident of rural Kodiak crosses paths with a brown bear. Their paths will cross more than once. I was hiking the mountain south of Cottonwood when I met a brown bear with a white blaze on his back, a four-pointed star in the rich dark fur. I quit the area at once. Next morning I avoided the mountaintop and hiked the seashore, but the bear had the same idea. There he was at Eagle Rock, same white blaze on his back, standing upright and gazing seaward like a captain anxiously awaiting his next commission.

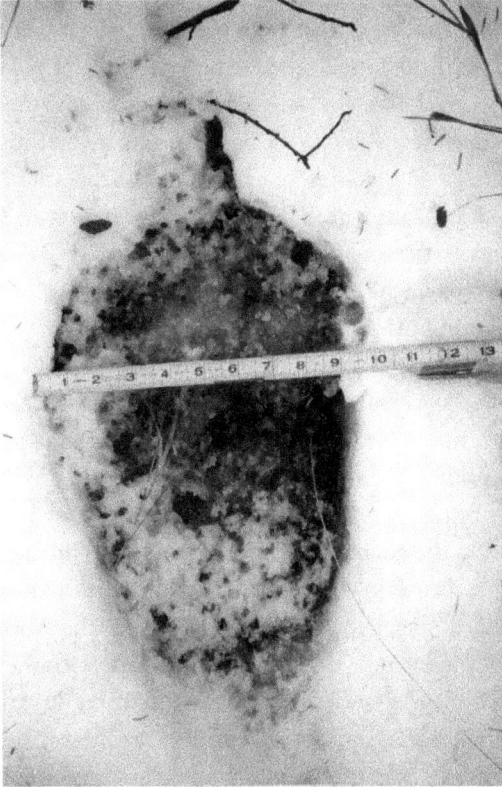

"THERE IS NOTHING LIKE A BEAR TRACK TO AROUSE THE IMAGINATION."

The taxonomy of the Kodiak brown bear has long been disputed. The Kodiak bear was once considered a separate species. Today the North American brown bear is said to include both the Kodiak bear and the mainland grizzly bear, but not all scientists agree that the Kodiak bear's bigger size and anatomical differences entitle it to its own subspecies (*Ursus arctos middendorffi*).

Kodiak bears have been isolated here since the glaciers retreated at the end of the Pleistocene, and it stands to reason they are genetically distinct. Kodiak has a subspecies of short-tailed weasel for the same reason: it lives only on the Kodiak Archipelago. The local Visitor's Guide informs us, "The Kodiak bear is a subspecies of the brown or grizzly bear and is the largest bear in the world," a declaration that will keep the tribes of Linnaeus warring for another century—and will annoy the champions of the polar bear, who insist that the polar bear is bigger than the Kodiak brown bear. These battles often come down to competing word choices and standards of measurement. Kodiak Island, measured in miles of coastline, is the largest island in the United States, but measured in square miles it is second to Hawaii. Taxonomically, the Kodiak bear is a flesh-eating carnivore, but in practice the bear is an omnivore who enjoys grass and berries and fish.

It's safe to say, I hope, that the Kodiak bear is a brown bear who inhabits the Kodiak Archipelago. He is one of the largest living land carnivores on the planet—the male can easily weigh over half a ton—so it's wise to remember he's out there. A paradox of living with brown bears is that you want nothing to do with them but it feels such a privilege to live among them. Without bears there wouldn't be the same air of wildness and consequence that hangs over the country, the same tautening of the senses that checks the dulling of habit, the same deep and real and fearsome context against which to joy in the finer pleasures of a wildflower or a bird's song. The special atmosphere of a place inhabited by these bears correlates, I suppose, with the overall scarceness of the bears, with their diminished numbers elsewhere, their virtual extermination from the vast range where they once flourished. Meriwether Lewis calls these bears, interchangeably, grizzlies and brown bears: "tremendous animals," he writes in his journal, whose ferocity could only be conquered "by a shot in the head." I am a bit brokenhearted when I read Lewis and Clark, not because I think them callous or cruel, but because I know their heroism was inseparable from their ignorance, from how much they didn't understand.

In the past, drawn by the mystique of the brown bears, I fought down an impulse to follow them. This strange pull, this gravitation, was strongest in my early years at Cottonwood, when I was alone at the homestead and more susceptible, if not more reckless. I stood in forest twilight admiring the fluid grace of a brown bear padding soundlessly by, the loft of its head, the smoothly moving muscles of its hip and shoulder, and I longed to follow the bear. I sometimes followed a ways. Today when I see a brown bear I act to avert a meeting, and I assume the same is true of the bears. They impress me with their size and majesty, in keeping with their mystique—"furious and formidable," Meriwether Lewis writes—but in truth a bear can be a base creature, a hunger-driven scavenger leading a dismal animal existence. The insects harass him and a raven's squawk startles him. For every anecdote of the bear's grandeur there's another that paints him a clown or petty criminal. A teenager bear broke into so-and-so's cabin and snatched a candy bar. A bear ate a bucketful of paint and a pipeful of Freon and when the owners came home they found him slumped across the open chest freezer.

It's hard to overstate the bears' influence on our lives at Cottonwood. Punctured tires, a torn inflatable boat, a ruined outhouse door—this partial list of the bear damage we've sustained over the years is the least of it. The bears became an everyday contingency, like the weather. We heard their nasal bawling in the bush, we heard their doggish panting when they swept past our window, or a bear heard us first and startled us by standing in the vegetation to better see us. Our choices at Cottonwood have been guided by the bears in significant ways—the decision to build a solar electric fence—and innumerable small ways, like which direction to hike on a given day. Every kind of brown bear is here, light brown and chocolate and golden in color, mature males, adolescents, females with cubs, the cool, standoffish bears of midsummer, the temperamental bears of autumn, bears by moonlight, bears in snow, bears on the mountain and bears down below.

Wherever I had lived in Alaska, even in the populated environs of Fairbanks and Anchorage, wild bears lived nearby and they sometimes clashed with people. But to live in the Kodiak bush, to share a roadless wilderness with the bears, a country in which the bears outnumber the people—this felt different. It felt total. And I was immersed in this new world right away. To round a bend in the trail and encounter brown bears—it's unnerving. Five miles east of Cottonwood, at Port Bailey Cannery, a brown bear was shot after it reared up on a cannery worker. When Martina and the children eventually joined me at Cottonwood, I became anxious about the risks. "There is nothing like a bear track to arouse the imagination," Adolph Murie writes, and how true it is. I had absurd nightmares of being chased by the bears. In one dream the bear yelled, "To hell with equal rights!" before he bashed the door in and came after me.

A large male and several females with cubs ranged through Cottonwood, and my glimpses of them kept me on edge. A bear moves with natural grace but is careless who hears him, and only a bear in the bush, heavy and unafraid, sets off such a slow, sustained snapping of branches. This was a sound I heard as I explored the country on foot or as I worked about the cabin, tilling the garden or painting the siding—

> A tramping in the woods that nobody
> but he could make alerted me, and I
> pricked up listening, all newborn with suspense
> to see where he'd emerge.
> I'd turned so quickly, apprehensive,
> disoriented, not knowing where he was,
> I was momentarily blinded by the sun
> high in the southwest sky.
> But when he came, it was at an amble,
> adolescent, just this side of frisky,
> from under the five or six big spruce trees,
> not knowing that the man
> who had dropped his paintbrush and backed away
> was just as startled as he. I repented,
> I laughed aloud and called him back by name,
> but, nameless, he didn't stay.

The most abundant bear sign, the commonest reminder of the bears' presence, is their droppings. "Bear sign" is an esoteric phrase that basically means crap. I must have been chasing a scout badge or entering a post-poetry poetry contest when I kept this catalog:

fresh sign, black and shiny, between gully and
     section line
enormous olive-colored grassy heap of bear scat
green and lumpy like horse apples
a gigantic pile of porridge
oozy wet & black
blue-black with berry seeds
drying mounds of seaweed-laden excrement

    A careful observation of bear droppings is no doubt essential practice for the Alaskan woodsman.

    Bear sign includes, more broadly, tracks and other evidence of the bears' presence: the hollows in which they bed down, the branches they rip from a tree, the raked earth and torn moss, the stray tufts of their hair. Bears shed their fur when they roll on the ground or when they catch on a branch. They also have favorite rubbing trees where they stand and scratch their backs. One such tree is a thin, whitish spruce, free of spurs and heavily scored by bear claws. Clumps of auburn hair stick in the spruce sap and cling in the creases of bark after the bear has gone. I whistled at a bear who was rubbing his back here and he looked over at me and squinted as if he couldn't believe anyone else knew the refrain from Tom T. Hall's "Old Dogs, Children and Watermelon Wine."

In the late 1990s brown bears were more active on the Kupreanof Peninsula than at any time in living memory. A reduced food supply after seasons of adverse weather, poor salmon returns, the climatic cycle known as El Niño—the peak bear activity was attributed to any and all of these phenomena. A staffer at the Kodiak National Wildlife Refuge speculated that the nature-pampered Kodiak brown bears would have to get their paws dirty and to scrounge for roots and grubs the way the grizzlies of interior Alaska always had to, and she warned me that the bears wouldn't go down easy for the winter, not before they ate enough food to store the fat and nutrients they needed to survive.

She was right. In the trying autumn of 1998, a season that extended into December, we saw or heard brown bears almost daily, and it put a strain on our family. At times Martina didn't forgive me for the homestead. Kody was a year old and Miranda was six years old, and we felt vulnerable. News of a mauling at Terror Bay reached us. The bears periodically ripped our tarps or ransacked a tote. They tracked the snow around the cabin. The delight we had experienced in September when a mother and triplets frolicked outside our window turned inexorably to jitters. I bought a cordless spotlight for the dark nights and I strung a tripwire alarm around our supply tent. It's no good for a cub to learn from its mother to poke around people's cabins, and we took precautions to avoid this. We kept a clean cabin and removed all our food waste. During hikes we carried a bear horn and a shotgun. I always carried the shotgun, even in rain, and even while packing my son on my back. "Coming through, bear, coming through!" To carry the gun and to dry and oil it every day was a chore, but I would not have forgiven myself for not having the gun as a fallback in an emergency. There is such a thing as a mean-tempered bear, a bear that in human terms is just plain mean, and while the mean bear is no doubt the exception, nobody who goes among wild bears should hold nature in so little esteem as to deny its exceptions. Willy Fulton, the pilot who in 2003 discovered the scant remains of bear researchers Timothy Treadwell and Amie Huguenard at Kaflia Bay, across Shelikof Strait from us, tells me that the bear that stalked him there and that made a meal of Treadwell and Huguenard was well known to be a mean-tempered bear.

Brown bears seldom attack people unless provoked, and the commonsense advice is don't provoke the bears, but in wild country it's not possible to eliminate every potential misunderstanding. Bears are individuals, with their own quirks and peeves. A foraging bear can be surprisingly oblivious, and no matter how careful you are, you may walk up on one. Bears have run from me, bears have ignored me, and most have behaved with calm discretion and moved on. The few bears that harassed us around the cabin were adolescent bears. I only once saw a bear that I instinctively felt was ill-natured, one that turned on us with a vicious scowl when it heard my family approaching on foot. To this day the bear's expression chills me when I think of it. He was occupied with some object in the grass, I didn't see what, but the glower on his face, his disgruntlement, went beyond possessiveness, and I only knew it was essential that we withdraw.

There wasn't an uninhabited cabin in the miles around Cottonwood that wasn't hit by brown bears that autumn. Gaping doors, punched-out windows and ransacked interiors were the tell. We saw two bears at it in November, batting around the items they had dragged from a tiny hunting cabin—a cooler, a funnel, a plastic storage container. At another cabin we found broken glass and bloody paw prints. Even Alderwood Lodge was hit, a wilderness lodge four miles east of us. The doors of bungalows and outbuildings hung open. A window was shattered over the lodge entry. The bear had smashed the front doorknob and broken the lock. He went straight to the ground-floor kitchen, padding around the long counter at which in better times the lodge guests relaxed over coffee. Flour and cocoa mix sprinkled the floor. Cupboards exposed, contents spilled out.

In town the brown bears were ornery, too. Kodiakans debated how to minimize the attraction of the municipal dump. A bear just digs *under* a fence, critics said, or the fence just keeps the bears *inside*. What about an electric fence? Skeptics offered eyewitness accounts of clever bears reaching between fence wires to get what they wanted. One man knew of a brown bear that had climbed into an electrified dumpster and was literally *cooking and smoking from the nostrils* but didn't leave.

The townspeople worried that once school started and the kids were out and about, there would be a mauling. After the winter's deep freeze, the spring's cold snap and a salmon return that was as disappointing as the salmonberry crop, the brown bears were hungry and on the prowl. Did the local bear population need thinning? A public meeting was held. A bear guide named Tom Stick proposed a solution: grant more hunting permits to the bear guides.

I had met Tom Stick in December when I helped him load an outboard motor into a seaplane at Trident Basin, the seaplane base in town. He told me that the Alaska Department of Fish & Game had tried to get him to bring a fall bear hunt to our peninsula to help ease the bear pressure. Nine months a year, Stick lived at his hunting lodge in the converted cannery of Port Vita on Raspberry Strait. He was returning now to board it up for the winter. Spectacled, quiet-spoken and underdressed for the cold of December, Stick wasn't anybody's stereotype of a professional bear hunter. He charged $9,500 for a fifteen-day bear hunt, and he told me he didn't clear a lot of money at it once he had covered his costs.

Bear hunting is a tightly regulated activity on Kodiak Island. The island's bear population is flourishing, and legal hunting has had a role in effective management. Frankly, the notion of management insults my sense of wilderness, but in the cause of wilderness I have made my peace with management at the expense of wildness. The Kodiak National Wildlife Refuge, nearly two million acres in size, is about as pristine a wilderness as can be had anymore, and bear hunters were among the earliest conservationists to work for protection of these magnificent animals in the years leading to the creation of the refuge in 1941. Nonresident bear hunters must hunt with a guide, but even in a guided hunt, there is no guarantee of coming away with a brownie, and hunters go home every spring and fall with tags but no bears. Bear hunters are a sporting people with a love of the outdoors, but there is a rowdy sort of bear hunter who gives the group a bad name. At the Kodiak Airport, I heard a successful bear hunter on the telephone describing his hunt to his girlfriend and serenading her as follows:

"I ain't smoked for three days, honey, and I'm walking kinda high. I'm gonna hide in the house and get my ass fucked up. Yeah, it was a nine-foot-six-inch bear. Way high up the motherfucking mountain. We had our snowshoes out and we slid down and dragged him down on our snowshoes. You'd never believe how steep that was. I had to sleep on the mountain that night, and last night I only slept three hours, skinning the hide out. Now don't expect me to go to work right away, honey. I'll see if I can get me a couple of joints first. I guess I wouldn't mind having a cigarette, but if I go back into a smoky room it's gonna be the end of me quitting. Buy me a steak and don't keep me waiting here, huh?"

Kodiak's Alutiiq people, the region's first inhabitants, hunted the brown bear with spears and with traps. They harvested the bear for meat, and they used the rest of the animal for clothing, bedding, tools and decorations. The Alutiiq consider it disrespectful and inauspicious to boast about bear hunting.

By the way, bear guide Tom Stick's hunting camp at Port Vita wasn't immune from brown bear mischief. A bear ripped the door off Stick's new refrigerator just when a party of bear hunters was due. Stick was said to be renovating his lodge kitchen, taking out the cabinets and putting in new vinyl. People gossip about such things here. On the radio, at the mail stop, at the boat landing, at the Coast Guard station, or in town at Safeway or King's Diner, people swap bear stories, either their own story or somebody else's, an honest-to-God bear encounter or an unusual sighting—the bear as big as a Winnebago—everybody quick to offer opinions on the best bear defense or the latest bear management plan. A photographer friend of mine, a lover of nature, recently launched a drone into the air to photograph mating brown bears, but the noise of the drone spoiled the romantic atmosphere and the bears uncoupled and fled in opposite directions.

With the brown bears of Kodiak Island, ecotourism and sport hunting and wildlife science have overlapping interests. Each contributes to the island's brown bear subculture. Our human fears and vanities, our hypocrisies and generosities are exposed in our dealings with these animals. Everyone here is affected by the brown bears, in their legend and in their reality, and life on Kodiak wouldn't be the same without them.

At Cottonwood our precautions in living with the brown bears have long since become reflexes. We keep a clean cabin, we stay alert, we call aloud in dense vegetation, and we do these things even in quiet years when we rarely see the bears. The brown bears are native to this place; these are their old haunts and trails, and as a rule I defer to them.

The Kodiak brown bear is the shape of the wilderness, a supreme incarnation of nature's power, a vital expression of unseen and omnipresent law. He's a shade of past epochs when fierce and giant creatures roamed the earth, and when I hear the bear or see him, I stop with a slight shudder and look around at my natural home, shaken out of my complacency and returned to my humanity, recognizing myself as a representative man in a wild and glorious country.

BUSH PLANES & PILOTS

The romance of the bush pilots springs from the legendary exploits of some of the Northland's early flyers, but the pilots I have known, dogged by bureaucratic regulation and hikes in the costs of insurance and engine parts, downplay the mystique of their profession and speak of their love of flying. To call them mere air taxi operators doesn't do them justice. These pilots put down on land and sea, they fly a captain to his boat or an injured fisherman off the boat, they fly a scientist to a remote wildlife or limnology study, they fly bear-viewing charters, they drop hunters at hunting camp, they shuttle mechanics, schoolteachers, carpenters, inspectors and tree fallers to wherever they need to go to get the job done, they fly island families to rural villages and tourists to ritzy wilderness lodges, and heroically they respond to emergencies and fly medical evacuations in often marginal conditions.

I was in the air with Dean Andrew of Andrew Airways when he surprised me by flying down Afognak Strait to pick up Ike Shepard, an old-timer suffering from congestive heart failure. The man couldn't breathe and was blue and white in the face. In town, Dean landed his floatplane in Lilly Lake to put the patient close to the hospital. A few months later I chanced to meet Mr. Shepard when he was normal in color and steady on his feet. He had recovered the air of one of those tough Alaskan birds who go on forever. "I'm glad to see you're doing so much better," I said. I didn't expect him to remember me—he was dying when we met, his eyes focused inward on that critical life event—but he certainly recalled the fateful seaplane flight when I reminded him of it.

Small planes are part and parcel of the Kodiak Island culture. There is no faster means of getting beyond Kodiak's limited road system and of getting back to town from the bush. It's expensive to fly, but expensive is a relative word. When you're crazed with cabin fever or suffering a medical emergency, you are happy to pay the pilot. A flying service is often no more than an owner-operator, a pilot with a Cessna 206 or a De Havilland Beaver on floats, and the overhead costs are high. Several pilots have confided to me how little money they make. Commercial fishermen and hunting guides have told me the same thing. They should all just quit and become writers.

Bush pilots tend to be youthful souls, far from the staid image of a uniformed United Airlines pilot. A seaplane jockey named Phil used to ride his unicycle around the docks before he pulled himself together and flew us to our homestead. Imagine a United pilot weaving through Terminal B on a unicycle with his arms out to the sides, his cap askew on his head, his long hair hanging down and a happy smile of accomplishment on his face. To be a United pilot isn't necessarily the ambition of an Alaskan bush pilot. "A United Air pilot doesn't fly," I was told, "he launches a flying computer." It's more thrilling to fly hunters to a mountain camp in the fall; it's more intimately gratifying to rescue a village gunshot victim and wing him to the hospital in town. In winter, these freewheeling bush pilots may stop flying to pursue earthbound pleasures in the Sunbelt, or they sign up for far-out flying adventures like landing tourists on glaciers or dropping skydivers over Belize or Dubai.

In bush Alaska, the coming or going of a charter plane is an event. A neighbor who learns you have a plane coming might show up to give you her outgoing mail or to pick up the booze or snoose he had arranged for the pilot to bring. If you have a satellite telephone or a satellite texting device, you can communicate with the front office of the flying service, but otherwise you set a pickup date ahead of time and hope they remember you. They don't, not always. I once sat on the beach a full day in the rain waiting for a pilot who just plain forgot me. Everybody makes mistakes, I guess, but I wasn't emotionally devastated when I heard a few years later that Uyak Air had shut down.

A relationship works both ways, of course, and a flying service can fire a customer. Penn Air did this to me. One April they delivered long-awaited supplies to our beach: a pre-hung door, seven sheets of half-inch plywood, seven sheets of T-111 siding, and fuel and provisions. The two-man crew turned the Grumman Goose in the shallow water, unloaded the cargo onto our beach and made ready to leave. The Grumman Goose, I should say, is a large amphibious transport with twin overhead propellers. The men laid our new door on the beach just behind the Goose. I should have seen what would happen, but they should have seen it sooner. They had no sooner throttled up the engines and got the propellers turning than our new door, caught in the blast of air, blew up off the rocks. The door nearly decapitated my daughter Miranda and cracked apart on landing.

The roar of the seaplane drowned out my yells, but I later phoned Penn Air from the pay telephone at Port Bailey Cannery and insisted they repair or replace my door. Too many communications ensued, but the upshot was that they gave us a new door. They didn't like to, and they grumbled about the angle and rockiness of our beach at Cottonwood and swore never to land there again.

A beach's orientation with respect to the wind and waves affects a pilot's decision whether to land or not. At Cottonwood, where our beach faces north, a strong northwest or northeast wind complicates a landing. Even small waves push a plane onto the beach. If the rocks are exposed, a pilot fears dinging his floats. "We're not pussies, we're just tired of taking our floats to the shop," Rolan Ruoss of Sea Hawk Air tells me, circling in the air as he reconnoiters our beach. The aluminum floats on Rolan's 1953 De Havilland Beaver are four-hundredths of an inch thick. It doesn't take too large or sharp a rock to dent or puncture them. Rolan, his right hand working the propeller and throttle and mix controls, descends into the wind and sets his floats in the water, and we bump and skid across the sea. Beaver 56Tango taxis to shore and we remove our headsets.

Incidentally, they aren't called "pontoons" in Alaska, they're called "floats." If you use the word pontoons, it will be as if you had said "poltroons" or "pantaloons" and you either won't be understood or you'll be taken for a poltroon or a pantaloon yourself. Don't say pontoons. It's a worse solecism than mistaking a snowmachine for a snowmobile.

There are two flight paths between Kodiak town and our homestead on Kupreanof Peninsula, one that cuts across the mountainous head of the island, through Sharatin Pass or Buskin Pass, where four white crosses mark the site of an old flying tragedy, and a second path that avoids the mountains by following the coastline north out of town and west toward Kupreanof Strait. High seas, gale winds and zero-zero fogs will undo any flight plan, but lousy flying weather doesn't always mean stormy weather. The sea might be flat calm, but the fog socks you in, or the sunshine sparkles, but the wind is insane. The Federal Aviation Administration mandates a safe cloud ceiling of five hundred feet, but I asked a pilot if he would fly at fifty feet in an emergency and he said, "Yes, if it was life and death. Rules and safety aren't the same thing," he added.

The stress of waiting for a seaplane in bad weather is a syndrome in itself. As the hours tick by, discouragement, anger and even paranoia set in. If someone in the party is ill, the anxiety of the wait can be overwhelming. My wife, Martina, suffered a respiratory emergency at our homestead, and I will see many tomorrows before I put behind me the anguish of fearing she would die on the beach before a seaplane got to us. Afterwards we never returned to Cottonwood without bringing a rented satellite telephone.

In bad weather I would rather be stuck in town than stranded on a remote beach or landing strip. In town I meet other travelers. Mainland Alaskans, European tourists, twenty-something backpackers, a state legislator, an Alutiiq Elder—I have met all kinds in the lounges of the flying services. People in transit are people in motion, en route, coming from and going to. Such people have stories to tell. The charm of adventure hangs over them.

A white-haired gentleman climbed out of a Piper Super Cub dressed to the nines in two-piece camouflage with a monster bowie knife on his hip. A deluded old-timer? With his arrow-straight posture and his dazzling complexion, the mysterious bushman looked to me as if he really had discovered the fountain of youth out there in the bush and been putting back a shot a day at least. Then there was the North Dakotan who, at a Rocky Mountain Elk Foundation fundraiser, had bid on and won a Kodiak Island deer hunt with the famed hunting guide Andy Runyan. The hunt had gone well and the fellow was on cloud nine. He couldn't stop babbling about button bucks and bucks in velvet and green bucks and stick bucks and the buck that got away from them—"probably Boone & Crockett," he assured me. Here was a traveler who wasn't going home disappointed.

PILOT JERRY BORSHARD, COTTONWOOD, 2019

Some pilots hang their wings up during the winter months when low temperatures, snow squalls, high winds and high seas make the flying unprofitable and sometimes dangerous. One of the few pilots who flew during the terrible winter of 1998–99 was Steve Harvey. His plane was a Grumman Widgeon, a rare and beautiful plane in which he took the greatest pride. I first saw the Widgeon in late December, when Harvey flew the mail run to Port Bailey Cannery and I happened to be on hand. To see the amphibious Widgeon waddle up on the beach like an exotic yellow and blue bird was a treat. Six weeks later, I had a chance to fly in the Widgeon when I was in town in icy weather and couldn't find another pilot willing to take me home to Cottonwood. Harvey's rate was $310 for up to 1,100 pounds of cargo. He was a thoughtful man with red cheeks and a head of tumultuous graying black hair. At our destination he touched down into a west wind and took a lot of saltwater on the windshield. This didn't bother him, since he looked on his beloved Widgeon as a boat. Being a boat, the plane didn't have a door up front, just a rear door on the port side. "The more doors you have on a boat, the more places you have that'll leak," he explained.

The Kodiak flying community is a small one, and the pilots know more about one another than they want to. As businesspeople they compete, but they also share weather reports and help one another in emergencies. When a pilot recently married, the congratulatory messages penned by his fellow aviators borrowed from the lingo of flying—"Wishing you a lot of thrust and little drag" and the like. The pilots know the scuttlebutt about which one of them has been suspended for bad flying and who took a dunk in the ocean and had to be fished out. With time I have become acquainted with some of the pilots and some of the operations managers and support staff at the flying services, and I inevitably hear stories about them. I hear, for example, that Willy Fulton quit flying planes and opened a bar in Montana, or that Willy Fulton blew his money opening the bar in Montana and was back in Kodiak flying planes again.

Willy Fulton is the pilot who in 2003 brought to light the fatal maulings of bear researchers Timothy Treadwell and Amie Huguenard in Alaska's Katmai National Park, a horror that became a national and international news sensation. Willy, flying a Beaver for Andrew Airways, arrived to pick the pair up as scheduled, and hours later he returned to Kodiak with their reduced remains in a plastic bag on board. In the interval he himself was stalked by the killer bear, saw the bear feeding on ("chowing down on," in Willy's words) human remains, helped to recover the scattered body parts, and was nearly caught in the barrage of gunfire when the authorities put down the rogue grizzly.

Movies were made and books were written about it. People capitalized on the tragedy and moved on. But Willy had to live with what he'd seen.

He didn't appear to wear the experience heavily, but how does such a thing not affect you?

In 2006, Willy announced that he was leaving Andrew Airways to live out his dream of sailing around the world with his girlfriend. "Sailing" was not just a figure of speech with Willy. He owned a sailboat in town and had sailed it past our homestead before. Willy loved the thrill of operating the sails in the wind. "Life is short," he said. "Flying is good work, but it gets to be a grind. When I'm broke I'll probably fly again."

We chatted on the docks at Trident Basin, the seaplanes bobbing in their slips around us. With his sweeping mustache and his broad smile, Willy had a cowboy's flair. Before coming to Kodiak Island he had flown for an outfit out of Iliamna on the Alaska mainland, and his roots were in Montana and Wyoming. His dream was to sail around the world, but he refused to frame his goals in precisely those terms. "It puts too much pressure on you," he said. "It's better to sail from port to port and keep going as long as you enjoy it."

Willy wasn't the only pilot to weary of the merry-go-round of summer flying in Kodiak. Pilot Dan Dorman knew the feeling well. With the long summer days and the crowding into those days of so much flying, there was little time for anything else. And with rising costs and a level of government regulation that bordered on sabotage, a pilot's morale was at risk these days. Dan feared that the old-style bush pilots were a dying breed practicing a dying art. "Used to be more of a Wild West mentality, in the good sense," Dan said. "Safety came first, but there were fewer rules and you could disregard most of them. Now we're smothered in it. You can be grounded if you get a warranty replacement by a shop that doesn't have a drug testing program." Dan had airplane repairs in mind because a grizzly bear had recently leaned on the elevator of his Cessna 206—Dan flew bear-viewing charters to the mainland—and bit a hole in the rudder.

Dan, the co-owner, with his wife Kim, of Highline Air, happened to be the son-in-law of our homestead neighbors, the Petersons. It must be convenient to have a pilot in the family. One day Dan dropped the school-teacher Mr. Provost at our homestead to check on the educational welfare of our daughter Miranda. Dan's wife, Kim, and their daughter Megan rode along in the floatplane. After dropping Mr. Provost at our beach, they taxied a mile up the coast to visit Kim's parents. Dan tied his plane to the Peterson running line, shared in the family lunch of fried chicken and potato salad, shot some clay pigeons off the cliff with his father-in-law, Richard, and after these midday amusements, leaving his wife and daughter to spend the night with Grandma and Grandpa, Dan taxied back to Cottonwood, picked up Mr. Provost and flew him home to Kodiak.

I never leaned on my acquaintance with Dan to get flying favors from him, but he one time landed on our windswept sea when I am sure no other pilot would have done it. A brisk northeast wind was blowing and the arm of land to our east offers only the slimmest windbreak. The oval of water in the lee of this windbreak was bordered by whitecaps. In this oval of water Dan put his plane down as gracefully as a dancer glissades across the floor in a ballet. I hadn't seen Martina in two months, and maybe Dan thought there was a conjugal urgency in our reunion. In any event he was determined to get her to me.

The Cessna 206, the Piper Super Cub, the Grumman Widgeon and the De Havilland Beaver—these classic bush planes shuttle me between worlds. When a pilot tips his wings in farewell after dropping me on the Kodiak shoreline, I couldn't be happier, but weeks or months later I'll be just as pleased when he buzzes the cabin at Cottonwood and descends to the water to pick me up and return me to the other world.

CABIN FEVER

How do you know if you have it? Irritability, feelings of entrapment, open-mouthed sloth, high-risk behaviors that present themselves as constructive alternatives to sloth, sociopathy, misanthropy, hallucination and psychosis are some of the common symptoms of cabin fever. When somebody's eating pistachio nuts and the crackling in the cabin becomes unbearable, there's a problem. How many times on a rainy day can you open and close every blade and attachment on your Leatherman or Swiss Army knife? You'll find out.

It bears repeating that our closest neighbor at Cottonwood lived a mile away. I had experience of living remotely for long intervals, but for Martina and the children the isolation was a trial whose novelty was bound to wear off. We enjoyed the pleasures of family life, the wonders of the wilderness and an uncommon liberty, but when your range of stimulations is as limited as ours was in foul weather, a demoralizing restlessness sets in and you begin to hear the call of town and of civilization.

After three months at the homestead, Martina and the children traveled to Kodiak town for some rest and relaxation. They rented movies, ate junk food, shopped and otherwise indulged in the higher things of life. My three days of solitude came as a relief. You can only step barefoot so many times on a plastic triceratops with a pencil sticking out of its gorge before you scream. The trip temporarily cured them of cabin fever, but I mean temporarily. Only high-achieving Buddhists are cured of cabin fever. The rest go into remission. Winter was cold and snowy, and with two young children in the cabin and nowhere to go in a storm, we were sometimes at a loss for things to do.

"Why don't we sit here and watch for a fly to land on the window," Miranda, six years old, suggested. Her mother and I exchanged glances of good-humored alarm. Miranda needed to trap an insect for her homeschool science project, but she had unwittingly articulated the lotus-eating world-view that undoes a high-minded homesteading ethic and turns homesteaders into fly-watching sluggards.

Another break was indicated, and Martina took the children to visit their grandparents in Hawaii. Surely Hawaii has an answer for the stubbornest cabin fever. They returned to Alaska refreshed and ready for the next bout of cabin fever, which arrived in March on a blast of cold air that marked, fittingly, the anniversary of Seward's Folly.

Cabin fever has much in common with everyday kvetching, with our unwillingness to be content. Adam and Eve are the prototypes. At Cotton-wood we were blessed with beautiful spring days, but we forgot all about them during the fifteen consecutive days of rainfall in June. Considering the hard winter we'd endured, the rain bitterly disappointed us. There was a peep of protest in my soul when I woke every morning to the drip of rainwater. Martina read books at night, finding consolation in them, and this brings me to the subject of books and book burning.

It's a fine pleasure on a rainy day to select a book from the shelf and to turn its pages and now and then to sip hot tea while gazing pensively out the window at the ocean. A good book sees us through sieges of bad weather and boredom. But as an antidote to cabin fever, books only go so far, and too much reading, or reading of a vexing nature, may exasperate the fever until what you really want to do is not to read a book but burn it.

This is exactly what happened to my stir-crazy Martina one summer when a series of nor'easters brought us nothing but rain and overcast. Rain ad nauseam, every day a copy of the day before and after. We combated our rainy-day crankiness by walking back and forth under the spruce trees. At this time the children were fourteen years old and ten years old, and as they had grown in size, the cabin had effectively shrunk. It rained full bore for days, during which Martina in the loft read the plays of Henrik Ibsen. We never got around to discussing the literary merits of the plays, but I inferred from her angry exclamations that the plays did not sit well with her. "This is disgusting," she said. She didn't mean it in a good way. "I'm going to burn this book," she said.

"You're what?"

"I'm going to burn this book."

"You can't burn Ibsen."

"I don't believe that just because it's a book it's somehow sacred and you can't touch it," she said.

The children watched their mother descend the loft ladder with the Ibsen in hand.

Miranda, mature at fourteen years of age, said, "Mom, you're always telling us not to treat books that way."

"I don't care what I told you—I want to burn a book."

"We don't burn books here," I said.

"Come on, we'll build a fire," she said, evoking a scene of jolly amusement as she drew her raincoat on. The children hesitantly followed her lead, crinkling their foreheads at me. They expected me to take a stand.

"Are you coming?" I was asked.

"Absolutely not."

Martina opened the cabin door.

"Wait," I stammered. "Not Ibsen."

"Then you pick one," she said.

I don't know why I chose the book I chose for the honorary immolation. It was a paperback novel I knew nothing about. Somehow the red cover struck me as combustible. I couldn't remember whether book burning was covered by the First Amendment, but I knew it was covered by Martina's freedom to do pretty much as she pleased at Cottonwood, and I think I loved her even more for her latest foray into the forbidden. We were about to cross another item off the list of things we hadn't done yet.

It was dismal outside, the hiss of rainfall diabolical. The paperback book came along passively, like an Incan princess who has been drugged before her sacrifice. I carried the chosen book to a dry spot in the spruce forest, shook gasoline over it and struck a match. We stepped back and watched it burn.

We stood in a ring around the burning book, the flames brightening our faces. Miranda remained baffled and somewhat indignant, but ten-year-old Kodiak was always game for a fire. We stirred the glowing mass and orange sparks flew up from it. We stirred the ashes one more time, and then, like a quartet of witches, we shuffled home and ate a hearty stew for dinner, under no illusion that we had extinguished for good the evil of cabin fever.

CANNERY

he first time I rafted alone through the notorious Whale Passage on Kodiak Island's north coast, I celebrated being alive by tying up at Port Bailey Cannery and buying a pack of Camel Lights for $2.70. I had already quit smoking cigarettes, but I made an exception. At the cannery store I asked Tammy—she was broke and up from Montana—what the heck was going on. Why were the cannery workers twiddling their thumbs? "Everybody's sitting around like there's no tomorrow."

"Maybe there's not," she said.

The cannery store sold food and sundries, not just the snack foods that the cannery workers favored, but also the milk and eggs and other staples that the fishermen stocked their boats with. The store being on the main dock next to the business office, Tammy had her ear to the source of important cannery gossip.

"What happened?" I said. "Fish stop swimming?"

"Fishermen stopped fishing," she said. The canneries had offered such a low price for a pound of pink salmon that the fishermen were meeting in town tonight to decide whether to strike.

"No kidding," I said. "I didn't know they had a union."

"Just started up. Caught everybody by surprise," she said.

Eight or ten rubber-booted cannery workers lounged on the dock benches or leaned against the railings, and when I stepped out of the store and lit a cigarette, they scrunched their eyes up and looked at me.

"Just heard about the strike," I said.

"Ain't no fish anyway," one of them said with a shrug.

"Red salmon run totally sucks, is what I heard," another said.

"I'm just here to detox," a third said. "I don't give a shit about the fish."
I felt like I was among my own people again. Like the man who has
wandered the earth in search of social justice and finally come home
because he couldn't even find a clean bathroom. Half a dozen cannery
workers rushed toward me when I offered cigarettes. I left them the pack
and went and said hello to Slim, the plant manager, who had just turned
into the office next door. Earlier in the summer—the year was 1997—Slim
had given me permission to tie my raft up at Port Bailey Cannery and to
shop at the cannery store and use the pay telephone. The cannery, owned
by Wards Cove Packing Company of Seattle, one of Alaska's major seafood
processors, was private property, after all, so I was grateful to Slim for his
indifference to my coming and going. He was always busy superintending
cannery operations and didn't pretend to be friendly, but he knew I wasn't
a fisherman, just a local homesteader, and figuring that I didn't have a dog
in the price dispute, he briefed me on the cannery's latest position. The
fishermen wanted 15 cents for a pound of pink salmon; the company offered
a nickel. One Kodiak cannery was willing to pay 15 cents, but they wouldn't
be able to handle the inevitable glut of salmon unless another company
like Wards Cove matched the price.

"And?" I said.

"I can't answer you," Slim coolly replied, "but I can tell you this." He
stopped in the doorway and nodded at the milling cannery hands. "The
ones being hurt when the fishermen don't fish are those kids. If this keeps
up, we'll have to send them home."

This was not an idle threat. When I returned to the cannery a few days
later, there was a grimness in the air and a dug-in fatalism in the faces of the
workers. Some of them were going home. From the company's perspective,
neither Mother Nature nor the fishermen were cooperating.

Tammy sighed and leaned her elbows on the store counter. "Not enough
fish coming in," she said. "If it doesn't get better, it's going to get worse."

"Your job safe?"

"Supposed to be through August, fish or no fish," she said. "Who knows?"

The wind had risen in the bay, a sign that I should head back to the
homestead. I had a yen for eggs and gave Tammy two dollars for a carton

of them, and she walked me across the dock and looked out at the water with me. "You'll get your eggs scrambled before you get home," she said.

She was right about that. The smell of raw eggs frankly revolts me, but that's exactly what I got on my raincoat that day after I stowed the carton of eggs in my waterproof float bag, thinking it would be cushioned by the clothes there. The seas were at my back, but in a raft you get knocked around, and when it was over I had just enough unbroken eggs for an onion and Tabasco omelet.

A round trip to Port Bailey Cannery, five miles east of Cottonwood, cost me a gallon and a half of gasoline. The cannery's pay telephone and its mail service, a twice weekly mail service by seaplane, were helpful to me when I needed to buy a tool or to talk with a supplier. When I ruined my power drill by leaving it outside in the rain, I used the cannery telephone to order a new drill, and a week later I boated to the cannery to see if my drill had arrived on the mail plane. Best of all, I could telephone Martina, and if she didn't answer, at least I heard her voice on the recording. In those days I was still learning how to be alone in the bush, and no matter how laborious it was to launch the raft by myself—it was laborious—I traveled to Port Bailey Cannery more often than I needed to just so I could see the people there.

There were fewer of them as the summer wore on. An enormous tramp steamer was anchored in the bay one day, and this was an ominous sign. A smaller boat, a Wards Cove tender, lay alongside it.

"Tramper's taking all the fish and salmon eggs we got," Tammy said.

"Taking it where?"

"Japan. Slim's emptying every freezer in the house." She led me next door and showed me a notice taped in the office window. *Cannery operations suspended as of July 31.*

"That's that," I said.

By the middle of August, the cannery was down to a skeleton crew. I roamed the premises and hardly saw anybody. A couple of Filipinos were tinkering in a bulbous metal skiff, talking softly in Filipino or in one of the Philippine languages. There was such a strong tradition of Filipinos working at Port Bailey Cannery, one of the bunkhouses was called the Filipino Bunkhouse.

PHOTO BY BUD CARTER

I found a letter from Martina in the mail crate in the cannery office.

"Sure appreciate you letting me get my mail here," I told Slim.

"Don't mention it," he said, not looking up from his paperwork.

"Cannery going to reopen?" I said. I had seen the Wards Cove tender picking salmon up from the local fishermen.

"No chance of that," Slim said. He didn't deny that Wards Cove was buying salmon again, but the harvest was being shipped to the company's Alitak plant at the south end of the island. I didn't want to irritate Slim by asking him how the company had resolved its price dispute with the fishermen, but when I went outside I found a relevant posting in the office window. Due to "an expected shortfall" of pink salmon, the price being paid to the fishermen had risen to 12 cents a pound effective August 1st.

Tammy joined me outside on the dock.

"What's the word?" I said.

"*Real* slow," she said, rolling her eyes. "Silver salmon and chum salmon runs have been lousy. Herring season was horrible. Fishermen gonna be hurting for money this winter."

"What about you?" I followed her into the store and bought a three-pack of Cracker Jack. I left one of the boxes on the counter for her.

"Still broke," she said. "Didn't get the overtime I wanted working nights on the line. It's been a crappy season."

In the third week of August I rafted back to Port Bailey Cannery to say goodbye to her. The cannery was deathly quiet now. I would soon head north to Fairbanks for the winter, and Tammy was moving on to a cannery in Dutch Harbor. She was glad to be able to say so.

Dutch Harbor turned out to be more than a one-time gig for Tammy. When I looked for her the following May at Port Bailey, the young woman behind the counter told me that Tammy had relocated to the Dutch Harbor plant.

"Good for her," I said. "Bet she cleans up there."

"Hopefully."

I introduced myself and we shook hands.

"I'm Alba," she said. "The foreman's daughter."

"You're kidding me."

"No. My father is José, the foreman," she said.

"I guess if I looked like you and worked in a cannery I'd be the foreman's daughter too," I said. "That's a pretty name, Alba. What's it mean?"

"It means dawn," she said. Alba's mother worked in the cannery kitchen, and her little brother was there, too. Alba had been coming to Port Bailey from Texas every year since she was a child. In round terms she looked to me about fifteen years old, and I didn't doubt that her mom and pop kept a close eye on her.

The cannery store stayed open that summer of 1998, but I didn't see as much of Alba as I'd seen of Tammy. Mostly I stayed at the homestead, finishing the cabin trim and interior. Martina and the kids would join me in August and I wanted the cabin to be ready for them. And Port Bailey wasn't as diverting as before because there weren't many people around. The cannery remained active, loaning nets and skiffs to the company fishermen; boats docked at the cannery; a fuel tender dispensed fuel there; but the fish processing operations, the canning and freezing lines, didn't reopen after their untimely closure last summer, and so the line crews didn't return, and without the workers there wasn't the old summertime liveliness at Port Bailey. The warmth was gone.

Even so, I rafted there to use the pay telephone and the mail service. I ordered a Stihl bar and sawchain from Jackovich Industrial in Fairbanks. I complained to Shakespeare Marine Technical Support about the lemon of a reconditioned radio they'd sold me. In the cannery store I bought an eight-pack of beef franks from Alba, and she went and got me a loaf of wheat bread from the cannery kitchen. It was a morning in June and I was her first customer of the day.

"You going to eat all those hot dogs?" she said.

"We're having a bachelor party, me and my neighbor," I said. "You know Richard Pederson[1]?"

"That old man? He's married, isn't he?"

"Yeah, it's just an expression. 'Bachelor party.' But yeah, his wife's not around. Mine neither."

"I knew you were married," she said.

"How'd you know?" I passed my hand in front of her eyes. "I don't wear a ring or anything."

"I just knew."

"How? Maybe I can do better next time."

Alba laughed and looked somewhere safe—at my split ends. "You got kids?" she said.

I made a peace sign. "Five and one," I said. "You?"

"No!"

Now it was my turn to laugh. "There's no hurry," I said. "Hey, I gotta make the tide, Alba. See you next time."

Port Bailey Cannery operated as a supply base for Wards Cove fishermen in transit to the fishing grounds of Bristol Bay and mainland Alaska. It also served as a regional headquarters for the tenders that freighted fish from the north island waters to the Wards Cove plant down at Alitak. But the heart of the old cannery, the canning and freezing lines, never restarted.

---

1 For simplicity, when I refer to Laurel Peterson and Richard Pederson as a couple—the Petersons—I spell the surname in accord with the example on their return address stamp. I am betting it was Laurel, the letter writer, who designed the stamp.

It would be some time before we understood how Port Bailey Cannery had been caught up in and doomed by the changing economics of the seafood industry in the 1990s, by the globalization of every segment of the seafood market, labor and supply as well as consumer demand. We saw the early signs, though. In September 1998, Wards Cove sent an appraiser to Port Bailey Cannery to determine the value of the plant machinery. According to Dennis Bell, the newly arrived cannery caretaker, the company wanted to borrow money on its hard assets. Why? Dennis, when I asked him why, gestured at his shabby clothes and his scruffy, blear-eyed face and said, "Do I look like they tell me?"

Nevertheless, Dennis speculated that Wards Cove planned to open a new cannery in Russia, where it already co-owned a plant with the Russian government. "Plenty of labor in Russia," Dennis said, "and the country's like Alaska, but industrially they're seventy-five years behind us, so there's still plenty of fish there."

Dennis and Barbara Bell lived in the modest caretaker's residence that overlooked the cannery from the hillside on the south. Their job was to maintain the machines over the winter and to mind the premises. They also monitored VHF radio channel 79, an important duty because Port Bailey remained a communications hub for the island's north coast. The Bells were people whose lives had been irrevocably touched by the ocean. Dennis had come to Alaska from Washington state in 1957, a deckhand on a halibut boat. His crewmate on the boat was Barbara's father. When Barbara visited Alaska, her father introduced her to Dennis, and they were married twenty-eight days later. "I thought any man who was okay by Dad was good enough for me," Barbara said.

After Martina and the kids joined me at Cottonwood, a boat trip to Port Bailey Cannery became a family excursion, an outing made memorable by the conversation and refreshments we enjoyed with the Bells, either up at their house or in the cannery's front office. Barbara had gathered boxfuls of paperback books and sweatshirts left behind by the cannery workers, and she let us pick through these and take what we wanted. We continued to make use of the mail service and the cannery telephone, and on mail days we crossed paths with peninsula neighbors whom we rarely saw otherwise.

Dennis had the job of weekly changing the oil in the Northern Lights generator, a 55-kilowatt generator that powered the dormant cannery in winter. The powerhouse also housed four diesel generators rated 250, 250, 400 and 420 kilowatts—enormous machines, yellow Caterpillars—plus a water system generator and circuit breaker panels for the entire cannery, the machine shop, the kitchen and bakery, bunkrooms, caretaker's house, the freezer compressors and so on, a reminder that a working cannery is like a small city. This is an aspect of canneries that always fascinated me, how the profit motive, or the motive to satisfy a popular appetite for seafood and to profit by doing so, led to the flourishing in remote parts of Alaska of these mechanized outposts of civilization. Two residences, apart from the caretaker's house, overlooked the cannery complex, the superintendent's house and a guest house, and below these, kitty-corner to the main processing plant, were the mess hall and living quarters for the workers: the Surf House, Island House and Filipino Bunkhouse. The cannery offices—front office, radio room, general store—were centered on the main dock, and a sprawling breezeway linked the offices to the cannery proper. In the breezeway a variety of boats and vehicles were parked: pickup trucks, four-wheelers, forklifts and seine skiffs. Port Bailey Cannery had a welding and machine shop, a wood shop, infirmary, laundry, battery shed, a "beach locker" where oil and chemicals were kept, and, at the edge of the dock where a boat could pull up to it, an ice house.

What we saw when we approached Port Bailey Cannery by sea from the west was the immense cannery itself projecting from the shore on pier and piles, a long white warehouse with thirteen square vented windows in its side and a tin roof. The several large, attached structures included a green-roofed hangar on which the seagulls often congregated. In front, at each of the seaward corners of the dock, a crane stood ready for lifting and lowering cargo. On one of the main facades the words PORT BAILEY were painted in huge black letters easily visible to the cannery crews arriving by seaplane.

Inside, the crews either froze or canned the incoming harvest of salmon. The freezers included five blast freezers that instantly crystallized the fish and a deep-freeze chamber that held above a million pounds of product at -30°F. The salmon, after being headed, gutted and washed on the slime line, were fast-frozen, glazed in a salt bath, packed in shipping boxes and moved into deep freeze. Five red compressors valued at $1.5 million compressed ammonia gas into liquid as part of the freezing process. There were tanks and valves and condensers at every turn. Water, power and refrigerant lines passed along the walls and overhead. As I explored the vast cannery, either alone or in the company of the various caretakers who came and went, I craned my neck looking up into its highest heights and farthest corners.

In May 1999 the Bells were replaced by the Garbers, John and Midge, another longtime Wards Cove couple, devoted to the company. A man like John Garber, who knew plumbing, electricity and diesel engine generators, who knew the working guts of a cannery and had the virtue of loyalty, was of tremendous value to a company like Wards Cove. When I walked the lines with John I learned details about the equipment that I never would have known or thought to ask. I had worked in canneries in Bristol Bay and Anchorage, I'd been a gutter, a giller, a spooner and a grader, I'd stood in slime lines and packing lines, cleaning and boxing herring, halibut and salmon, and I'd manned freezer lines, hefting my share of fifty-pound boxes, but these were low-level jobs of the sort in which the laborer, cut off from the greater design of the cannery, is too timid to ask questions for which he expects no answers or is too indifferent or muscle-weary to care.

Port Bailey Cannery had seven giant retort cookers for sealing the newly canned batches of salmon. The retort operator turned a wheel to open and shut these massive vats, each of which accommodated many hundreds of cans. The trays were slid in, a red light went on, and the cans were brought to a temperature of 260°F for seventy-two minutes. The heat was generated in an oil-burning boiler that stood upright in the middle of this array of vats. The salmon had been prepared beforehand, of course, on a mechanized butchering line that hadn't changed much since its invention early in the twentieth century. The despicable nickname of the machine, though, the "Iron Chink"—the machine was patented under this name—has fortunately gone the way of the prejudice that spawned it. The incoming fish were headed, tailed, gutted and pressure-cleaned by machine, then cut into can-size pieces. A salt pellet was dropped into each can, and a lid put on. Even with the automation, it took a shift of twenty-four souls to run the twin can lines. The workers guided the salmon through the cutting and filling machines, scraped the guts and trimmed the meat by hand when necessary, graded the salmon and removed the valuable roe to the egg house.

An entire can line was missing now, a few rollers left behind on the floor and some power cords dangling from the ceiling. John Garber told me that the apparatus had been shipped to Russia for Wards Cove's new venture there. As the company looked abroad for cheap labor and unexploited consumer markets, it streamlined its business at home by closing and consolidating plants. Alaska's seafood industry had been bleeding a hundred million dollars a year. The watchwords were efficiency and cost-cutting. In April I had seen several tenders leaving Port Bailey Cannery with fishing gear for the upcoming herring and salmon seasons, but also with dry goods taken from the shelves of the cannery store where Tammy and Alba used to work. If there's a sure sign that a cannery is dying, it's the closing of the company store. By the summer of '99 it was clear that Wards Cove meant to rid itself of Port Bailey Cannery. John Garber never gave me the skinny on a cannery sale, but once as we walked in the breezeway he pointed at a sixteen-foot Lund skiff and told me that Wards Cove would let me have it for a couple of hundred dollars if I wanted it.

John Garber was a large, kindly, patient man with a head of white hair and a Lincolnesque beard. He had commercially fished with a thousand-foot driftnet and had maintained entire canneries and fresh-frozen plants, but he still liked to fish from the dock with a simple rod and reel in the hope of catching a simple codfish, which he considered "not bad eating, if you scrape the worms off of 'em." Before John got too busy with his summer duties, we would sit on the dock and chat in the spring sunshine. I enjoyed hearing stories of his gold-mining operation on remote Tugidak Island in the Gulf of Alaska. Tugidak, one of the Trinity Islands south of Kodiak, a government-owned island protected for its harbor seals and other wildlife, officially has no human population, but John and Midge Garber, when they weren't caretaking canneries in the offseason, had lived on their Tugidak Island gold claim, a leasehold, since the 1980s. The gold was powder, not nuggets, and the work of separating it from the black sand of the beach was labor-intensive, to say the least. John used a four-wheeler and a trailer at low tide to move the sand, and at high tide he sluiced the sand to extract the gold. This amounted to moving tons of sand for a pittance of yellow metal. When I met John, the price of gold had fallen from $400 an ounce to $275, and the work no longer paid. "A guy does well to take out twenty ounces a year," John told me, "and you might use four ounces of that, or twelve hundred bucks, to charter to town and back to sell your gold."

John's wife, Midge, emerged smoking a Lucky Strike cigarette, and she sat with us on the dock and turned her face up in the sunshine. The fleece cap on her head was superfluous, but I have noticed that after winter some people wear a favorite hat out of habit or a feeling of security. A mutual acquaintance had advised me that Midge Garber had an "active imagination," and I suppose this was intended as a warning. It could be that living on isolated Alaskan islands and haunting out-of-the-way canneries does this to people, gives them an active imagination. Or maybe some of us, no matter where we live, are disposed to counter emptiness and loneliness with dreamy imaginings. Midge told me that having "copped out of the corporate world," she didn't plan to return to it, and when I asked her what corporate world she had copped out of, she confided to me that she had worked in government intelligence for twenty-six years. A grandmother, Midge had blue eyes and short blonde hair that converged to a point over either cheek. In her gaze a sharp intensity alternated with a lost-my-train-of-thought abstraction. With her ever-present Lucky Strikes and her convalescence from various ailments, Midge was perhaps not an undemanding woman, but John always appeared devoted to her and attentive to her needs, even when it meant forklifting a couch through the window of their house or launching the runabout to take her to sea. Midge's other protector was a light brown Yorkshire terrier named Woody who must have come into the world hot-style, biting its mother and snapping at its siblings. That Yorkie was a terror.

Port Bailey Cannery got busy again in early June before the commercial salmon fishing opened. The cannery remained a base from which the company loaned skiffs and nets to its fishermen. The *Viking*

Star and other boats docked at Port Bailey one day, and John was so busy helping the crews that he forgot to put his lower teeth in. There was an enormous red building called the web loft at the east end of the cannery complex, essentially a warehouse for lines and nets, the floor crowded with pallets on which folded salmon seines and herring seines were stacked, and here a fisherman might hang a fishnet from overhead cords to inspect and repair it. But despite these spurts of activity at Port Bailey Cannery, the decision had been made in Seattle to shut it down, and there was no talk of processing fish here again. The price disputes with the fishermen, the labor actions of the up-and-coming United Salmon Association, the financial and moral drag of *Wards Cove Packing Company v. Atonio*, an epic legal battle in which Wards Cove had been embroiled for a quarter-century—these added uncertainty to a market already challenged by the spread of aquaculture and foreign competition. The drive to consolidate was relentless. The *Blazer*, a Wards Cove tender that held a hundred thousand pounds of fish on ice, carried the local catch south to the company's Alitak cannery in Lazy Bay.

John Garber and I pondered what we would do with Port Bailey Cannery if we could buy it. With its bunkhouses, its docks, its anchorage and seaplane beach, the place had a fantastic appeal. Its greatest glory was its setting near the foot of Kupreanof Mountain in Dry Spruce Bay. John envisioned a summer camp for disabled kids. I had in mind a wilderness retreat or halfway house for "ornery" kids. We liked each other's ideas almost as much as our own.

I never saw John angry or despairing when he made the rounds of the fallen cannery. Wearing a Gold Miners Association of America cap, John was calmly Calvinistic about things. "You have one million fish one year, ten million the next," he said. "How do you prepare for that? You can't. It's too unpredictable. Right now, down at Alitak, they're going full steam because they've taken all the work this cannery used to do. At the moment there are more fish than you can say grace over, but the writing is on the wall. The future is in farmed fish, and Alaskans will have to join in that industry or lose out." In John's opinion, commercial fishing was as doomed as one-man gold mines.

After the Garbers left, another couple came on as caretakers, Brian and Melinda from San Antonio, Texas, and they were followed by a local couple from Kodiak. To me the cannery had become a melancholy place. When I wandered the cannery premises, I noticed the smaller things now, the details that evoked the people who had worked here and the routines they had followed: the hand dip station, the earplug dispenser, the cage full of rubber gloves, the warning signs about the machines and the dangers of moving parts. I could just about hear the clangor of the machines and see the fish-laden belts going by and feel the blast of cold air from the freezers. But mostly it was the absence of the workers that affected me, affected me as powerfully as if they had all been suddenly present, all the cannery hands who ever worked here, expended muscle and spirit here, all of that energy coalescing in a single great shout—an outcry—a crescendo, and then that too died away and I was alone in the echoing silence.

In the end the cannery was a ghost cannery, an echo of itself, killed off, finally, by the same modernization and the same balance-sheet logic that at one time had animated and made of it a thriving world. In its twentieth-century heyday, the cannery was a factory producing countless tons of canned and boxed salmon that fed countless people around the world. Port Bailey Cannery was sold for a comparative pittance in 2003, its grounds suspected of being contaminated by fuel and other hazardous wastes. The subsequent owners have met with mixed success in transforming the sprawling property into this or that profitable enterprise.

CIVILIZATION

I was never without light at Cottonwood. When the cabin was a mere shell and I rose shivering in the darkness, I read Cervantes by the light of a hissing gas lantern and amused myself before dawn. After my family joined me at Cottonwood, we relied for light on low-watt, 12-volt fluorescent lamps. We worked and played games by this light. The lamps drew their power from a pair of deep-cycle, 6-volt, lead-acid batteries, the same batteries that powered the 12-volt pump that delivered water to us from a 55-gallon polyethylene barrel in the southwest corner of the cabin. Every day or two we burned in a generator a small amount of gasoline to produce the electricity needed to recharge these batteries.

Although we homeschooled Miranda, her curriculum paralleled the curriculum of other first graders and followed the traditional stepping stones of civilization. We were free to petition the heavens with any jabberwocky we wanted, or not to pray at all, but Martina said her simple grace at meals, a grace she had learned in childhood, and I, a civilized, tolerant man, though not a baptized Christian, valued the deliberate pause as an opportunity to reflect.

Education, lights, running water ... it sounds incongruous that on moving into the Alaskan wild we so quickly adopted the rudiments of civilization. But I never set out to reinvent human nature, only to get reacquainted with it in myself. It's impossible to live in a vacuum and it's foolish to define self-reliance so extremely that to rely in any way on the goods and services others make available to us disqualifies us. We sprouted our own alfalfa, but we imported the alfalfa seed. We hunted the meat we ate, but we purchased the ammunition and rifle.

Coffee doesn't grow in Alaska, but most mornings at Cottonwood I enjoyed the indulgence of a pot of coffee percolated on a propane stove. The coffee traveled to Kodiak Island via the trade routes and market hubs that underpin civilization. The propane stove came from Sears. Would I consider my homestead life to be more authentic if I had never graduated beyond the Coleman camp stove? No, I would consider myself guilty of a willful drudgery. Why would the purist in me be satisfied with the iconic camp stove? To stay close to earth I should gather sticks in the morning and warm my knuckles over a smoky campfire. In doing this I would do nothing good for my marriage, but at least I would be pure. My wool cap would be carded, spun and woven by my own hands. The error in this portrait of purity is that I'm no monk and I never took vows to do without coffee and cocoa and cinnamon.

The difference between our lives at Cottonwood and the lives of most of our countrymen was a difference of proportion and perspective. We enjoyed none of the fashions and mass entertainments of the day and in turn were spared the manic harassments of advertising and the excesses of the mercantile economy. We knew enough about late twentieth-century American culture—frenzied, innocent years spawned by the merger of high finance and high technology, a minor Gilded Age wedged between the Blue Dress and the Dotcom Bust and terminated by the fall of the Twin Towers—to know that we lived outside of the mainstream, and we lived this way by choice, in the cultivation of our values or in the quest to recover the values we felt had been lost. What we craved was something basic or rudimentary, "some vigor of wild virtue," in Ralph Waldo Emerson's phrase. To maximize our joy in life, to actualize our time together, we focused our lives by simplifying them. And to grow in self-awareness, to grow beyond what our institutional educations had given us, we immersed ourselves in the nature that originated us. But we didn't live in a skin tent and treat our lacerations with bear dung while thumbing our noses at the masses of the lower latitudes. We used a small inverter to turn our 12-volt power into the familiar household current, and on this electric current Martina powered the IBM laptop computer (not a casual purchase in 1998!) on which she kept our homestead inventory. Our radio antenna was a Shakespeare antenna. Our medium-weight casting rod was a Shakespeare rod. Several of our machines burned gasoline. This catalog of possessions isn't meant to sound boastful. But my shame doesn't last long either. As much as I love the wilderness, I am inescapably a carrier of civilization. My schooling gave me the language to critique my civilization and perhaps even inspired me to try a life far removed from the loci of that civilization to see what the distance might do for my inward health and happiness.

At Cottonwood we relished our modest comforts because we knew what their absence looked like, there having been nothing here beforehand but wilderness. The costs of transportation to the homestead added value to every tool and foodstuff that made the journey. We took nothing for granted. Being hands-on responsible for the electric generator, we didn't run it longer or burn more fuel in it than necessary. Because we supplied our water, we wasted none. By providing water and light and education on our terms and at our cost, we ended up not with less appreciation of civilization but, I think, with more.

On leaving Cottonwood I hoped we wouldn't lapse too easily into the habits of lazy consumption. Our nervous systems slowly adjusted to the jagged edges of advertising and the ridiculous braggadocio of television. We were astounded by the luxury of the on-demand amenities in our hotel room. A telephone five steps away, not a five-mile boat ride! A reliable electric current twenty-four hours a day! Water faucets with perpetually hot running water! It got better all the time. Our own flush toilet! In exchange for an honest-to-God flush toilet we surrendered the freedom to step outside and piss where we pleased. Two-year-old Kodiak was the least willing to sign on. He turned into a corner of the hotel room and cheerfully wet the carpet, marking his territory, as was his custom. What did Kody want with pissing in a porcelain pot and washing it down with gallons of good water?

Civilization and wilderness are fundamentally incompatible. The advance of one is the recession of the other. Frederick Jackson Turner, the historian of the American frontier, describes civilization as being disintegrative of wilderness. Civilization values the growth of cities, the farming of crops, the ranching of livestock; it values settlement over wilderness, and it finally commodifies the wilderness and overruns it with visitors. Civilization harnesses nature and excludes what it can't use, and where it finds wilderness in its midst, it stamps it underfoot as you and I would stamp flames out, fearful what they might grow into. Wilderness is civilization's fantasy, its wish fulfillment. The "nature spaces" incorporated into the opulent headquarters of today's technology companies have more in common with the Gardens of Babylon and Versailles than they have with wilderness. The energy and aerospace companies, those other bulwarks of civilization, continue to encroach on and to shrink our wild spaces. What civilization can't exploit is fenced off, driven out or exterminated. When my children spilled food at Cottonwood where the brown bears might smell it, I reacted with swift discipline. But here in town, where I didn't worry about brown bears smelling the spill and lumbering through the hotel looking for it, and where in any case the maids were employed to tidy up, my caution was vestigial, and the children crumbed on the floor and dribbled on the bed with impunity. Why worry? Let the kids be kids.

Historians apply the word *civilization* to any remarkable apex of human prosperity and its foundational culture, no matter how uncivilized by our lights or how savage the culture may have been. To appreciate civilization we need to appreciate our stake in it, but it isn't enough to be glad about suspension bridges and art museums; it also behooves us to recognize the threats to civilization. The dangers to our own civilization are manifold: megaquakes, supervolcanos, asteroids, environmental and climatic upheaval, pandemics and superbugs, technological implosion, cyberwar, nuclear war, fiscal collapse, domestic rebellion, moral exhaustion ... several of which threats originate in nature, in raw nature and the eruption of forces beyond our control. Nature in its superordinate reality puts into humbling perspective the frantic world of human interests. Our civilization is tenuously erected on a substrate of wilderness, the wilderness inside us and the wilderness outside, and the principles of nature apply to a civilization as they apply to an untenanted wilderness cabin. I've seen it happen again and again in Alaska. Decay sets in and nature reclaims what belongs to it. I have used these terms loosely, *nature* and *wilderness*, but they aren't equivalent. We can have nature without wilderness, but we can't have wilderness without nature. Nature is ineradicable. Wilderness is lost by those who never knew what it looked like, but the rules of nature, of wild life and wild country, don't disappear because wilderness does; no, not though many a technocrat and schoolteacher would have it otherwise.

Our civilization may be superior to most or all that preceded it, but I don't always like what I see. In town again after sixteen months in the outback, I find in the hotel lobby a recent edition of the *Anchorage Daily News*. My complimentary coffee in hand, I settle down for an engaging read. How dispiriting it is! "U.S. the world's top arms dealer." President Clinton's prosperous America the world's top gun runner! We had just been bombing the hell out of the Balkans, so it worked out profitably for all parties except the murdering sods we targeted. There was lots of giddy chatter in those days about the stock market, and the public were encouraged to invest money not only in the internet companies but also in the defense companies, i.e., the arms manufacturers. This too is civilization.

But even when I didn't like what I saw, it was impossible for me, returned to civilization from bush Alaska, not to marvel at the far-reaching inventiveness on display around me, at the networks of communication and transportation that people had built, at the intelligence these relied on and the cooperation that underlay the prosperity, a prosperity that enriched the community and the state as well as the nation, a prosperity more democratic than an imperfect humanity had ever known. My optimism that evening at our celebratory back-to-civilization dinner at Henry's Great Alaskan Restaurant was unfeigned.

After dinner the children wanted to return to the hotel room and watch television. Their indulgent mother went with them. I wandered the Kodiak waterfront toward the City Dock, and I tramped back to town along Shelikof Street. Across from the internet café, I stopped at the railing and looked out at the boats in St. Paul Harbor, remembering our leave-taking of the year before. Two hot mochas and a box of fishing line ... this was our last-minute purchase before we boarded the cargo boat and embarked for Cottonwood Homestead and our life in the bush, a life at the edge of civilization but not outside of it, or not beyond the pale of the taxing authority. Our year at Cottonwood had gone quickly, and toward the end Martina and I discussed whether to make our homestead life a permanent one. She almost said yes. Some days were gifts, she said, echoes of paradise, and, fresh from her healthy exertions, she couldn't imagine living anywhere else. Life at Cottonwood had strengthened her commitments and helped her to see what she wanted and why, she said, and she would cherish her time there as one of the best times in her life. But we had two children who had to make their way in the world, in the civilized world, and she didn't want to risk hobbling them by bringing them up in the isolation of the homestead.

I understood her. Our choices, hers and mine, had led us to Alaska and to the Kodiak wilderness, but to impose such a life on the children, a life so far out of the mainstream, to start them out in this way, didn't seem fair. The truth was that I wanted to stay at Cottonwood and she didn't, and the only thing I wanted more than to stay at Cottonwood was to be with her and the children, wherever they were. This too is civilization.

Civilization's interests are so tangled that when we invest money in a company that manufactures explosive weaponry we might be indirectly funding a medical breakthrough that saves lives in the country we're bombing. We don't get a line-item veto with respect to civilization, but sooner or later most of us get a reason to be grateful for it. One night at Cottonwood, Martina suffered an attack of anaphylaxis that nearly killed her. We never knew what triggered the attack, but the doctors later compared it to a full-blown asthma attack. Not being asthmatic, Martina didn't have available any of the emergency measures that a person with experience might have brought to a remote place like Cottonwood. As a result she nearly suffocated. The attack came in the dark of night, with repetitions into the next day as we tried to get a seaplane to pick us up. The flying conditions were poor and I couldn't rouse anyone by radio. In our desperation we were reduced to shaping an SOS on the beach using driftwood for the S letters and a wooden palette for the O.

It was one of the nightmarish nights of my life, and the children were naturally terrified. Our relief was just as great when a seaplane arrived and we got Martina to Providence Medical Center in town. The doctors medicated her, and her breathing normalized. You feel older and wiser and tenderer after such an ordeal. The dark cloud lowers and passes on.

Civilization isn't ghostly pyramids or glittering opera houses or smartphone assembly plants. Civilization is much more than that. Civilization is people, a grandly working homestead of hundreds of millions of people who come together to build and operate flying machines and municipalities and well-stocked schools and hospitals. After our near disaster at Cottonwood, we never returned to the homestead without renting a satellite telephone for maintaining an alliance with, and a lifeline to, our civilization.

COTTONWOOD

The cabin is salmon-colored with a green pitched roof and a radio antenna standing off the west end of the roof. It occupies a meadow of moss and fireweed that overlooks the ocean on the north and is overlooked by a mountain on the south. The Kupreanof Peninsula's land pattern is one of mountains and glacial valleys, the coast lowlands rising steeply inland or in places opening into wetlands. Dark, rolling spruce forest alternates with mossy swales and meadows bright with forbs and wildflowers. Thickets of alder and salmonberry are common, shrub willow omnipresent. Creeks and numberless rills course through the country, the direction of their flow determined by the mountains that run the interior length of the peninsula. Wild animal trails web the peninsula from sea level to the top of Outlet Cape at land's end.

The Sitka spruce is the dominant tree here, and in most places it's the only tree except for the common alder. Hard by the cabin the spruce forest looms up like the prow of a great ship which during a storm bears ominously down on us. We also have a grove of black cottonwood trees down the middle of the homestead where the ground is low and damp. Fisherman Mike Resoff tells me that his father, a fisherman, fished offshore here and called this area the Cottonwood Set, and that's how the homestead got its name, because Mike suggested the name Cottonwood for our radio handle. Seen from the water, the cottonwood trees stand out for the fair green of their summer foliage and their burst of yellow in the fall.

Raspberry Island, across Kupreanof Strait from us, is a long, rolling mountain with gentle peaks and laps of land that catch the sunshine and the snow. Whether the sea is satiny blue or gray and tempestuous, whether the sky is clear or buttermilk or overcast, it's always Raspberry Island we see when we look out the north windows in the morning. This isn't strictly true. In a heavy fog we won't see Raspberry Island or much of anything else. The marine weather is swift to turn, and if we're at sea in the raft, we usually won't go farther than the middle of the strait, say a mile and a half out, though we occasionally motor across to Raspberry Island and explore the spruce-shadowed beaches.

Behind the cabin, the land rises dramatically. Spruce trees cluster on slopes that are emerald green or golden brown or ermine white with the season. I have names for my favorite ascents of the mountain—the Chute, the Keyhole—and names for certain terrain formations on the summit—Bristle Top, High View Dome, Three Cartridge Dome, Shangri La Lakes. Brown bear and Sitka black-tailed deer range across the mountain summit. There is much seclusion and beauty here, much deep breathing and wide gazing.

The view from the mountaintop is to either shore of the peninsula, to Kupreanof Strait in the north and to Shelikof Strait and Viekoda Bay in the west and south. South lies Uganik Island, and to the west the horizon is crenelated by the snow peaks of the Alaska Peninsula. This prodigious land remains the home of the Alutiiq people, the region's first inhabitants, whose ancestors paddled to the archipelago more than 7,500 years ago. Some Alutiiq also use the designator Sugpiaq, meaning "real person."

Over time the volcanos of the mainland have rained on Kodiak Island the ash that makes up a large part of our soil here. It's a clayey soil, and if I dig a pit or a posthole in it, I will likely reach, four feet down or so, a table of trapped water that has drained through the soil but not penetrated the glacial till below, a layer of ground rock left behind by the glaciers that twenty millennia ago overlay this land.

Kupreanof Mountain, a 2500-foot peak named for one of the governors of Russian America, rises starkly to the east of Cottonwood. Even in June this mountain, its top often hidden in clouds, weeps long lines of snow. The mountain's steepness supports nothing but rockslides of black scree until, lower down, the vegetation takes hold and the greenery fills out over the shoreline. Kupreanof Mountain stands as an imposing northern bulwark, but a mountain has many faces, and this one, if approached from the east,

has a gentler aspect, ascending gradually like the broad back of a whale and without the forbidding bluntness of the north and west faces.

When President Franklin Roosevelt established the Kodiak National Wildlife Refuge in 1941, it included the Kupreanof Peninsula, but in a turn of the horse-trading that has characterized the history of realty in modern Alaska, Kupreanof Peninsula was withdrawn from the refuge in 1958 by a public land order—Alaska statehood was imminent, and Alaska Native interests were in play. This turn of events made possible a modicum of human settlement and therefore has a bearing on my presence here.

The country is so vast and its vegetation so profuse that it's easy to miss the cabin on its hill, and I have overflown it in a seaplane without seeing it on the first pass. It is wonderful to arrive on a sunny day when the warmth of the mother planet exudes through all the tips of the grasses. I will soon be at work transporting my supplies and removing the bear guards from the door and windows, but there is time for all of that, and I like to linger on the beach for a while, glad to be back and steeping my senses in it, smelling the salt murk, feeling on my skin the spritz of the waterfall, and watching a salmon leap and an eagle glide by. To return, to find myself here again, it is to pick up the thread of a marvelous dream.

On the cliffs at Cottonwood, where the land fronts the sea, life is embroiled in earth and rock. The tendony spruce roots are not always strong enough to hold the soil in place, and the trees sometimes descend or tumble onto the beach. The beaches are littered with boulders of shale and slate and speckled granite. The boulders buttress the sea cliffs, but not stably, and blocks of stone fall and shatter below. The dark hues of the shale and slate match the plumage of the bald eagle and add to the brooding primevalness of Kodiak's north coast.

Time has strengthened my attachment to this place. With time I note where the cliffs erode, where a bog has spread or shrunk, where a sapling has flourished. I know where the marsh violets gather and where the white anemone blooms, where the stream runs deepest and how far from its mouth the wild chive grows, and I know where the hares frolic and by what trails the bears come and on which rock the seabird suns itself. Where the devil's club musters, where the deer hide molders, where the sea tides conspire to entrap me, where the red sun blazes between mainland peaks at sunset—all of this I know. It seems to me that a love for the land doesn't precede a relationship with it but comes with the achievement of one. Acquisitiveness is different, a kind of lust, a feeling I have known as well. The love comes through study and respect, the reading of signs and fathoming of moods. I believe it's a two-way bond between me and the land and that the land responds to being loved well. It's so with Cottonwood and me. I will never possess this land, and I understand that, too. The land possesses me and we are one.

DEER

After my father died, my mother designed a memorial card in which she incorporated a Hokusai image of a solitary deer accompanied by this haiku of Buson—

Calling three times,
then no more to be heard—
the deer in the rain

—and this image radiated through my thoughts as I witnessed the ordeal of the black-tailed deer in winter. They staggered through the snow and scratched for food and starved. Some of them descended to the beaches and subsisted on seaweed. The beach was land's end for the deer, and for some it was the final shore. A deer lay down and died while the otters and ducks swam by. In the beauty of the day there was this cruelty.

Carcasses came to light as the snow melted: skin and bones at the far end of winter's beaten path. One day, a brightness of rubies drew me into a glade where the blood-dyed ribs of a deer protruded from the sunlit moss.

On a warm day in late April—better news—I met a pregnant doe feeding on seaweed. She looked nearly ready, bulging in the barrel. Head lowered, her ears folded back, she nibbled the algae. Then she raised her face and stared at me, her ears stiff and pointed to either side, a green leaf of sea lettuce hanging from her lip. At length she turned and ambled off, her black tail pressed down firmly on her rear. She had been eating more than just the tender sea lettuce. The hollow brown stalk of a bull kelp—rap on it with your knuckles, you'll see how tough it is—gleamed with the chisel marks of her teeth. She had gnawed up and down the length of the stalk and eaten the outer tissue.

As a species, the Sitka black-tailed deer is a transplant to Kodiak Island, and I find this remarkable because their presence seems so natural here, coeval with the land itself. I suppose their native habitat, the coastal rainforests of southeast Alaska and northern British Columbia, is comparable to Kodiak Island. They have an air of belonging, of being intimately tuned to the rhythms that order their lives here. The deer are masters of the quiet, whether stepping through the forest or browsing in shrubbery, and for every time I have hiked past a deer and known it, I am sure to have gone by many times unawares.

They are diverse in personality: skittish, playful, trusting, bold. These are anthropocentric words, yes, but the words correlate with behaviors we recognize in other species. Curiosity is a deer turning to me when I click my tongue or wave a cow parsnip leaf. Loyalty is a deer lingering at the side of its slain companion. Innocence is a spotted fawn imitating its mother's caution by staring into the distance—but staring in the wrong direction. The deer have grace and dignity without the brute kingliness of the Kodiak brown bear or the out-of-reach hauteur of the bald eagle. They are gentle. They endure.

For two months one summer we had a regular visitor to the homestead, a Sitka black-tailed deer named Sawbuck. He was breakfasting on fireweed and salmonberry shoots one morning, and he subsequently returned twice a day, morning and late afternoon. Curious, friendly, a black diamond at his brow, Sawbuck nibbled the irresistible greens at the edges of our dooryard. If we startled him, he leaped back in reflex, but he always reconsidered. If I helloed him, if I spoke to him at all, a reluctance overcame him, his brown eyes raised toward me, his ears twitching and nose quivering, and I think he may have struggled with himself, this wild deer whom the children had named Sawbuck, trying to decide who he was and who he wanted to be in life, knowing in his heart of hearts that he was getting too close to us humans.

At the June solstice Sawbuck's antlers were just emerging from his head, but a month later his velvet antlers had grown and branched. Martina was baking blueberry muffins one morning when she opened the cabin door and found Sawbuck standing there. We almost set a place for him at the table. He appeared one last time at the end of July, just before the start of hunting season, and after that we never saw him again. It amuses me to say he was giving himself a running start, but the hunting pressure is minimal here, and he likely moved on by instinct, heading uphill as his hormones and the shortening days dictated.

Kodiak's deer population rises and falls according to the winter's harshness and its effect on the mortality and food supply. A hunter's harvest limit varies accordingly. We ate a lot of venison when we lived full-time at Cottonwood, but I never thought of deer hunting as just a meat harvest. To hunt is to find and kill game, true, but in this it becomes an intense negotiation between the hunter and his world, between nature and the self. Every cross-country hunt has a corresponding inner hunt that shapes the mind and emotions of the hunter.

Early one morning after an autumn hunt, I woke to the pelting sounds of a gusting wind, the sort of wind that frees the spruce scales from the cones, and as I listened, I worried that the game bag was getting wet or that it would blow down from the tree and the brown bears would find it, so I went outside and checked. Everything was fine. The sky was clear and starry, and the venison hung securely on its branch.

Inside I lay down and laced my fingers behind my head, and as I reviewed the hunt from beginning to end, every step of it came back to me. This always happens after a hunt. It's a way of spending time with the deer again. Spirit time. I didn't need the binoculars, because the deer stood in the open, almost black against the snow. The crust on the snow made it impossible for me to descend toward him in silence, and he knew I was there. He led me on an extended chase down into the valley and through the willows in the valley bottom. At the end I hunkered in the willows and the deer lost track of me. He hadn't thought I would stick it out for so long. I got up on my knee and made the shot.

SAWBUCK, IN JULY

I took the quarters, the backstraps, the tenderloins, the rib meat and what was good of the neck. Every now and then I straightened my back and scanned the area for brown bears. It must have been forty degrees out. A stream wound through the snowy valley, and the spruce forest swept down to the sea. Afterwards I washed my hands in the snow.

In the fat years the deer are plentiful, and in the lean years the deer are scarce. I have hunted in lean years and come away with no deer at all. I once spotted a mature buck in dense vegetation, but I was above him on a ledge with no easy way down, so I didn't take the shot, not knowing that I wouldn't see another deer that year. The die-off of deer would have been catastrophic for my family if we had truly depended on the hunt for food and faced famine instead. This is true for the brown bear as well. The introduction of deer to Kodiak Island has enriched the brown bear's diet, but a deer comes as a windfall of meat, not a prey on which the bear depends for survival. To reckon with nature isn't only to glory in it, it is also sometimes to suffer with it. An elderly acquaintance recalls that his father saw the family through the Great Depression by hunting deer and pheasant "out of season," that is, by obeying a commandment of nature more deeply rooted in us than the regulations of a game board. This is the truth within the truth and the law within the law. Nature is hard on the living.

As a matter of fact, I saw a lot of young animals that year—fox and kits, bear and cubs, beaver and kits, a young eagle dragging its talons through the water as it practiced hunting at sea. And I went away with a feeling that things were well with the wilderness. But even in the best of times, the balance is precarious, and I covered a lot of ground that year without seeing another deer.

Sometimes nature has the Edenic sweetness that we wish it always had. I came to a standstill one day because of a deer in my path, and she wasn't alone. Two other does and three fawns were in her band. We were surrounded by fireweed, willow, wild rose and salmonberry, and at the margins, alder and cottonwood. What happened next was a sort of coming out, a showing off of their babies to me. In no hurry to be gone—they first had to know what sort of creature I was—the deer stepped gingerly around me and nosed the fireweed stalk that I bent toward them. Their moist noses glistened. They were in a trusting, maternal haze and believed only good of the world, and at that moment so did I.

DIVIDENDS

After the children were born, Martina, a practical and provident woman, matured with great rapidity. I was less hasty about it. On the other hand, she would never have shuttered her office in Fairbanks and come homesteading with me if finances—money—had been her life's priority. Our homestead expenses were low, near subsistence level, but we did have expenses: a seaplane charter, a new tool, the groceries we sometimes ordered by mail. The mortgage on our Fairbanks house was paid by the tenants, but we had no income, and while most of our homesteading costs had been met up front—we arrived at Cottonwood with a year's supply of provisions and fuel—a profit-and-loss analysis of the homesteading, one which factored in "lost income" and the absence of a "wealth-building strategy," would have yielded bleak results, and with two young children to care for and no health insurance, I think we understood we had little margin for error.

In these circumstances the dividend payments we received from the Alaska Permanent Fund came as a bonanza. For our family of four, the payments totaled above $6,000. That's a lot of money to get for just living in a place. My one-year-old's income that fall was the same as mine.

The Permanent Fund is a profit-sharing investment fund set up by the State of Alaska for the benefit of Alaskans, and because it is capitalized by oil revenues, many Alaskans metaphorically hold their noses when they cash their dividend checks. I'm sure the activist is out there who tears his check in half, drops the pieces in the trash and high-fives himself in the mirror, but I haven't met him. Some Alaskans look on the annual dividend as hardship money, a compensation for Alaska's high cost of living. Critics see the payment as hush money, i.e., payees are being bought off by the oil companies and their allies in Juneau and Washington. I don't understand the hullabaloo. At bottom, all social organization works on the principle of hush money, of buying off and being bought off, of giving up X in exchange for Y. It's called the social contract.

Homesteading, in which the homesteader drops out of the prevailing economic system, is not something the homesteader does to get rich, certainly not rich in the conventional pocketbook sense. But there are riches and there are riches, and for us, Kodiak Island proved a treasure island which, in experience, in self-reliance and in love of nature, in love of all creation, enriched us beyond measure. And later, when we had given up our Alaska residency and no longer received the dividend checks, we never stopped drawing strength and sustenance from our lives at Cottonwood. On this we draw lifetime dividends.

I heard about a multimillionaire who bought a palatial vacation retreat on nearby Raspberry Island and who repaired there one week a year. I was fascinated by this, I mean by the notion that one could travel from the Lower 48 states all the way to Raspberry Island for a week and in that interval restore oneself or do anything more than snap a photo, snag a salmon and pant for breath. I felt a wry compassion for the man. The land bestows riches on anyone who abides on it and sinks muscle and heart into it, the riches of simplicity and freedom and a life grounded in natural rhythms. But such riches are withheld from the hurried multimillionaire, not because he is rich but because of the way of life his riches have imposed on him.

I might say the same of my billionaire hedge fund friend in Manhattan. He, knowing of my Alaska connection, emailed me the itinerary of a yacht trip he proposed to take through Southeast Alaska. He asked my opinion of the journey, and in my opinion it looked marvelous. He showed a laudable thrift in keeping the projected cost of the cruise under a hundred thousand dollars. The itinerary doubled as a detailed invoice, so I had an idea of his investment in the journey. As he traveled he would know what each leg of his journey was worth.

"Honest to God," you'll chide me, "it makes no difference how much money a person has. Let others root in the dirt if they wish. If I were rich I'd keep lavish digs in Venice, Vail, New York and Alaska. It's better to shuttle around Alaska in a luxury yacht than never to see it at all. A tycoon enjoys nature as much as anyone does. Rich men and women give millions to research and philanthropy. You don't understand how satisfying it is to be so disgustingly, filthily rich!"

I agree with much of what you've said, and I couldn't have said it better. I think I understand how my billionaire friend feels about his attainments because we discussed it one afternoon over chai lattes in Brentwood. He expressed his feelings using two familiar phrases. He felt he had "won the lottery," and he gloried in his freedom to "live off the fat of the land," ways of speaking figuratively about life that suggest ripeness, joy, plenitude and good fortune. My wealthy friend's characterization revealed both his modesty and his sense of the miraculous, and for me it didn't take too great a feat of empathy (though I had never walked in his Prada shoes) to understand what he meant by his words, because in conversation I might have chosen identical phrases—winning the lottery, living off the fat of the land—to summarize my own happy exuberance about my life in Alaska.

A man who grows a multibillion-dollar hedge fund out of seed money has every reason to feel pride and vindication in his achievements. But to say of a man who has spent his adult life taking long and short positions in equities, placing currency bets, leveraging his way into boardrooms and squeezing threepenny earnings beats out of corporate officers, to say of this man who earns and burns through millions of dollars in minutes, to say of my talented friend that from the deck of a passing yacht his feel for the shore will be superficial and that he won't fathom the glories of a landscape in a ten-day luxury tour, not merely because the ten-day term is inadequate but more importantly because he lacks the training for it, the deep exposure to the place and the conditioning of his senses, to say these things of my friend is not, I think, out of line. I might sit in the VIP room at Sotheby's or tour a high-speed trading operation or make the pilgrimage to Davos once in my life, and my financier friend, seeing me in any of these situations, might with justice observe, "He can't possibly know what sort of game we're playing here."

We could each of us learn, of course, but the point is that by following our inclinations we had come to very different places in life.

In my case it was far out of the economic mainstream. It's a measure of how far out of the mainstream I and Martina had drifted since our salad days in college that the Wall Street and internet manias of the 1990s were nearly lost on us. From our bush outpost we got wind, occasionally, of the national obsession with the stock market and the fortunes being made in the internet companies, and while we thought it generally a good thing if people were better off than before, we ourselves had more or less escaped the cash economy, and we didn't regret it. We were laying up other treasures.

Martina, who had closed her one-woman law office in Fairbanks, saw her coming to Cottonwood with me, her opting for the homestead life, as a bid for peace and emotional focus, for an unencumbered family life. "Whatever I'm doing, I'm always thinking of something else," she said, and she wanted to change that, to live the fullness of each moment with her children, to live consciously and from the inside out. To do the opposite, to live from the outside in, is what the everyday economy, the cash-and-credit world of retail sales, taxes, margins, credit scores, interest rates, all of the little tricks we learn for coming out ahead, for taking in a little more so that we may spend a little more—to live from the outside in is what the cash-and-credit world, incessantly warping us with impersonal and pecuniary pressures, forces us to do.

I inspected a boat one day with a friend who had determined to buy it. The boat was a 30-foot, extra-wide, all-weld aluminum skiff with an inboard Volvo engine. My friend didn't want an inboard engine and had no intention of paying the asking price of $9,000. At the bank he withdrew $6,000 and hid a thousand of it in his pocket. He explained to me how the deal would go down. "I put five thousand on the table," he said, "and I spread those bills in front of him so he can't look away. If he says, 'Six and it's yours,' I'll take it."

The seller never even held out for the extra grand. My friend ran that Volvo engine into the sea, jettisoned it, sealed the hold, hung his favorite outboard motor off the stern, and sailed his new skiff happily into the sunset. He had perfected a technique of reverse cash merchandising whereby his $5,000 became the desired product. He sold the mouth-watering five grand to the other fellow for the price of a boat. The cash was the prime mover in the deal, and other notions of value and fairness were pegged to it or forgotten. The seller became the buyer and didn't know it.

In the dollar economy, we get played like this more often than we realize. We keep our eye on the cash where we once considered the worth of a thing or the dignity of the labor or the loving relationships we had gone to work to preserve. Around and around we chase a prize we never get enough of, and we're soon running for the sake of running, afraid to stop running lest we lose our place to another.

At Cottonwood we respected the virtue, the necessity, of thrift, but beyond that we had no conscious economic agenda. Nevertheless, working for ourselves and in isolation from the larger economy was, I believe, a precondition for our feeling as wonderfully free as we felt at Cottonwood— and for receiving the immaterial dividends that came with that freedom. Just to do that, just to get off the economic treadmill instead of jostling to get on it, not to treat everyone and everything that crosses your path according to its perceived material worth, according to whether and how much it sets you up and advantages you—just to do this expands the sense of belonging in a wholesome order and, by increasing the joy you take in small things, prepares you to discover the invisible treasures around you.

Martina sometimes took me to task for my understating the importance of moneymaking. She acknowledged my arguments in favor of, the "selling points" of, a small-is-beautiful life in the wild: the healthful immersion in nature, the making the most of our youth, the unique education for the children, the incalculable rewards of living for a season unburdened by the social deadweight that attaches to us at birth and that we carry to our creaking ends: all of these, the moral and spiritual dividends that our life at Cottonwood profited us, she acknowledged, but she nonetheless feared that we were falling into poverty, slipping "backwards" in the way her immigrant parents would have meant the word. We debated the economics of Cottonwood Homestead as we debated the laws of nature and of survival, and as always I was indebted to her for engaging me in robust and thoughtful discourse.

I have many times in my homestead solitude breathed the good air and looked on the wildflowers and the forest and heard the birdsong and ached in my heart for my loved ones and thought *I am a wealthy man*, and this though I had very little in the way of cash reserves; not just wealthy but almost impossibly privileged in being the beneficiary of so many blessings; grateful that this fullness that brought me such joy and that I valued as priceless had come to me as a boon not by inheritance, unless as a human inheritance, not by any of those skin-deep parameters that obsess a limited mentality, but by sympathy and inclination, and by listening to myself, by rarely being satisfied with the first answer that came my way, and by the sum total of the many qualities that compose who I am.

EAGLE

If there's an animal that evokes the north coast of Kodiak Island for me, it's the bald eagle perched in a seaside spruce tree. The eagle's size, its plumage, its simple but regal features make it unforgettable. The eagle lights on a bough or a driftwood snag, a crag or a grassy clifftop, and pairs of them guard our beach with the imperial disdain of centurions. They seem to do nothing but watch, keen-eyed and aloof, all-seeing and inscrutable, revealing nothing.

Eagles are predators and scavengers, and what they watch for is food, but it doesn't diminish their superiority that they eat meals like the rest of us. An eagle holds himself so frostily upright, it's a wonder he doesn't fall backwards off his perch. A primmer, more erect posture you never saw. I'm an underling, a shlub on the beach compared with him and his lofty gazing at the horizon. If he notices me, it's by glacially turning his head and eyeing my carcass, and if my existence irritates him enough, he'll step off his branch and glide to a superior perch.

When I am beachcombing, I may not be aware of the raptor's presence until I see the shadow of her outspread wings or hear the rustle of her feathers above me. If I unwittingly approach her nest, the eagle shrieks at me and dashes overhead. They don't like to mingle with the lesser birds, but if we're cleaning a catch of fish on the beach, an eagle may condescend to land and, always the patrician, she'll stand apart while the seagulls squabble among themselves over a length of intestine.

The eagle's aquiline bill and priestly plumage—black habit, white collar—contribute to its noble image. The eagle's totemic majesty is such that I was disappointed the first time I heard one open its mouth. The cry was laughably high-pitched. I had expected something defiant and heaven-resounding, a Wagnerian wail worthy of the name eagle, and what I got was a soprano bleat.

With time I grew accustomed to the icy shriek of the bald eagle. This is what angels would sound like without their human hormones and their trumpets. The cry of the eagle is a pure celestial echo, a distillation of the skyey heights it flies.

It's hard to think of bald eagles as frisky and sociable, but their dour demeanor changes during spring courtship and breeding. Eagles answer to the same god Eros as the rest of us. The eagles of Kupreanof Peninsula wheel in topless columns, soar in linked spirals, whistle in exultation and tag one another in the sky. Their spring frolics are a delight to watch. I've seen couples tumble earthward with their talons entwined. Eagles are said to be life mates, romantically loyal and sharing in their parental duties.

We encountered a dozen or so eagles by a mountain lake one morning, and they appeared to be playing a game or running a flight clinic. At least half of them were juvenile eagles. One by one, the eagles flew across the lake, skimming just above its surface, and disappeared over the precipice beyond. Every bird took its turn until the last bird was alone on the lakeshore. The eagle shifted its feet and flapped its wings but refused to fly. As the minutes went by, the other eagles whistled and clucked in encouragement or impatience. An adult eagle floated overhead and surveyed the situation. Finally the holdout took flight. In a few wingbeats the eagle cleared the lake and soared out over the green cliffs. It was a balmy July morning, the rock ridges bright with the blooms of Kamchatka rhododendron. When the eagles had tired of riding the winds, they lit directly on the green slopes. We had never seen bald eagles so sociable. We at first assumed there must be a carcass in the area, but the eagles were simply celebrating the day as we were, no other explanation necessary. It was good to be an eagle and good to be alive.

On a freezing winter day at sea level, the eagles watch impassively from the spruce trees. The wads of snow caught in the tree branches give the eagles a wintry camouflage by reducing the conspicuousness of their white-feathered heads. Their dark torsos blend in with the slates and

olives of the shoreline. Bald eagles don't need much camouflage since we humans left off massacring them, but the concealment helps when they still-hunt for prey. These raptors aren't as shiftless and cowardly as high-profile observers like Ben Franklin and John J. Audubon made them out to be. Police in the Netherlands recently trained bald eagles to intercept enemy drones. Eagles don't just feed on whatever carrion they find lying on the ground; they are active as thieves and hunters, too. I watched an eagle steal a fish from an unsuspecting fisherman on the Kodiak docks. The eagle dropped off its lamppost, grabbed the cod or sculpin in its talons, and flew off with it. People ask if bald eagles really swoop down at sea and catch live fish in their talons the way nature

programs show on television, and the answer is yes, they do, with grace and devastating efficiency, and they fly on, cool and unruffled, barely breaking a wingbeat.

The "baldness" of the bald eagle refers not to an absence of head feathers but rather to the whiteness of the head feathers. The eagle's surname, *leucocephalus,* means "white head." Young bald eagles don't have the distinctive white head feathers of the adult and so they aren't "bald" except taxonomically. These eaglets, mottled brown and gray and white, look just-got-out-of-bed messy. They may be large, but in color they lack the severe simplicity and striking contrast—white head, white tail, black trunk, yellow bill—of the mature baldy. I use these colors advisedly. From a distance the bald eagle looks black, but the eagle feathers that I have observed on the beach are chestnut and charcoal in hue, not black.

It is all the same to the bald eagle. To the eagle on its branch over the sea; to the eagle in flight, propelled by the power of those massive wings; and higher still, to the eagle soaring overhead, to the eagle drafting on the winds, it is all the same. The eagle gives the impression of having transcended its nature, of having achieved a supreme knowing and needing nothing at all. Hearing those piercing whistles, I search the sky, but the eagle is far, far out of sight.

FIREWEED

When I lived in interior Alaska, I couldn't imagine that country without the wild rose, and on Kodiak Island I feel this way about the fireweed. The blooming fireweed, its pink spires gracing meadows and hillsides, is a principal in the Alaska wildflower pageant. In a matter of weeks in July and August, the fire of the fireweed spreads from a bloom to a blaze to an island-wide conflagration. The fireweed lights and colors the land. A pinkness tinges the world as if drops of fireweed elixir had been added to the sun.

We have a dwarf fireweed that flourishes on the sea cliffs and two shades of tall fireweed, a rare pale pink and a rich magenta. Sometimes a brown bear traverses the hillside above our cabin, only his back visible among the fireweed flowers. The pollen of the fireweed, pastel green in color, dusts my jeans and coats the oiled barrel of my shotgun. Fireweed blooms relatively late in the season, glorifying the summer while auguring its end. The early-blooming iris hangs withered while the fireweed draws hosts of hungry bees.

When the fireweed bloom climaxes in early August, a heavenly pink suffuses the land, a pink amplified by the wild rose, pyrola, rose purple orchid and other flowers. The clouds are pink at sunrise, the pink reflects in the silky waters of the strait, and pink morning vapors wreathe the cabin. Pink flora, pink cloud, pink water, pink flush of air and land and sea, a pink shot through with sun and birdsong, a sunshot, songshot pink, bushels of bright sound and color, everywhere this joyful pink, this beeful birdfulness, this frenzy of delight.

It passes too soon. Fireweed petals shower the earth. The tips of the stalks flower into September, but the flush is gone. The leaves and stems redden with the fall. The seed pods split and spill their cotton. Masses of white down are blown aloft.

A yellow cast creeps into the country. Autumn's palette is laid on thick. The ferns brown, the cottonwoods yellow, the fireweed rusts and rattles. The frost blights the stalks, the wind fells them, and the animals trample them underfoot.

The winter fields are crossboned with fallen fireweed. It's a dreary sight. But in May as the willows fuzz and the fiddleheads unfurl, the burgundy fireweed shoots appear. The young fireweed are tender on the tongue—now's the time to pick a few and eat them. In another month they'll have grown to two feet. Four feet. Five. The slender stalks of the fireweed, laden with ripened buds, nod in the wind, disclosing hints of the pink within. And the green hills are again bright with fireweed.

FOX

Even if you've never seen a wild one, you know a lot about foxes if you have a dog. Foxes are companionable, curious, forgiving, inordinately fond of food, and sometimes shameless. Wild foxes normally keep their distance, but there is often a bold fox who traipses from the four-wheeler to the burn barrel to the sawhorses and investigates everything. He plumps down in the sunshine at our trailhead, scratches himself under the chin, and watches us go about our chores. We look up and there he is, lying there like a dog.

One rebel wanted to spend all his spare time with us and even made himself comfortable on the outdoor furniture. His disapproving mother did the equivalent of grab him by the ear and march him home, or she chastised him—pssht!—from the cover of the red-berried elders. This freethinking fox is the only fox I ever fed out of my hand. I had always considered the hand-feeding of foxes to be a bridge too far, but I was showing off to my children and finally crossed it. This speaks to the winsomeness of the fox as much as to my own moral weakness.

There is something archetypal in the gesture of a human being throwing something to, or at, a fox. I suppose canines evolved getting pelted by rocks and insults if not by savory bones and reassuring commands. A ratty-looking, long-snouted fox spent a lot of time around our cabin one summer, and he wasn't being curious or sociable, he was one thing: hungry. And when all they want is food, they skulk. I tossed a block of wood to him and he chased it down and gnawed it like a crust of bread. It's hard not to give a fox a little treat in a spirit of sharing, and I followed up the wood with a round of pilot bread. I had found a fox carcass on the bluffs, mummified by the salt wind, and another set of fox remains in the woods, and I suspected there was disease or famine in the population. With a deep freeze the previous winter and a late cold snap, the tundra voles had been killed off, and the foxes may have suffered, too. For that matter, the short-tailed weasel, a vole "specialist," must have famished. All three of these mammals are indigenous here, but that doesn't proof them against a harsh winter. A harsh winter has ripple effects on all the species.

These are red foxes, technically, but don't let that fool you. They come in red, black, silver and every combination. Their wildly variable color is a reason we lose track of the fox generations from one year to the next. In a given summer we'll recognize individuals and families, but with all of their reproducing and color-changing, they get jumbled in our minds. A young fox may be deep black while its parent is red or gray.

There is nothing cuter than a fox kit romping in the Shasta daisies and making excited puppy sounds at its mother. They aren't so cute when they grow up, but that's true of most of us. They may become sneaky and low-down, or blasé and cynical like city coyotes, or they become obnoxious petty vandals, digging where they please, leaving turds in your stuff and looking dryly at you, like—*You wanted the wilderness experience.*

I've seen foxes in their prime, though, foxes that bring honor to the species. I remember a handsome, barrel-chested fox standing on the ocean cliffs with a limp hare in his jaws. His posture was Napoleonic. In color he was a silver-tipped black fox. It was getting toward Bastille Day and he was having no trouble staying thick through the trunk. To this animal, Charles Darwin's world was no indignity. When he heard me, he turned and stared at me, and with the hare secure in his jaws, he bounded into the willows.

I saw this prince of foxes a couple of mornings later. He wandered up the game trail in the streaming sunlight behind our cabin and lay down and rested in the dry moss of the hillside. Gazing on the world, the fox appeared to do nothing but relish the moment. You may or not believe in free will, but I won't rule out a degree of free play in the consciousness of the so-called lower animals. I'm not saying this fox was a theoretical physicist, but I believe he was basking in being alive that lovely summer morning, taking joy in his foxhood, perhaps reflecting on his recent hunting successes or making plans to travel by one trail that afternoon instead of another.

I remember a gorgeous noble female, too. She was black-gray-silver with red in her tail and penetrating yellow-orange eyes. Her pups trotted up behind her on the beach and peered around her at me and my son. With a bark she warned us to keep our distance. We followed the family up the beach and over a grassy bank to their den, though where exactly the den opened we didn't see. The furry pups disappeared inside and their mother stood guard outside, watchful and erect. She stood hidden in the tall beach grass, but whenever the grass swayed in the wind, I saw her yellow-orange eyes staring at me.

The eyes of a wild fox can be spooky-bizarre or hauntingly beautiful. They're like the stones in the Art Nouveau costume jewelry we wore in the vibrant decadence of youth. On some nights the foxes' bloodcurdling shrieks rise over the countryside. I've been awakened by their screeching and lain with a palpitating heart until it ended. When people say Bigfoot has a cry like a woman being murdered, they might be hearing foxes. A couple of foxes were roughhousing outside the cabin one night, the big fox mauling and ripping the throat of the younger fox—really killing it, I thought. Apocalyptic screams came from the victim. The terrible noise subsided after the big fox lost interest and let go. I'm not a hundred percent certain the screaming wasn't hysterical laughter. No wonder the snowshoe hares fear these devils.

Foxes yowl, yelp, bark, shriek, howl and otherwise communicate, and knowing their kinship with dogs, I shouldn't be surprised by their vocal versatility. One July the yowling and yelping of the foxes was unbearable. They were hyenas. Night after night the maddening chorus persisted. I was searching for the culprits one evening when an earthquake struck, a long one, and the foxes fell silent. From the radio I learned this was a magnitude 6.4 quake centered in the Alaska Peninsula. I recalled a week or ten days earlier we'd had a 6.3 quake centered southeast of Kodiak. Was it possible the month's active geology had inspired the baying of the foxes? In any event, after the second quake the foxes didn't have much to say.

Foxes are feisty, finicky, fun-loving and family-oriented. When we've had a good day of fishing, the foxes come down to the beach to congratulate us, always keeping an eye on what we throw away. Before they take any scraps, they'll sidle close to gauge our reactions. When a fish carcass floats in the tide, the fox vacillates between reaching for the fish with its mouth and its forepaw and quick-stepping backwards to avoid getting its feet wet.

Foxes have families to feed, and we never saw a prouder, more prancing fox than the fox heading home with a fresh halibut carcass in his mouth. He clasped the unwieldy carcass by its edge and tried to keep it from swinging against his fur. He returned later for the salmon carcass, hardly believing his good fortune. An annoying pink strand hung from the salmon carcass and slapped him in the chest. He *hated* that. He stopped, laid the fish down, rearranged it, then grasped the neat package in his mouth and trotted down the beach with it, and never once took a bite for himself, so proud of his trophy that he couldn't bear to diminish it by biting into it before he got it home.

GOLDEN-CROWNED
SPARROW

The three-noted song of the golden-crowned sparrow, minor in mood but not melancholy, evokes the music of a slowly moving brook on a summer afternoon. It echoes over the Alaskan hills, over lakeshore, stream, spruce wood and alder thicket, and in the mellow clarity and round simplicity of the song, in its sonic purity, there is balm for the body and soul.

We start seeing these sparrows in May, when they arrive to breed after traveling up the West Coast. We watch them scratch at the soil and kick up the spruce litter in their hunt for seeds and insects. The golden-crowned sparrow is, for the most part, unremarkable in appearance, though easily distinguished, in the breeding adult, by its yellow crown. They warm up to their song, and in June we hear every day its strange, free-floating ventriloquy. The beauty of that triune whistle, the notes quavering and bending in their descent, is exquisite.

Come July there's a chaotic change in the sparrow's repertory as the chicks learn to fly. What sounds like the cacophony of a flock of birds is a single family in training, hopping and winging about, the chicks giddy and calling in excitement, the parents anxiously tracking the chicks' progress, a scene repeated by many other families in many other groves.

This is a stressful, perilous time for the sparrows. Their nest abandoned, the chicks must live on the fly. Flight school is a branch-to-branch affair of fluttering wings and high-pitched aspirations. Avian Aeronautics, Navigation, Migration Theory, Basics of Biofeedback, Electromagnetism, Wing Maintenance and Feather Care—all of these subjects must be mastered by the fledglings and mastered at a breakneck pace.

Flight Training: A Case Study

July 27

3 p.m. We discover at the edge of the spruce grove a brood of golden-crowned sparrows, four chicks huddled side by side on the tip of a fallen spruce branch. The chicks, sheltered from the drizzle by a single cow parsnip leaf, are wide-eyed and unafraid until my own little ones, seven and twelve years old, lowering themselves to the ground, get too close and the startled chicks scatter. Three of the chicks hop into the grasses and fireweed that border the spruce grove, while the fourth attains the top of a cow parsnip stalk, where it is met by its mother. She feeds the chick by tucking a treat into its mouth, and this precocious youngster flies away and we never see it again.

The remaining chicks regroup on a horizontal twig six inches off the ground. Their crystalline cries—*tsetsetse cheecheechee*—sound whenever their parents draw near to feed them. The chicks sense the parental approach and turn up their orange mouths to receive whatever is given. They eat and they hush. When mother and father return, the chicks, open-mouthed, squall again. The cycle repeats. Bystander birds watch these doings in curiosity. The children and I, readily tolerated by chicks and parents alike, crawl close in observation. The chicks, six inches off the ground, doze side by side on their perch. Even with their eyes closed they fidget for position.

When we leave them in the evening, reluctantly, we feel we're leaving them to the protection of dumb luck. A fox or other predator could easily scoop them up and make a meal of them.

July 28

9 a.m. The fledglings have survived the night's dangers. We are relieved to find them on the same low twig. By noon, the trio are hopping across the ground doing what look like cardiovascular exercises. The flying lessons begin in earnest. Short bursts of flight are followed by longer courses and deliberate climbs. The training takes them outward and upward, so that at 3 p.m., when the chicks break for a nap, they are thirteen feet up in the spruce tree.

It's a big, hospitable Sitka spruce whose evenly spaced branches my children climb with ease. Climbing the tree is like climbing a sturdy ladder, and it occurs to me, as the birds flit and fetch another branch, that my children are in these high branches for the first time, too. We take turns at the prime viewing spot. I, standing on a spruce branch, hooking my arm over another branch for support, am on a level, or my face is, with the dark-browed sparrow chicks on *their* branch. I am less than an arm's length away.

The chicks tremble and groom and nap without fear of us. "Sleep, chirp and eat," my daughter sums it up. They peck at the lichens on the tree bark or at the spruce needles while they wait for mother and father to return with more vittles. The parents forage in the surrounding grove, or they hunt farther afield for buds and insects. Sometimes the hungriest or lustiest chick strides to the end of the branch to meet its parent, and in reward it gets all the food.

The parents feed them constantly. All afternoon and evening they shuttle back and forth with the meals.

July 29
11 a.m. The chicks have found a new perch, twenty-two feet up in a neighboring spruce tree. We locate them by zeroing in on their cheeping and flurrying, on the wing-beating and twig-bobbing when one of the parents arrives with nourishment and the open-mouthed chicks jostle on their branch.

From this new base they fly sorties among the spruce trees. Not three weeks old, the chicks have ascended from an earthbound helplessness to a height above twenty feet. The rapidity of their growth is breathtaking. And once again I am conscious of the parallels between our species. Our training days on the homestead are as noisy and chaotic, as seemingly chaotic, as theirs are. My little ones develop more slowly but not less surely than the sparrow chicks, our tasks—to hit a target, to recite a poem, to design an energy bar that will reward entrepreneurship—our tasks apparently more complex than a sparrow's, but as humans we're equipped to meet our challenges as the sparrows are equipped to fly. Our lifespans do differ, of course, but in shape does a human life differ so very much from a golden-crowned sparrow's?

For these stout young birds, there are no higher rungs on the ladder of independence; there is only the open sky, and we don't expect to see them again.

July 30
11 a.m. A vigorous twittering in the spruce grove. Our trio of chicks occupy a lofty branch, stirring the air with flecked triangular wings while holding out for a meal. My daughter, binoculars in hand, reports seeing a worm twisting from the mother's bill. The first chick bites off a piece of the worm, the mother holds the curling victim to the next chick, and so on. They don't stay long.

July 31
The grove is empty and silent.

August 5
Encore! The sparrows have returned from a five-day absence—call it a field trip or a trial migration—and the twittering resumes in the spruce grove. However, we count only two sparrow chicks, one resting on its branch and the other pacing back and forth like an impatient teenager. Neither parent arrives.

    Goodbye! Goodbye all!

GRIEF

The fourth anniversary of my father's death coincided with my first summer alone at Cottonwood. I had been aware of the impending anniversary, but in the way we have of fending off these thoughts because too close and stubborn a remembrance does us no good, on the day in question I forgot the anniversary and I didn't remember it again for several days. The weather, when I did remember, was overcast, gray and rainy, and the paneless window spaces, the black tarpaper on the unfinished roof, the plastic sheeting that shrouded the cabin and rustled in the wind—these impressions together with the recollection of his death put me in a profound gloom, and I sat for a while and considered my grief.

He was a traveler, my father, and would have been interested to know what I was doing here on Kodiak Island. I had inherited some of his wanderlust, no doubt about it. I wondered how much of my recent impatience with clockwork living, my taunting of the void, had originated in emotions of grief and stricken loneliness; how much my retreat from the world was in grief for the world; and whether that grief, whatever its measure, would find healing here at Cottonwood. To learn to accept death without giving up the gusto for life—surely this is one of life's secrets. In any event, grief is universal, not original with me. I thought of my young family in Fairbanks, my wife and daughter and newborn son. Today I missed everybody dearly.

I decided to call on my neighbors, the Petersons, the only year-round residents in these parts. I hadn't met the Petersons yet, but a few days earlier somebody had left at my trailhead an arrow formed of spruce sticks—the arrow pointed west—and after I had recovered from the strangeness of coming on this unexpected artifact, I reasoned that it must be the Petersons who had left it. So today I changed my shirt and hiked west for a mile, keeping close to the sea cliffs and passing through spruce forest, and I found Laurel Peterson at home with her visiting mother Eve. Richard, Laurel's husband, an electrical lineman near retirement, was away on a summer job.

What a homestead the couple had built! The single-story frame house was in itself unspectacular, but here in the bush my impressionable eye saw it as a wonderful mirage. I drank a soda and had a tour of the gardens. Laurel had arranged a bench and some rocks in an arbor with a view of the ocean, a memorial to her first husband, Don, an educator and experienced hunter who had died of hypothermia during a hunt gone bad. It was indeed Laurel who a few days earlier had left the mysterious symbol of an arrow at my trailhead, and she laughed when I told her of my surprise in finding it. I offered to get her mail for her while her husband Richard was away—"getting the mail" meant a six-mile boat trip from her house to the local salmon cannery—and so, a few days after this first meeting, Laurel returned the visit by hiking to my cabin to collect her mail from me.

She brought gifts from her garden, and it seemed to me that I had never eaten vegetables more robust, vividly colored and zesty on the tongue. It's true I was easily impressed, having been subsisting on a skeleton menu, but those green onion bulbs were as shapely as round onions; the carrots, after the first orange crunch, dissolved sweetly in my mouth; and every turnip, heavy around as a piece of ordnance, was boldly striped like the flag of a sovereign nation. When she had emptied her backpack of a vegetable medley that included zucchini and radish, she filled the pack with the mail I had picked up for her at the cannery. Her mother, Eve, she said, was blind—I hadn't noticed—and this explained the audiobooks that had arrived in a red cloth envelope from the Fairbanks Public Library.

Not long afterwards, having the excuse of bringing more mail to them, I returned to the Peterson homestead. We talked at the dining table in the bay window, or Laurel and I talked and Eve occasionally interposed. Eve's blindness was barely noticeable, but the dodder in her hand was distracting. At first I thought she was dabbing a crumb of zucchini bread off the table, but five minutes along she was still dabbing at it. "The tremor gets worse when she's anxious," Laurel told me. "It goes away at night when she's sleeping. The blindness is from macular degeneration. Mom's health took a turn for the worse a few years ago, after Dad died."

They were running low on medicines and on the cans of nutritional supplement that Eve drank, and I assured them that I would pick up the arriving mail shipment. The next time I called at their house, Laurel's young granddaughter Megan was visiting. The child had been dropped off by her father, a local seaplane pilot. I sat with Laurel on the back porch and drank a soda while she shelled peas from her garden and while Megan rode a training bicycle on the graveled path beyond the garden fence. Megan disappeared behind the tall August fireweed that bordered the garden, and we heard her happy exclamations and the scrape of gravel against her bicycle tires.

It was sunny out, seventy-two degrees by the thermometer on the cedar post, an exceptionally fine day on Kodiak Island, but in the recent winds Laurel sensed the coming of autumn, and she pointed to the gladiolas and the tall bachelor buttons as evidence that the growth cycle had peaked. The flowers and vegetables grew with a leafy exuberance that I preferred to too much trimming. The retriever lay on the porch, snuffling forward and eating peas as they spilled from Laurel's hands. Mother was inside having her "quiet hour" during which she drank a glass of wine and listened to an audiobook. "I sometimes have to remind her that she's eighty-seven years old," Laurel said. "She was always a wizard at shelling peas, and she's frustrated because she can't do it now. Being blind and with the old-age tremors, by golly you bet things are going to be different."

Eve was unable to live alone in Montana anymore, and Laurel and her brothers were in the process of deciding how best to see to their mother's future.

The training bicycle lay on its side in the grass where Megan had abandoned it, and she was now in the garden helping herself to ripe strawberries. My young daughter Miranda would have eaten the strawberries as passionately as Megan did, squatting and gobbling them out of stained and sticky hands.

Later at Cottonwood I stood on the sea cliffs in a driving wind thinking of them, of the generations young and old. Second by second the waves were born and flowered and died on the water's surface, and it seemed to me that I saw in the vast, foaming sea a dynamic allegory of life itself, of the phases of our lives here on earth.

In Fairbanks for the winter, I received a letter in the mail from Laurel Peterson. She was flying south to Oregon with her mother, who would enter a care home not far from Laurel's brother's place in Tigard. Given the realities, this was the best arrangement for the family, but Laurel's outlook was shaken, and when I returned to Kodiak Island in May, she conceded that she was finding the bush life increasingly difficult as she aged. Although she had never expected to leave Alaska, she and Richard were considering it.

She recalled an incident from long ago in Dawson City, Yukon, where she and her first husband, Don, visiting the historic town, had met an old-timer who had crossed the Chilkoot Trail on foot during the Klondike Gold Rush. For the price of some tobacco this fellow recounted his tales of those bygone days, and he led them through the barn where he had collected rusty antiquities of the period. "We all become that man," Laurel told me, not letting her anecdote go to waste. "We all become the old-timer who crossed the Chilkoot Trail on foot during the Gold Rush."

Laurel had a heart attack a few weeks later, down in Portland. She had traveled to Oregon to visit her mother, and in Portland she was undergoing a battery of tests whose purpose was to ensure that she *not* have a heart attack. She recovered well enough, but back home on Kodiak Island, her dog died, and her mother-in-law, Richard's mother, died in Montana.

Grief is how life processes the inescapable passing of what it holds dear. Sooner or later we all learn what we must. I notice that with time my late father, my physical father, becomes rather like a doll I've outgrown or a character in a book that I've returned to the shelf, something outside of me that once was quite close to me. But the memory of my father, as distinct from my remembered father, I mean the totality of the moments I shared with him, the aura of that totality as distinct from some fixed and unchanging corpus preserved in my brain, continues rich and full of living qualities, mellowed and accessible but never insistent or frantic.

Laurel's mother, Eve, died down in Oregon. Laurel brought some of her mother's ashes back to Alaska, and while sprinkling them on the beach at the family's old fish camp, she found a hollowed stone that she recognized as an Alutiiq artifact, a seal oil lamp, and she took solace in the symbolism of the discovery—the sea, the lamp, the flame, the loop of grief—particularly on a gorgeous July day when the blooming fireweed lit the island.

At a blustery day's end I watch the sea, thinking of people absent or passed away. My homestead solitude is occasionally troubled by ghosts. But around me the berry canes are laden with ripe berries, and the shaggy ranks of the plant kingdom rebel at every gust. The lowering sun, covered and uncovered by the clouds, shines undiscouraged, and the sea in its ceaseless threnody ceaselessly soothes me.

GULL

I can't help but love the seagulls, though they do so much to make themselves unlovable. The cry of the wheeling gulls, their flocking on the beach, a gull's solitary vigil on a fogbound jetty—these are impressions of my California childhood. Our long acquaintance makes me forgiving. If I empty a bag of slop into the tide, the gulls pretend nonchalance before they squabble, flap, snap, growl and glare up bitterly at their airborne rivals. Let a salmon head fall on the beach, the gulls angle toward the godsend, waddling closer and flashing their wingspans until the chief among them, the generalissimo of the seagull clan, the Bully Big Chief Jolly, big in status and big around the chest, combatively turns on the presumptuous lesser gulls, who back away in retreat.

To the east of Cottonwood there's a grassy islet known as Egg Island, and if I stop my raft at this little rookery, I risk an angry uprising of seagulls. It's a noisy place, a rank pungency overhanging it, the grass nests and rock ledges whitened with bird droppings. If you have ever been spooked by Alfred Hitchcock's *The Birds*, you won't like what happens next. A low-flying posse of long-legged, yellow-billed squawkers attacks you, or they chase you like the Furies and bomb you with Jackson Pollocks until you swing your tiller around and throttle out of there.

They don't take guff from anyone, those gulls. I've seen them drive bald eagles from their airspace. They'll fly out of their way to hector an eagle. Gulls are scrappy, high-strung and maneuverable at close quarters, and while a bald eagle may not lose a fight to a seagull, it emerges from it disheveled and with its grandeur diminished, rather like America after it tangled with Libya—no offense to the seagull. Gulls are sneaky, grasping, quarrelsome, thick-headed, bottom-feeding lowlifes, but they also have patience, courage, tenacity, endurance and resilience. A glaucous-winged gull perched on a rock or a timber and gazing seaward has a nobility or at least a piratical dignity.

When I first noticed the red spot on the seagull's yellow bill, I mistook it for a drop of blood left after a meal. A gull coasts by in solo reconnaissance, or they plunge from the sky in twos and threes, or they float in massive rafts at sea. In a storm wind I can't tell the intrepid seagulls from the flying foam. Their mantles outspread, buffeted by the gusts, they are always on the hunt for something to eat, and their reputation as survivors is deserved. The sharpness of a gull's senses is staggering. I once flung a fish gut off my knife when there wasn't a seagull in sight. The fish gut floating on the ocean was effectively invisible, but in no time a gimlet-eyed seagull dropped out of the sky and took it.

As low-tech fish finders, the seagulls point the way for us. If we don't know where to try our hooks for halibut or salmon, we search the horizon for gulls. The gulls often congregate over the schooling fish, the sand lance and herring that are tracked by the game fish. If a whale happens to be surface-feeding on a shoal of fish, the shrieking seagulls, seizing the opportunity, drop around the whale to catch the gleanings. There might be a dozen gulls circling and kerplunking in the water, or a frenzied, feeding mass of them, but our chances of catching a fish improve if we follow the gulls.

Seagulls embody the spirit of waterfronts everywhere. In bays and shipyards and ports of call, among creaking gangways, rippling flags, ropes, pulleys, cranes, nets, musseled pilings, drifting algae, the smell of fuel and creosoted timbers, wind and salt and pitching seas, the roar of engines, the shouts of sailors and longshoremen, ships embarking across every sea for every corner of the earth, at home in all of this, witness to the buzz and raillery of the waterfront, and to its lonely languor, too, ubiquitous, floating under piers, combing the beaches and boardwalks, bobbing in the wakes and gliding over the roadsteads, tiptoeing across bulwarks and bridges, wheeling over maritime ghettos, picking through the sewage and garbage, beggar, thief, mime, carnival barker, baggage handler, cannery rat, master recycler, diseased artiste, working-class poet, scoundrel, glutton, graverobber, compass bird, bargeman's beauty, sea dog chanticleer, fit company for cormorants and crows, haunter of noxious backwaters, shrieker, cackler, hustler, fomenter of discord—perched atop it all, biding its time, treading from foot to foot, much abused but never defeated, this is the seagull.

FIN WHALE WITH GULLS, KUPREANOF STRAIT

HAPPINESS STEW

The first salmon I caught at Cottonwood was a pink salmon, just the right size for a no-leftovers meal. I washed the thin fillets at the creek mouth and carried them to the cabin, where I boiled a handful of rice on the camp stove and dropped in a cube of bouillon. Before the rice was done I laid in the salmon fillets and added half a tin of tomato sauce to simmer. I jiggered Parmesan cheese over it and ate it hot from the pan.

Even a pink salmon is a gourmet fish when it's that fresh. Afterwards I sweetened my breath with a bowlful of salmonberries. Homestead living isn't all salmon and salmonberries, but I ate some of each that day.

In those days I cooked on a Coleman camp stove and ate my meals outdoors, but I knew that the cooking patterns would change once Martina and the kids joined me at Cottonwood, and I worked to ready the cabin for family meals.

For a satisfying dinner after an eventful day outdoors, here's my favorite recipe for Happiness Stew:

Boil a chopped potato in a pot of water. Throw in a cube of bouillon. Add garlic powder, lemon pepper, or whatever you've got. Don't stint on the wild chives. If you're recently from town and have fresh carrots, add them; they won't last forever. Now add a three-ounce can of tuna. Drain it or not, suit yourself, but don't burn yourself tasting ahead of time. The water boils off and leaves more or less a casserole. Add Parmesan cheese or Tabasco to taste and eat directly from the pot.

Whenever I returned to Cottonwood with supplies from town, I brought eight or ten loaves of wheat bread and ate peanut butter and jelly sandwiches and cheese sandwiches until the bread and cheese gave out.

Other foods that I relied on, easy to keep, easy to use and inexpensive, were alfalfa seed, lentils and mung beans, jerky, coffee, dry milk, cereal, minute rice, dry soup, dehydrated fruits and vegetables, and saltines and pilot bread. I always brought fresh produce from town, a few pounds of apples, carrots and potatoes, but never as much as I wanted, being limited by weight in what I could bring on the seaplane, and Kodiak's high cost of produce being a factor, too.

In August, just before my family arrived at Cottonwood, I installed a gas range and we cooked with propane after that. Before long, Martina was baking bread from scratch. Rye, wheat, pumpernickel, you name it. To bake from scratch was something she had always wanted to do, and the children and I had every reason (muffins, pizza) to encourage her. Hot homemade bread and venison are the foods I most associate with our homestead life at Cottonwood. For a tender venison stew I used a recipe from Russell Tinsley's *Hunting the Whitetail Deer*. The key is to start cooking the stew early, before you're hungry for it, and to first brown the cubed venison in shortening.

Apart from our wild harvest of meat and fish and berries, we imported food to the homestead. The ideal foods were lightweight, with a long shelf life. We added all sorts of ingenious stuff to our larder: burgundy powder, honey powder, molasses powder, vinegar powder, margarine powder, cheese powder—awful stuff, really, most of it. Yams and refried beans were the best freeze-dried bulk foods. Broccoli, bell pepper and carrots were among the useful dehydrated vegetables. I used dried celery and carrots in a braised heart of venison that tasted rich and tender like corned beef.

Betty Crocker's *International Cookbook* gave us ideas, but we were creative at our peril. We prepared a curry of venison backstrap substituting milk and cornstarch for sour cream, and the results were decidedly mixed. For our daughter Miranda's birthday cake, Martina devised a Black Forest cake with a frosting of cocoa powder, vanilla coffee creamer and powdered sugar. The taste I leave to the reader's imagination. I have repressed all memory of it.

The snowbound days of winter were good for family meals and family bonding. We ate three meals a day and we shared every one of them. In a one-room cabin there is nowhere to eat by yourself, and we had none of the high-tech distractions that people complain about. The only distractions were the sight of a whale spouting in the strait or a family of brown bears outside the window or an aurora borealis too gorgeous to ignore. Martina or Miranda said grace, Kody mimicked them from his booster seat, and I basked in the glow of thanksgiving without fretting the theology. I had many reasons to give thanks for this world and for the gift of a life in which to catalog its beauties. In feeding my body at Cottonwood I always felt I was feeding my soul, too, and that's what I am trying to say. Food in itself doesn't make me happy, but as an enhancement, adding gusto to the moment, the right meal aids in the digestion of life.

And what meals we had! I ate with zest, always:

Hot blueberry muffins for breakfast, potato soup with wild chives for lunch, pasta and fried venison sausage for dinner.

Home-style cinnamon buns, Dutch green pea soup with venison sausage and hot pumpernickel, spaghetti with fiddleheads and olive oil.

Oatmeal, fish chowder, homestead pizza, Scandinavian rhubarb pudding.

Pancakes, venison stew, snail fritters.

Oh, those fritters! We gathered the snails at low low tide and cooked them to tender perfection using a seafood fritters recipe from Virginia Pill and Marjorie Furlong's *Edible? Incredible!* Those snail fritters were every bit as delicious as the clam fritters we used to fry from Kenai Peninsula razor clams.

In summer, as the days lengthened, we ate at a later hour. We dined on pan-fried halibut at eight or nine o'clock and we worked outside for a couple of hours and we came in at ten or eleven o'clock for hot chocolate chip cookies or salmonberry crisp or Krusteaz maple-walnut scones. This reminds me of a story I shouldn't tell. Occasionally we got to town and shopped for groceries, and if we bought a premix for baking, say a pancake or scone mix, we generally went with the value brand Krusteaz. The name Krusteaz, it's fair to say, leaves some latitude for pronunciation. One isn't entirely sure how to say it. In my ignorance I pronounced the word Krusty-Az or (spelled otherwise) Crusty Ass. And because I did this unthinkingly for many weeks at the cabin, because it sounded not incredible as a pronunciation, and because Martina is a clean-minded woman, over time she adopted the usage and never gave it another thought.

For Thanksgiving dinner we were invited to the homestead of our neighbors, the Petersons. Laurel and Richard planned to serve turkey, Parker rolls, Montana canned pea salad and sparkling apple juice. Our contribution was to be baked scones, a berry pie, raisin chutney and mashed yams. The day having arrived, we hiked a mile to the Peterson place and hung our jackets in the entry. The children settled into their activities; Richard and I, talking guns, found our way to the armchairs; and Martina and Laurel, sharing baking lore, drifted into the kitchen to put the finishing touches on the meal.

Cooks don't always admit to using premixes, but when Martina broke the ice by admitting to Laurel that the yummy-looking scones were actually Crusty Ass scones, the women entered into an enthusiastic exchange of opinions and brand comparisons. I distinctly heard the words Crusty Ass echoing across the room as Martina several times extolled the virtues of the brand. Laurel never stopped smiling, but she finally interrupted the conversation to ask a question. "Do you mean Krust-*ease?*" she said.

Martina fell silent and her mouth fell open. She looked over at me, sitting blamelessly in my armchair, and I naturally jumped up to see if there was anything I could do to help them in the kitchen. I was sure there would be.

HERMIT THRUSH

A sound of water welling up in a spring or fountain and spiraling down in rich silvery tones. A quavering silence. A renewal of the musical phrase. And again an answerless silence, a breathless waiting. And the starting up again, the melancholy outcry.

A bird of the northern summer, brownish in plumage with a spotted breast, the hermit thrush is unassuming to look at, but when he opens his bill and sings his evening song, a shiver of rapture runs through me. The song weaves a spell over this place, a mellow gurgle, a haunting vespertine echo. After an interval the incantation repeats, or the thrush mews on its branch at midnight and all is quiet in the boreal forest. Sleep is at hand.

We are old friends now, the hermit thrush and I, but at first I didn't know what bird this was that so enthralled me. I left off my chores and searched the trees. That such an unprepossessing creature could be the source of such poignant sweetness seemed incredible. There he was on his branch, calling me to meditations, fluting of anguish, grief and solitude, of evanescence, love and infinite longing. When I found this bird celebrated in Walt Whitman and Edward Abbey, I understood why.

We start hearing them in the spring when they arrive at Cottonwood and the surrounding woodlands. I have worked outside on spring and summer evenings with the hermit thrush for my unseen companion. They are by nature retiring, but a memorable exception was the hermit thrush who regularly lit on our cabin post and batted his red-brown tail up and down as though he were painting with it.

The hour before midnight is the special hour of the hermit thrush. Across the wistful reaches of the night I hear his song. With the slow-motion tremolo of dream, it rises from the evergreen wood and carries over the streamside cottonwoods. It's a song for aching hearts, for the worshipful and lovelorn and forgotten, for hermits in their wild chapels and poets at dusk.

The beauty of the song is uncanny, as close to perfection as I know. Opposites fuse in that liquid beauty. Why should the song of a diminutive thrush move my restless heart? What deep harmony binds us?

It's by no means a cheerless song. Life, though excruciated by doubt and defeat, pours its heart into a beautiful lament which it repeats undeterred. There is always, pushing up through blue regret, through every sinking gyration, a resistance, a heartbroken indignation that the world is as it is. This is the song sung from every branch. Yearning is possibility is life's glory. Lament becomes hosanna, and in that hosanna the best that's in us is encrypted.

The song trails off, dissolving in velvet twilight. The hermit thrush quiets, submerged in a healing silence, eyes open and seeing. Then the blood and breath quicken, the bill is lifted, and by and by the thrush sings again, and in the resumption of his song he finds his answer.

HIPPY RIG

When Bea Hagen, of Fairbanks and Manley Hot Springs, let us take her old Hoover electric washing machine on the ferry boat to Kodiak Island, she was entrusting to us a cherished memento of her past. It was her gift to us as we embarked for our homestead on the Kupreanof Peninsula. Bea and her husband Al had used this machine years earlier at their placer gold mine on Cooney Creek in interior Alaska, and in giving it to us, Bea smiled nostalgically on her own endeavor as she smiled prospectively on ours.

In its day, the Hoover Model 0512 was a beauty: a yard high, a couple of feet wide, sixteen inches deep, a compact, top-loading, twin-tub washer-wringer that would stash under a tarp and plug into a generator when you wanted to wash your clothes. If you were game enough to own an electric generator, you were game enough for the Hoover 0512, and if you were such a stick-in-the-mud back-to-the-lander that you scorned all machinery, God bless you, you could take your stick out of the mud and beat your clothes clean on the riverbank.

In our case, there was nothing in the Hoover that a couple of small-is-beautiful homesteaders with a five-year-old and a one-year-old objected to. We were grateful to Bea, who valued her years in the bush as a highlight of her youth and who even today applied the experience as a touchstone in her daily life. And so the well-traveled hippy rig ended up with us at the northern tip of Kodiak Island.

Unfortunately the hippy rig had aged over the decades and wasn't in the finest fettle. Alaska's climate is hard on plastics and rubbers. The machine's agitator still worked, driving the wash tub, but as soon as winter arrived, around November first, the spin belt broke, meaning that the spin basket wouldn't turn and the water wouldn't get wrung out of the laundry.

The clothes just sat there, a sodden mass in the basket. We squeezed the water out by hand and hung the clothes to dry inside the cabin. In Kodiak's wet atmosphere, the wash would never have dried outside in November, and even inside, the laundry, strung on a sagging line from one corner of the cabin to the other, was musty and slow to dry.

An extra spin belt for the antique Hoover was not something I had thought to bring to Cottonwood. I had generally been meticulous in my planning. I had brought many spare parts, knowing there are no hardware stores in the bush. I had considered food, water, transportation, communication, even education. But clean laundry was not something I had numbered among life's essentials, and until Bea suggested we take the Hoover, I frankly hadn't given a thought to how we would wash our clothes or whether we would wash them at all. Clean clothes? Who cares!

Your wife cares, dummy. Over the coming weeks I learned just how much she cared. When we started out in life together, Martina and I were content to drop a few coins at the laundromat and to hold hands or eat chop suey while we waited for the clothes to wash and tumble. Now this! For the first time in my life I understood that fresh, clean laundry was a *good* thing. Not just a value-neutral concept, it was *desirable*. It could make a woman *happy*. Its absence could undo a *marriage*. Never mind the why of it, she cares! She cares that the cloth against her skin isn't wretchedly filthy and foul-smelling. Get used to it!

It's not that she objected in so many words to hand-washing in freezing water, for the sake of her beloved children, heap after heap of urine-stained linen and muddy denim. But with the other challenges that occupied us at Cottonwood—wintry weather, troublesome brown bears—the chore of laundry added to her doubts about the value of how she, a professional woman, had chosen to spend her time. Fortunately we had packed disposable diapers, and Martina quit using the washables while I worked to restore the hippy rig to health. I rapped on its brown metal housing. I knelt and peered at the surviving shred of a wiring diagram. There was a timing motor just under the control panel and a corroded wash motor. The washer belt was bubbly and brittle. The spin belt, as I say, was broken.

My thoughts and emotions were in conflict as I stood back and considered the Model 0512, sitting humbly under its spruce tree. What a marvel! I felt a surge of affection for it, admiring its simplicity and ingenuity. It was brilliant. The Hoover engineers hadn't sat around designing the perfect washing machine for hippies—why would you invent a washing machine for people who didn't wash? No, in tenement houses and tumbledown farmhouses and suburban bungalows across the USA, people—graduates of the tub and washboard, customers of the Sears catalog—had depended on machines like this. This was their step up in the world. Indoor plumbing, women's lib, the spread of hygiene, labor-saving inventiveness—in its cultural genes this appliance carried the aspirations and strivings of an older America. How far washing machines had evolved since then was a measure of our national prosperity. These various insights cheered me, but I felt mildly dejected by the fallen condition of the hippy rig. Rodents had chewed its yellow wire insulation. I thought of the young Bea Hagen using the Hoover at her gold mine on Cooney Creek north of Manley. "We were covered with mud after sluicing gray bedrock every day," Bea recalled. "Our clothes were permeated with silt. I used the Hoover outside, with cold, silty gray water splashing everywhere, and it never let me down."

Of the many young people who streamed north to Alaska in the 1960s and 1970s, Bea was one who had washed up in Alaska for good. Today she was a green thumb, a pet lover, a wife and attorney. In some ways you never stop being a hippy, but in other ways, in ways that might at one time have baffled or shocked you, you become like other people. Stuff like clean laundry matters. I walked around the old hippy rig and squeezed its shoulder, preferring to focus on the good times. In some ways you never stop being a hippy, but the props and stage machinery of hippiedom were no more.

In mid-November, when our daughter Miranda needed some teeth pulled, Martina chartered an air taxi into Kodiak. Here was the hippy rig's chance to spin again. I gave Martina the broken spin belt, advising her, "We need a twenty-six-inch belt to drive the wringer. They'll help you match it at the shop. But listen, this machine has seen better days.

If anyone in town carries propane dryers, I hear they're expensive, but if you really want one …"

Three days later, a seaplane lands at Cottonwood and Martina and the kids smilingly descend. Among the goods they have brought from town is a fifteen-dollar electric dryer exhumed from the Salvation Army thrift shop. Under Martina's observant eye I help the pilot to wrestle this white elephant onto our beach. From the beach I winch it up the bluff and four-wheel it uphill to our clearing. Martina imagines the Salvation Army dryer to be a diamond in the rough, so I keep quiet about it, but it's more than cumbersome, it's a damned hideous monstrosity, totally out of keeping with my vision of the homestead, and I throw a tarp over it so I won't have to look at it.

In a small town like Kodiak, finding a replacement spin belt for the obsolete Model 0512 turned out to be a fool's errand. I tested the belts that Martina had purchased in town, but neither one fit snugly enough to drive the spin basket. The only thing that moved was a rusty bolt that broke off in my hand. The Hoover's agitator still worked, though, and Martina was determined to wash some clothes. In filling the wash tub from a tote of standing water, we made the mistake of not removing all of the surface ice from the tote, and this ice was then turned into crushed ice by the action of the agitator, with the result that Martina had one of her famous "Why did I go to law school?" soliloquies as she picked ice chips out of her panties prior to wringing them.

After all the hand-wringing came the moment of truth. I untarped her fifteen-dollar Salvation Army dryer, front-loaded it with an armful of wet laundry and shoved the door shut. As soon as I plugged the dryer into our purring electric generator, the generator went into convulsions. I swear that dryer sucked more watts than Houston, Texas. The generator sputtered and nearly perished getting enough juice to the dryer. For forty-five minutes Martina kept a cheerful eye on her diamond in the rough while the laundry bumped around inside it. In her mind she was already pressing the warm fluffy cloth to her cheek.

After forty-five minutes I reached into the cavernous dryer and felt a mass of laundry as wet and stone cold as it had been to start with. "Did you happen to test this thing before you bought it?" I asked her. We hung the wet clothes on the sagging indoors clothesline and went back to ducking our heads. Next time I was in town I bought some O-rings at Alaska Hydraulics to try as spin belts for the Hoover, and in the coming months I experimented with rope belts and wire belts, but the hippy rig continued in bits and pieces to fall apart, and by the springtime we had given up on it.

Not given up morally, of course. Morally the hippy rig remained a wondrous device, a Chitty Chitty Bang Bang of the imagination, a time machine, an amphibious breakthrough in the technology of the human home.

In May it got warm enough to hang our laundry outside again. We had done as little clothes-washing as tolerable over the winter, and our dirtiest garments we cleaned the easy way by dropping them in the burn barrel and setting fire to them. I rolled the Salvation Army dryer into the four-wheeler's trailer and delivered it to the out-of-the-way homestead dump known as the Diaper Burying Ground. To this day the hippy rig occupies a place of honor at Cottonwood, a wise and owlish presence in the spruce grove behind the cabin. I recently gave it a whirl for old time's sake and am happy to report that the agitator still works fine.

INSECTS

Our neighbor Laurel Peterson, repeatedly stung by yellow jackets while picking salmonberries, sicked her husband on them. Richard, unable to pinpoint the yellow jacket nest, laid detonation cord in the area and blew everything up. This explained the loud boom we heard in the distance. Laurel's wasp problem was solved, but I wonder if she didn't lose half her favorite berry patch, too.

I better appreciated their predicament after our ten-year-old son Kodiak ran afoul of a yellow jacket colony while berrying by our cabin. He was at first perplexed by the angry buzzing, and at last he screamed and fled the thicket in tears. I waded into the thicket in long sleeves and gloves with a mosquito net over my face, located the weird papier-mâché spaceship of a nest—the nest was at ground level among the salmonberry canes—and dropped a lit seal bomb on it. A seal bomb, by the way, is a glorified firecracker, fluorescent orange in color, half a foot long from butt to fuse tip, distributed by the California Seal Control Corporation, and labeled a dangerous explosive by the well-meaning bureaucrats who decree such things. A fisherman gave it to me to throw at a brown bear if I was ever in a bind. Fortunately I never had to rely on it—the thing was a dud.

Dodging wasps, I seized the globular gray nest in my hand, flung it into our clearing and set fire to it. I regretted the remedy, much as gentle Hector Crèvecoeur in *Letters of an American Farmer* regrets directing "fire and brimstone" at the ferocious wasps in his hayfield, but like the wasp I am territorial and I wasn't willing to surrender our berry patch. Later, after a rainfall, I inspected the burnt nest and found a dozen greasy wasps crawling underneath. My regard for these loyal, tenacious creatures was never higher. Regarding the proper nomenclature, my daughter Miranda, home-schooling at Cottonwood, schooled me as follows: "Bees and mosquitos are insects, Dad. Bugs are insects, but not all insects are bugs. Spiders are arachnids." I understand that bugs and insects are not technically synonymous, but for the purposes of this entry—"Insects"—I may use the terms loosely.

With so many small creatures at large in the Kodiak wilderness, biters and suckers and stingers and crawlers and hoppers and flyers, to trap a live one in the Critter Cage for Miranda's science project was never a challenge. The challenge was rather to avoid the bugs. In Fairbanks the authorities had sprayed the town with mosquito dope in summer—a controversial practice—but here at Cottonwood we were on our own. I relied on my body hair to repel the insects, and on my sweat and my thick-skinned insensitivity, but these methods were unavailable to Martina and the children. It galls a mother to see her little ones bullied by the insects. During mosquito season Kody wore calamine lotion to bed every night, and Miranda took after her mother in viciously scratching her bites until they bled.

Martina became the family expert on floppy hats, mosquito nets, chemical repellents—all the regalia and paraphernalia of bug protection. Some nights at bedtime she sprayed a restaurant-grade bug repellent into the cabin. My objections counted for nothing. Few things are more detrimental to a sound night's sleep than mosquitos on the loose at night. I gathered bouquets of fleabane, hoping the plant had the natural repellency implied by its name, but the mosquitos only whirred more zealously at our door. In June it was time to hang a mosquito net in the doorway.

"All this scratching for the privilege of living close to nature," Martina observed one day with her usual acuity, jumping to her feet in the moss. How many romantic picnics were never consummated because of the uninvited bugs. Sometimes it seems the only thing separating us from paradise is a no-see-um. The famously short poem "Fleas" puts it succinctly: *Adam had 'em.* Just as I pop a luscious berry into my mouth, I notice the bug in it.

LITTLE BROWN BAT

The insect I resent above all is the one that crawls inside the lenses of my eyeglasses when my hands are occupied. I shake my head from side to side to dislodge the intruder. Insects can turn an hour's recreation into a misery. Casting for fish on a muggy morning, I am bait for the beach gnats. My fellow mammals don't much care for them either. The bear scratches, the fox scratches, the deer scratches: they flick their ears and scratch scratch scratch. No wonder it's such a pleasure at twilight to watch the swallows and the little brown bats feast on the insects.

The dragonfly, Alaska's state insect, is nicknamed the mosquito hawk for the good reason that it hunts and devours mosquitos. Alaska's schoolchildren elected the dragonfly, the four-spot skimmer dragonfly, the state insect and elevated it over the second-place mosquito. A marvel of nature's engineering, the dragonfly has been studied by scientists for the biological sophistication of its eyesight and its flight. Its flying skills have earned the dragonfly comparisons to Alaska's bush pilots—high praise for the bush pilots.

A large dragonfly landed on my head in the middle of Kupreanof Strait, more than a mile from the Kodiak seashore. This was in July near the peak of the dragonfly's life cycle. The colors of my cap, terra green and goldenrod, warm and inviting against the gray backdrop of the sea, may have attracted the keen-eyed dragonfly. It settled on my cap and stayed there as I moved about the raft, helping my wife and son with their fishing poles. A sedge darner, the creature had lustrous green and yellow markings along its head, thorax and abdomen, the colors patterning its length with the magnificent geometry of a totem pole. How do I know so much about a dragonfly that perched on my head, only peripherally visible to me? Martina, when she wasn't laughing at the spectacle of an enormous, four-winged dragonfly bestriding her husband, took pictures of it. The dragonfly was a female, and I later wondered in what urgency or distress—the day was cool, we were far from land—she had settled on my green cap as a place to drop her eggs or to rest her wings or to die.

Next day, I sat in the same raft in the same body of water, waiting for a fish to strike my line. The tedium lifted when Martina and Kody pointed their fingers at me and broke into laughter. An inchworm, they said, was making its way across the green peak of my cap. The inchworm must have ambushed me in the vegetation prior to our getting under way in the boat. Ensconced in the green fleece of my cap, a stowaway, it had ventured to sea with us. I only hope this moth-in-the-making found somewhere safe to complete its metamorphosis and join its fellow insects on the peninsula.

I was in the creek bottom one June under the cottonwood trees when a swarm of flies engulfed me. These were wicked-looking flies with long wings and red legs. In their humming approach I had a second's warning before I was inundated. They bounced off me in clusters, their numbers so great that I shielded my face to protect it. A panic arises, an animal revulsion, an imperative to escape. The noise in my ears, the metallic twanging of tens of thousands of wings, the collision of our bodies, the living maelstrom in which I felt trapped—I turned and fled, my face and neck pelted as I ran toward the sea, violently exhaling to expel one of the flies from my throat.

These may have been a species of March fly, but nobody knew for certain, and the local people called them "El Niño bugs" in reference to the summer's unusual weather, a way of explaining an invasion of insects that nobody had seen here before. After a few days the winged hordes vanished.

Entomologists tell us the many wonderful things that common flies do for us, but I dislike flies. Even so, I prefer to live in peace with the flies and to do no needless harm to any insect. For many of these creatures I feel great affection. I love the tall spiders that brave the spring snows and trap the flies in their webs. Life is hard and short, and I never heard a homestead spider complain about it. They shelter under the cabin and die there in quantity, and in spring it's my melancholy task to sweep out their weightless bodies and disperse them in the wind.

I love the patient beetle that plods the moss and the knotty spruce log. And the million white butterflies that arrive like waves in a northwest wind. In June, in the bright, buzzing heyday of summer, the Winnie-the-Pooh bees, yellow and brown, bump and bumble from blossom to blossom. Wild chive flowers sway like purple Taj Mahals where drunken bumblebees forever try to light.

Impossible to forget these fascinating, complicated, often annoying little creatures we share the earth with. The insects are everywhere. Their numbers and energy are immense. Reclining in the grass on a summer's day, I close my eyes and listen to the hum.

JOY

Through the woods and down along the beach we hike, and at low tide we cross the land bridge to Eagle Rock and eat cashews and raisins while we annoy the red-billed oystercatchers, and the children dig for treasures while their mother and I fill the backpack with broken cockles and pumice for the garden, and Kody counts the starfish and is fascinated by the "lessons" his sister gives him on the sea life. We hear porpoises breathing, see otters lounging and eagles peering down at us, and the kid's obsessed, too, by the "woods," the fabled "forest" he hears about in fairy tales—"Are we in the woods now?"—and we laugh and tell him yeah, boy, we're in the woods alright, and we pile onto the four-wheeler and joyride around the cabin, and during the midday rainshower we play Old Maid and Pokémon, and afterwards we swing on the fishing buoy and snack at the Dream Restaurant on "pizza" (tree bark) and "fudge cakes" (mud) and Miranda and I climb the spruce tree and, giggling, throw spruce cones onto the outhouse roof while her mom's inside, and I figure nine years old is old enough to learn to shoot a .22 rifle but the first lesson doesn't go good and Miranda runs crying to the cabin, and her four-year-old brother keenly eyes me—"Hell, no, boy, you gotta be older," I say—and we bathe in the sunshine and hike down to the beach again and float barks in the freshwater pool where the stream empties, we eat ready-to-eat meals watching the waves break and the kids couldn't be happier because MREs are like Cracker Jack to a kid. I remember being nine years old one December day when school was out for the holidays and Mom and Pop made a fire in the windy noonday at the seaside; she buried potatoes in the hot ash and we dug them up and unwrapped the foil and ate them hot from our hands. And even though he's only four years old, going forward I'm sure he'll have memories of Cottonwood—he's a good sport and comes along joking on every adventure, and we hike through the seven-foot fireweed and knight the wildflowers with names like Joy-After-Winter and Color-in-the-Gloom and Sweetness-in-the-Chest, and the children roll down the hill on their sides and dizzily stagger about—*whoo!* smiling *whoo!*—holding each other, and Kody asks are we in the forest yet, and we eat sandwiches and soup for dinner and skip stones in the sea and catch a polka-dotted Dolly Varden on a quarter-ounce Pixie, and Miranda, holding around my waist, wants me to sing "Michael Finnegan" and "Mercedes Benz" as we drive full throttle up the trail, and I guess I'm too hard on them sometimes, like the time I yelled at her not to miss the otters off our port bow—it wasn't her fault she couldn't see around the edge of her too-big lifejacket. Joy should be light, not heavy. They beg me to tow them in the trailer—Dad! Dad! Dad!—so we pad the trailer with floats and they bounce around laughing and screaming back there, and their mom, kneeling in the drizzle of evening, cuts the grass with her clippers so the kids won't get wet and itchy, and Miranda asks her if she's cheerful, and Martina says, "I don't know if Koreans were made to be cheerful," and I keep quiet but I'm thinking, *If this isn't happiness, I don't know what is,* and Martina asks, "Do you know any Koreans who are cheerful?" and I say with a shrug, "But I don't know many Catholic Koreans who *admit* to being cheerful," and she considers this and smiles and goes back to clipping the grass, and I'm thinking it's like pink clouds at midnight on summer solstice, you can call it day aborning or day undying, but it's much the same thing, isn't it? The tide's always ebbing or flooding somewhere, yesterday's footprints fill with saltwater, the stone cliffs erode, laughter recedes into silence, the little ones grow and forget and we fret and can't hold on, but when all is said and done, something remains of it, something must, *is,* an essence of sorts, and though I wonder in outrage how something so valuable can be so vulnerable, how the source of such aching joy weighs so little in the balance, how something so palpable simply vanishes, disappears as though it never existed, I say, but yes that's the point, it cannot, *cannot;* the most durable of lies is that nothing endures, a partial defeat is not futility nor futility a purpose, and though I don't know how or where, something for good and ever lasts of it all, and laughing I hike the broad hills of my dreams, and I shout at the heavens of joy everlasting.

KIDS

L ife isn't always a thrilling bear story; sometimes it's just a potty story. One of the satisfactions of homesteading in the Alaskan bush was to live in close quarters as a family. The joys and sheer fun of parenting are matched by unprecedented cares, and this is true anywhere. What added wonder to wonder was to watch the children grow in the middle of a wilderness, the cradle of life on the planet. Birth, growth, reproduction, decay, death—these processes were going on around us all the time in the plant and animal worlds, and we were in the thick of it ourselves. As the animals came and went with their young, the deer and bear and fox, the otter and beaver, I felt how fitting it was that we had little ones, too.

In the one-room cabin in which we lived at Cottonwood, the living spaces that by convention are partitioned—classroom, rumpus room, bedroom, kitchen—these spaces were for us integrated. On a single table we ate meals, homeschooled, did arts and crafts, butchered venison and played board games. As it was spatially, so it was temporally: we spent all our time together. All the work, play, learning and loving happened in the cabin and surrounding acres. The hours we didn't spend in traffic or in commutes to work or school we spent with one another and with the natural mysteries around us. We had nowhere else to go, true, but these circumstances offered rare privileges. For Martina, who had suspended her work of lawyering, the total, hands-on time with her children was, she later said, the paramount value of her time at Cottonwood, an immersion in mothering that cemented natural bonds of affection and replaced the preconceptions of prejudice with the truths of experience.

Our son Kodiak was fourteen months old when he arrived at Cotton-wood. He barely walked and barely talked. A year later, he was hiking miles on his own feet and had grammar and an extensive vocabulary conditioned by our surroundings. Words like grass, flower, duck ("quack-quack") and fish ("blup-blup") were among the earliest he learned. New words followed in clusters, his verbal curiosity undiscriminating and fed by novelty of experience, his language growing and mind awakening in interaction with the physical world, the more the better. He had no sooner split wood with me than he had the word "mau" (maul). From the mobile vantage of the baby carrier in which he rode on my back, he surveyed the world and pronounced the names—"skoo" (squirrel), "ego" (eagle)—that corresponded to what he saw. Toddling on the beach one day, he surprised us by drawing our attention to a sea otter—"Od-doo!"—a word he had never previously uttered, evidence that he could learn a word, store it away and produce it at the appropriate moment. With the passing months he recognized the trails and features of the landscape. Observing that we were on the return leg of a hike, "House," he said, making the leap of association. "Windy," he said, recognizing the feel and sound of moving air, the sight of the bowing trees. "Deep snow," he remarked one March day as I trudged through it, grunting with him on my back.

I detected a flourishing intelligence in that little head of his. As we walked the low tide, he called up experience, analyzed possibilities and suggested a course of action: "Too muddy, Dada. Walk grass." When I swatted my hand through the air, "Dada, dead fly?" he asked. And as his utterance grew in complexity, he became quite a mimic. He smacked his hands together at mealtime (prayed), jabbed his face with wildflowers (smelled the flowers), and declared, as he bounced his hookless fishing pole on the water, "I got sum'pin." His mouth, lips and tongue, his facial muscles didn't always serve his will, or they couldn't keep up with his expanding vocabulary, and the pathways linking his hearing and speech weren't entirely in sync, so that he confused his *d* for his *g* and his *t* for his *k,* and there were certain words he never managed to get to the end of. How he struggled to say *oystercatcher.* Even so, within a year he knew all of the wildflowers by name, and he had his favorite: the shy maiden, or "sigh maiden," as he called it.

Around his second birthday Kody went through an upheaval that his mother identified as the terrible twos. The prominent word in his vocabulary at this time was "no." If he was dressed, he wouldn't undress, if he was undressed, he wouldn't dress, if he was outside, he wouldn't enter, if he was inside, he wouldn't leave. He was a tantrum and a half. He tripped, fell, scraped himself and dropped things. I saw a grim, hard look in his eyes, a glare of raw will that meant business. If I carried firewood, he wanted to. If I pulled a tarp, he wanted to. He tried to seize the chainsaw out of my hands. He toddled off with the hammer and struck the wall with it. He repeatedly reached for the key in the four-wheeler's ignition, and we finally came to an arrangement whereby he would be permitted to start the engine with my lowly assistance.

Because we lived in close quarters, the boy's emotional distress was catching, and his six-year-old sister cried in sympathy. Miranda understood that beneath his tearful crankiness he was still her sweet baby brother who had emerged from their mother's bellybutton. She harnessed her brother's fury by involving him in his birthday preparations. Kody became the important personage who brought her the colored strips of construction paper that she fashioned into decorative paper chains. Grasping the stapler in her hands, she squeezed it shut on the overlapping ends of each new link. For his birthday she gave him bean bags sewn of polar fleece stuffed with black beans. "Guess how we're using all the black beans, Dad," she whispered. The child who is sensitive enough to attend to the needs of her baby sibling will be a bit wiser a bit earlier in life, I think.

Miranda wasn't quite six years old when she arrived at Cottonwood. Her story was different from her brother's. She had gone through kindergarten in Fairbanks and had left good friends behind. Now she homeschooled and lived in a wilderness cabin with her baby brother and her mother and father. She liked to read, and in rainy weather she read the miniature Moby Books classics at the alarming rate of one a day. For much of the year she sharpened her wits over the Narnia chronicles of C.S. Lewis. An English smartness crept into her speech. "Rather green and rather tart" was how she described the taste of an early salmonberry.

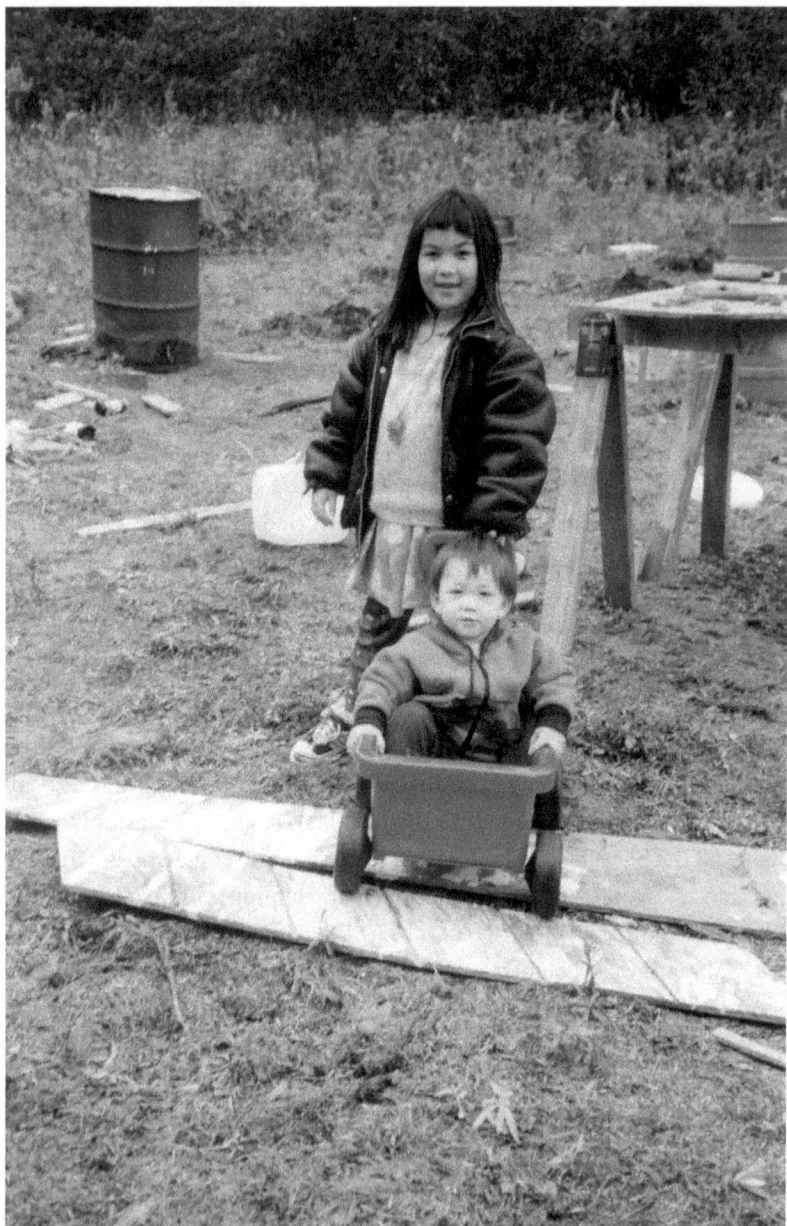

COTTONWOOD, 1998

Miranda, though well past the terrible twos, knew how to dig her feet in, and she more than once conveyed to her parents that our family hikes were no better than forced marches. Exceedingly tolerant of her little brother, she wouldn't be stepped on and made it known when he had presumed too far. I often saw her dreamily smiling, absorbed in one of her alternate worlds, but with her heavy eyebrows and her great brown eyes, she was capable of the profoundest scowls. We often relied on Miranda to mediate between us and her brother, and when the two of them were outside she shouldered the responsibility of staying alert for the crackle of vegetation that might signal the approach of a brown bear.

Our wild surroundings and our explorations in them enabled Miranda to draw parallels between our world and the worlds of her reading adventures. With windblown hair she knelt in the bow ("fo'c's'le," she called it) of our inflatable raft, a rope in her hand, laughing as we surged across the sea, and watching for the moment when at last she could cry in triumph "Port Bailey ahoy!" The end of the school year she celebrated by staging an adaption of *Prince Caspian*. Script, costumes, scenery—she managed the production herself. The tail of Prince Caspian's horse, a mass of seaweed, doubled as the Hag's hairpiece. "I've never heard of a hag with short hair," she explained, tapping her pencil on her cheek. The matinee was rained out, but the next day's opening went splendidly. Our neighbors the Petersons hiked a mile to attend, and they and their dogs each paid the quarter ticket price, so that the little impresario took in a dollar for the show. The audience sat on driftwood stumps, but the production was experimental in that we all played at least one role. Later, at the cast party, we enjoyed refreshments of "champagne" (Crystal Light) and apricot nut bread.

Emotionally and physically the children grew, and in succeeding years we measured the changes in them against the steadier homestead backdrop. They developed with an organic velocity, an inner necessity stimulated by whatever was around them. The Lascaux-like sketches on the cabin walls were replaced by hand-drawn maps. They folded animal origami, they fashioned three-dimensional crabshell puzzles, they recorded observations of the insects and tidepool creatures, and they planted wildflower seeds and harvested wild greens.

One summer Miranda concealed herself under a tarpaulin stretched between the four-wheeler and its trailer, and there in the blue light of the tarpaulin, sheltered from the insects, she read *Anne of Green Gables* and *Flowers for Algernon.* Her knot-tying skills morphed into an interest in codes and disguises. She knotted a secret code into a rope, and when she had done practicing her sheet bends and bowline knots, she tied herself into knots, disguising herself as a "limper," say, by lashing a stick to her leg and filling her shoe with beach pebbles.

Both of the children had short-lived obsessions, which they cast aside like crowns woven of beach grass. They learned to cook homestead meals, to fillet a halibut, and to release the clay pigeons that I shot out of the air. And they themselves learned to shoot. And the summer came, as I knew it must, when Miranda had other responsibilities and wasn't able to join our little platoon at Cottonwood. And in this inevitability I knew her brother Kodiak would follow.

Life's passages, parenting among them, stimulate feelings and behaviors that come naturally to us, a process that merges consciousness with the roots of human experience. This is why so many find in family love an answer to the supposed meaninglessness of life. Meaning has genetic substrates. Meaning, the emotional component of a purposeful drive, is felt, is known in the bone and nerve, not argued, or not convincingly argued, through logic and proposition. Meaning is inward, like faith.

Before going to bed at night, I always took a turn outside the cabin, and seeing in the window the lamplit faces of my wife and children, I had a sense, in the darkness of the hour and the vastness of the wilderness, a sense accompanied by a fearful shiver, of our fragility, our vulnerability to the natural forces that exceed our control. But it was never a prostrating fear or one that didn't include an element of exhilaration, and an element of relish, too, of liking it very much and being willing to testify to the essential goodness of the arrangement.

LORD OF THE DANCE

We pushed back against the dark and isolation with music and dance. It was our little light, our little voice in the wild. George Frideric Handel could have played organ music on those masses of blue ice that overhung the sea cliffs in winter. Rock 'n' roll tunes, folk, the classics—our jamboree was eclectic. Just to make sounds, human sounds, just to spend our breath in singing was what mattered, and we spun every occasion into a holiday. D cell batteries and a disc player gave us band and orchestra, and we ad-libbed our own chords for good measure. Mine is a quiet nature, and a little percussion goes a long way in a one-room cabin. A two-year-old picks up any two things, smashes them together and he's suddenly a symphony cymbalist.

Traditional American Music, one of Miranda's homeschool units, came with audio recordings of favorites like "America the Beautiful" and "This Land is Your Land." It was a joy to relearn the old lyrics alongside the children. I sang Woody Guthrie's anthem way back in grade school. While the kids learned fresh what we had learned as children, I was unlearning much of what adulthood had taught me. The little ones play at being us and we play at being gods, and that's how we get into trouble. I had my cares, my adult cares, yes, but when I gazed around at the wilderness or surveyed civilization from afar, I frankly didn't feel much older or wiser than a child.

Another song in the homeschool songbag was "Rock-A My Soul." I sang this grand old spiritual whenever I was on the mountain, quartering a deer or hiking home through bear country with a pack full of venison. I sang it loud. The point of singing aloud in bear country is to make yourself heard.

The song that meant the most to me while homesteading at Cottonwood was the Shaker dance song "Simple Gifts." Nature's beauty and sufficiency; my gratitude in living in this place with my family; and the rightness I felt in being here: these found in "Simple Gifts" a soulful, uplifting utterance. The melody, repeatedly cribbed and remixed over the years, sometimes goes by the name "Lord of the Dance," but whatever the name, no lyrics speak as intimately to me as the original ones of Joseph Brackett, and to this day, whether it's Judy Collins or Aaron Copland rendering it, the song thrills me and stirs in me a fine, sweet, melancholy regret for our purest intentions and our never wholly lost potential.

Around Thanksgiving is when the song most resonates. The yellows, reds and browns of the season, the lengthening nights and morning mists, the crackle of frost underfoot and the rattle of dried vegetation: the autumn reminds us of time's passing and the terms of mortal life on earth. In the cold months we drew together, glad for the warmth of the fire and the food that sustained us. We hiked the brown hills and the undulating grasses, across the gullies and under the trees, our son and daughter between us, and I often felt transported, and whether it was the Shakers or the Puritans or other settlers or immigrants anywhere in other times, people like Martina's family, who had set out from Inchon in South Korea, or like my own forebears, who came from Malmö and Odessa and forgotten Romanian villages, pioneers and refugees looking to begin their lives anew, people facing challenges much harsher than my own, I nevertheless felt a bond with them, with all of them, with anyone who gains a toehold in a strange and not always hospitable country, humbly proud, cast out but chosen, toiling, toiling for themselves and for their families and communities, not sparing themselves but striving to further their lives and to stay free and faithful and dignified in doing so. We are each handed a tambourine on our way into this world, and it's up to us to strike it.

MAGPIE

I've praised the gifted songbirds, I've exalted the bald eagles and trash-talked the seagulls, but day in and day out it's the crazy corvids, the magpies and ravens, who are my company at Cottonwood. In autumn when the leaves fall and the fair-weather songbirds have departed, the chortling magpie remains. Like the eagles, the magpies and ravens are year-round residents, seemingly unperturbed by the winter's rigors, but they lack the chilly aloofness and the regency of the bald eagle and are better described by their warmth and bantering playfulness.

If I have killed a deer and am caring for the meat, it won't be long before the first responder, a magpie, lights on a nearby branch. Another magpie arrives and they bicker over the scraps. They are gregarious birds; hence the superstition that a single magpie is a bad omen but a pair of them bodes well. If a second magpie never shows up, the natural order of things must be screwed.

Magpies, like their cousins the jays, are expert camp robbers, and indeed they resemble, with their black and white plumage, the masked bandits of cartoons. In diet the magpie is exceedingly omnivorous. The disorder known as pica, in which the human sufferer indiscriminately eats everything—furniture, dirt, dog hair—was named for the magpie, whose Latin name is *pica*. We used to accumulate our son's diapers outside the cabin, but we stopped doing this after it became clear that the ripening diapers attracted brown bears. The only other species drawn to the diapers was *Pica pica*, the elegant magpie. After I removed the diapers, a magpie traipsed across the spot looking for them, her long black tail feathers tracking the snow, something like the train of a lady's gown. She turned her head from side to side, searching for the treasures, and petulantly flew away.

By human standards, magpies are amoral opportunists. They are said to be highly intelligent, capable of recognizing people and even of speaking English. I never got far in conversation with a magpie, but one summer I befriended a raven who didn't just like me for my cracker crumbs. I was still hauling my drinking water from the beach at that time, and whenever I went there to fill my five-gallon cubitainers from the waterfall, this sociable raven descended from the sky and took wing baths in the freshwater pool. Whenever I showed up, she showed up.

Like ravens and crows, magpies have shadowed human beings for ages, harassed and impressed and amused us, and an abundant folklore has developed around them. The word *piebald*, meaning splotched or two-colored, e.g., black and white, corresponds to the word *pie*, which in Middle English means magpie and derives from the Latin *pica*. Dictionaries often give a bonus meaning for magpie: a chatterbox, a person who won't stop talking. I checked my Theophrastus to see if by chance he sketches the character of a Chatterbox, and he indeed sketches both the Garrulous Man and the Talkative Man and compares the latter to a bird, an inanely twittering parrot or swallow.

I associate the black-billed magpie with a staccato yakking and jaybird chattering, but the raven is master of a wider register. On a quiet morning at Cottonwood, my family asleep in bed, the ocean as still and serene as an old silver mirror, a raven belts out three protracted squawks, wakes everybody up, and settles into a mocking single-note chuckle. That is so raven.

The raven is the repeat offender who goes scot-free because he's a juvenile and knows it. The raven is the church vandal who scolds his captors for their lack of charity. Sometimes the ravens mass in the trees and hold a cawing rave, cawing with harsh gusto for minutes on end. The cackling of these bad-ass birds can be so maddening I want to murder them. I have thrown spruce cones at the ravens to shut them up, but ravens aren't a bird I am wise to be annoyed by. They rejoice in the prospect of getting on my nerves. They know me and they know my tricks. They take just enough hops to stay out of reach.

MAIL

The errand known as "going to the post office" took us half a day or more at Cottonwood. There was no post office, but the federal government contracted with Penn Air to fly a mail plane to and from Port Bailey Cannery, about five miles east of us. This plane, a floatplane, ran twice weekly in the summertime and less in winter, always depending on the weather. For a seat fare of $65, a passenger could catch the mail plane back to town.

To use the mail service was never as simple as jumping into the boat and motoring to Port Bailey Cannery when we felt like adding a letter to the outgoing mailbag or seeing if anything had arrived for us. Since we didn't keep our boat in the water, we had to ready it for every trip. To launch the boat, to winch it up the beach afterwards, to remove or remount the outboard motor—it all took time and effort, and we needed the weather to cooperate, too. No mail is worth drowning for. We didn't travel in high seas, and for that matter, fog or wind often grounded the mail plane in Kodiak.

To receive a cherished letter or a package rewarded the efforts. I had been alone three months at Cottonwood when a package arrived from Martina, and by the time I had rafted home from the cannery, put up the boat, climbed to the cabin and dug the parcel from my float bag, I was about bursting with excitement. In the box I found photos, homemade granola, instant vegetarian burger, foil-wrapped chocolate chip cookies, and, in a sticky gallon bag, a recycled water bottle sealed with duct tape and containing ... Kahlúa!

If I needed supplies at the homestead, I used the pay telephone at Port Bailey Cannery to order what I needed. The item eventually arrived in the cannery mail. The process could be frustrating to the point of absurdity.

Every hitch in transportation set me back another week. On one occasion the mail plane arrived empty because the Penn Air crew had forgotten to load the mailbags.

It turns out that you can't ask someone to mail you something at a remote Alaskan cannery and expect it to simply arrive. I ordered gun racks and a winch mounting kit from Cabela's, but the saleswoman wouldn't guarantee delivery unless I gave her a street address. Never mind that we don't have streets on the Kupreanof Peninsula—it was a matter of fooling the computer, she said. The body of water that we travel by boat is the Kupreanof Strait, so I suggested to her the Kupreanof Highway, and her computer fell for it. That's one stupid machine. The gun racks and winch mounting kit eventually arrived in my name at Box KPY, Port Bailey Cannery, Kupreanof Highway, Kodiak, Alaska 99697.

For our family of four a boat trip to Port Bailey Cannery to get our mail had the air of a holiday excursion. Lovely traveling weather, light adventure, the pleasure of meeting neighbors—these contributed to the festivity. There might be weeks of mail waiting for us at the cannery. There might be fresh food sent to us by the good people at Safeway—potatoes, carrots, cheddar cheese—foods which in Kodiak don't spoil in transit. While waiting for the mail plane, we conversed with neighbors about the unreliability of the mail plane, how to build a banya, how to score an emergency medical appointment in town by saying you're "in from the bush," the pros and cons of gun control, the merits of Liquid Nails, whether the President was a sleazebag, whether a tin of Copenhagen would set off security alarms, and so on. From these outings we arrived home reinvigorated, happy to have caught up with the gossip and the news.

In December we received from Martina's parents a care package containing a potent stew of Korean delicacies. Somewhere between Hawaii and Alaska the cardboard box fell apart and was salvaged by the Post Office equivalent of an oil spill containment team. God bless the postal worker who lifted that box dripping with garlic juice and chili marinades. They bagged the original box in plastic and enclosed it, swaddled in insulated packaging foam, in a second box which they addressed by hand and sent to us at no extra charge. Since then I am more apt to rise in defense of the Postal Service than to join others in derision. The foods which my parents-in-law had mailed to us, the recognizable foods, included pickled garlic cloves and sesame leaves, dried cuttlefish, dried seaweed, pepper leaves, a three-pack of pickled daikon radish, a bag of beef soup stock, a bag of stale shrimp chips, a bag of rice crackers and a bottle of tonkatsu sauce, which I splashed onto my venison cutlets that night at dinner. With a pot of rice to go around, we ate a feast, the children especially buoyant because the day's mail had included early holiday presents, which we permitted them to open.

In winter the freezing temperatures made the boat trip to Port Bailey Cannery time-consuming and potentially dangerous. Icy weather impeded the operation of the motor. Wear as many layers of clothes as you like, you will be cold in an open boat in winter. It took us eight hours, the heart of a winter's day, to travel to the cannery and back, and we finally stored the boat and motor and did without mail until spring.

Richard Pederson, our neighbor, had taken a post office box in the village of Port Lions, southeast of us, and I sometimes rode with Richard in his skiff. The aluminum skiff slammed up and down in the waves, and these trips were hard on the sacroiliac. Port Lions had an actual post office, a flag-flying post office that sold postage stamps and hung posters of wanted criminals. Naturally, the price of a first-class stamp had risen since I had been away from the world, and in Port Lions I traded my 32-cent stamps for 33-centers and gave Ginger, the postal clerk and notary public, a handful of pennies to cover the difference.

When you arrive at Port Lions on a flood tide, you can beach your skiff on the waterfront near the post office. It's convenient. But one beautiful morning in January, Settlers Cove was iced over. Richard assumed the ice was just skim ice and hit it at full throttle, expecting to break through it. Instead, we climbed up on the ice with a nasty thump and slid across a thick pan of it. The outboard motor kicked up and the Prevailer battery spilled forward and sparked out on the aluminum floor. We ended up high and dry, seventy-eighty feet from open water.

"Looks like hell finally froze over," Richard said.

We were using the oars to break free of the ice when a Good Samaritan with a power skiff saw our plight and repeatedly eased his bow onto the ice on either side of us to free us. The Good Samaritan later hit Richard up for fifty dollars, claiming he had broken his propeller in helping us.

In the springtime we resumed our family mail runs to Port Bailey Cannery. Through a combination of air, land and sea transport, the mail worked its way to our homestead cabin on the north coast of Kodiak Island. Miranda, assigned a homeschool project on the glorious nation of France, received from the French embassy in Washington, DC, a thick packet of information that she had requested. She was enormously pleased. The Postmaster General at the time was William J. Henderson, and I would like to thank Mr. Henderson for enabling a six-year-old in rural Alaska to communicate with the French embassy in Washington. Let me also express my admiration for the dedicated pilots who fly the mail planes in bush Alaska. I might as well acknowledge the entire Postal Service for their visionary persistence in an enterprise that only visionary persistence would describe as cost-effective. Alaska's mail plane is a sort of flying post coach, a descendant of the early stagecoaches that carried mail and people across the American continent and with pluck and bravado joined us together and helped to forge a national identity.

NEIGHBORS

When I was young, descending to the airport of any great city, I was big enough in my heart's aspirations to wish that I knew all of the people who lived below in the countless houses we overflew. I marveled that there were so many people in the world, each with a life story, with attachments and interests of the utmost importance to them, and I wondered how it would be possible for me to know them all.

Of course it wasn't. It is morally possible to love all of humanity, and it is possible for a cleric, an entertainer or a politician to connect with multitudes, but to live in an actual city among millions of strangers jostling in their day-to-day pursuits of their interests and to maintain at the same time a more than generic acceptance, a high level of caring about them as individuals, this doesn't seem to be within our capacity as human beings.

It isn't a judgment on our relative goodness to point this out, or to observe that for most people, the non-mystics among us, there is an upper limit to the number of people we can closely be surrounded by and still feel close to. Neighborliness, the relationship of cordial solicitude that exists among people who live near one another, may be less often realized than idealized. Neighborhood is hardly even a spatial term anymore. Twenty-first century neighbors are likely to be virtual neighbors, identified by their proximity in cyberspace, not in physical space. The correlation between neighborliness and numbers might actually be an inverse one: the bigger the population that engulfs us, the more alone or alienated some of us feel. In the Alaskan outback, where people are few, each individual looms larger than is the case in a populous capital. Where humans are few, a person's humanity becomes the salient and attractive feature.

BUSTER AND LIBBY'S CABIN, 2017

Not all solitudes are the same, and the number of people around us is only one determinant of the kind and degree of solitude. My solitude as a bachelor was different from my solitude as a family man. Physical isolation differs from existential aloneness. On this island in the Gulf of Alaska, it isn't the walls of buildings or of social prejudices, it isn't the numbing randomness of a day among strangers that distances me from other people; it is physical geography, true distance measured in mountain ranges and miles of ocean. I am so far out of earshot at Cottonwood that no stigma attaches to my celebrating my solitude as loudly as I please. I discharge the revolver when I feel like it. Nobody complains. I miss people, certainly, and I never equate solitude with freedom because I never equate freedom with the absence of human attachments. This would be disastrous. "It may be true that he travels farthest who travels alone," Teddy Roosevelt writes, "but the goal thus reached is not worth reaching." What sustains me in my solitude are the bonds of my affection for others. I miss people as individuals, but to be honest, I never miss the mindless hive, the multitudinous sidewalk that is more often a backdrop for aspirin commercials than a source of fellowship.

City and country differ in the expressions of neighborliness that are peculiar to them. In a city I might live for years next to somebody I know next to nothing about. In the bush I will consider someone a neighbor whom I've never even met but who owns a tiny cabin ("so-and-so's place") in the miles of unfenced wildland through which I hike. Helping a neighbor to recover a boat that has slipped its moorings, loaning the neighbor a fishnet, stepping outside to try the neighbor's new .50-caliber revolver, sharing a vegetable harvest from the garden, repairing the neighbor's door after a brown bear has destroyed it—such acts of neighborliness are peculiar to a life on the Kodiak seaboard, not to a life in, say (with the possible exception of the .50-caliber revolver), Chicago.

Until they moved out of Alaska, our nearest human neighbors, Richard and Laurel Peterson, were the only full-time residents for miles around. Their homestead was separated from ours by woodlands and streams and dense thickets, but in spite of the distance and the obstacles, they were more neighbors to us than the neighbors we used to hear bicker and abuse their furniture behind the common walls of the urban apartments we had occupied. I introduce the Petersons elsewhere in this book ("The Petersons"), and I note various neighbors throughout, but here I profile three other local families.

The Flerchingers

Ed and Britta Flerchinger lived on a 99-year land lease on the southeast shores of Afognak Island, the second biggest island in the Kodiak Archipelago. On the VHF radio they went by the handle "the Narrows," this being the passage of water that separates their corner of Afognak Island from Little Raspberry Island on the south. Britta was an Alaska Native (Alutiiq, through her mother), as was their son Tuggy, a Tlingit they had adopted in his infancy, now a young man with his own land allotment, a forested parcel from which the family took their lumber.

Ed Flerchinger, who had come of age in northern Idaho and had made a living and lost a finger as a mechanic, had along the way acquired the skills of handy inventiveness that are the envy of one like myself, who champions self-reliance but never mastered the trades. I believed the man could do anything. What a spread they had! The very dock where they moored their boats had been built by the Flerchingers. They had fitted the dock with a davit and hydraulic power winch that enabled them to lift an engine or a heavy generator into or out of a skiff. Even the aluminum pulley blocks had been fashioned by Ed. *That's* self-reliance. In the marine supplies shop in town, those magnum pulley blocks would have cost the rest of us two or three hundred dollars.

Aluminum welding was just one of Ed's talents. He padded around the compound in his house slippers showing me the highlights: the knee-operated log splitter, the larder with its twelve inches of sawdust insulation that kept the temperature at 36°F in winter and 42°F in summer, the shallow water well, the trio of generators (4, 5 and 8 kilowatt), the fuel room, the machine shop (a four-wheeler, tires removed, was hoisted up on a pair of sawhorses), and the wood shop where Ed had carpentered his own gun cabinets and the spruce wood wainscoting of the living room.

I sometimes heard Ed and Britta chatting on the VHF radio with our neighbors, the Petersons. Ed and Richard talked politics and building projects, Britta and Laurel, gardens and family. The husbands teased the wives and vice versa. Longtime friends, a generation ahead of me, the four made light of their ages. "We were in Port Lions having our free senior citizen dinner." "There's a new diabetic in the family." "Oh, you didn't know so-and-so had died." "I haven't completely lost my memory yet."

Ed Flerchinger was a stout man with stout opinions which he stoutly articulated, and whenever I visited the Flerchingers at the Narrows—I sometimes rode with the Petersons in their skiff—I sat in on exhilarating discussions of American culture and world affairs. A subject that often engaged the company was the First Amendment, and as a writer I was asked my thoughts on the subject. It's hard to make a case for the First Amendment,

I replied, when so many are making the case for its abridgement, but in the name of all good things we must try. We drank coffee and conversed at leisure until dear Britta rose and removed the tin of cookies from the window where the warmth of the sunlight had caused the frosting to run. It was typical of Britta to notice such a small thing as this. I am one who prefers to fetch a cup of coffee for a woman than to be served it by her, and Britta fussed about us more than I liked. She sometimes rested her chin in her palm and gazed out the window with an air of melancholy. A gentle, considerate woman, she gave me apples and oranges to take home to my children, knowing that we seldom got to town from our homestead.

Tuggy, their son, was a silent, practical young man, but I am told by people who knew him in his boyhood that Tuggy ran with the wildest. Today on a fair day in Kodiak you might see Tuggy taking to the road on his motorcycle. Mechanically gifted like Ed, Tuggy was also an accomplished duck hunter, a well of information about the local waterfowl. There is always a subject that turns a quiet man talkative, and for Tuggy it was duck hunting. Kodiak Island offers some of Alaska's best duck hunting, he insisted, because of its sheltered inland waters, and he drew my attention to the pintails and loons that wintered in the anchorage behind the Flerchinger dock.

I had assumed that Tuggy was quiet by temperament, but his throat cancer may have had something to do with it. It defied my sense of fairness that a man as young as Tuggy should be so afflicted. He frequently traveled to the mainland to get a CAT scan or a dose of radiation. A year earlier the doctors had given him antibiotics for what they had misdiagnosed as tonsillitis. His neck swelled up and it was hard for him to breathe when the tumor pressed on his windpipe. Tuggy eventually underwent a surgery that left him with a stoma, a hole in the throat, and today he talks with the greatest difficulty.

The past is far away now, but even from this distance I smell the lemon-almond fragrance of Britta's fresh-baked kulich bread. When we sat at the window and watched the birds at their feeder, there was so much we didn't see. What are the skills of a master builder, what is the love of a good woman, against the fate that awaits us?

Ed and Britta Flerchinger have passed on, and Tuggy survives with a vacancy in his heart that time overgrows but no surgery cures. Ed had

LAND OF BEAR AND EAGLE

wanted to have his prostate removed, knowing there was cancer in his genes, but the doctors wouldn't do it, and sure enough the cancer manifested—an aggressive, fatal form of it. Shortly after Ed died, Britta had a painful flare-up of diverticulitis, a condition for which she had previously been treated. She checked into the hospital in Anchorage and died in surgery on the operating table.

How strange it is! Nothing was more real than our lively conversations, nothing warmer and more savory than her fresh-baked kulich bread.

The Lundgrens

On the day we met Faith Lundgren, she and two of her daughters had boated to Port Bailey Cannery to meet the mail plane. We had boated there for the same reason, and afterwards it was invariably on mail day at the cannery that we saw the Lundgrens. They lived a short skiff ride from the cannery in a rambling house on the far side of Dry Spruce Bay. Over the years, as their family grew in number—there were six children now—they had added to the house while subsisting "off the grid," independent of the public utilities like electricity and running water.

Faith Lundgren was a capable, spirited woman, the sort of woman who stands up front and tells you up front where she stands. Her devotion to her family was praised by all who knew her. With her husband, Ken, she had brought up five daughters and a son on the shores of Dry Spruce Bay. Three of the children had been delivered there by Ken himself. Later I learned that there had been another child, a first son, stillborn after Faith contracted the intestinal infection giardia from a tainted water source. The child was buried on the property.

Faith homeschooled her children through middle school, and they boarded in town to attend high school. A woman who has homeschooled six children has effectively gone through school seven times, and it surprised nobody when, years later, Faith became a schoolteacher in town. Ken Lundgren, for his part, didn't think much of schoolteachers, complaining that they set themselves above the rest of us. Ken liked to tell the anecdote about the schoolteacher who pumped gasoline for his boat and went off without paying for it. "I'd understand if it was a fisherman who did that," he said, "but a schoolteacher!"

A mustached fisherman in Xtratuf boots and a worn raincoat, Ken was lately having trouble finding reliable employment. He had worked years as a cannery mechanic and a fisherman, but with the downturn in Alaska's fishing industry and the closing of Port Bailey Cannery, gainful work was hard to come by. The bush life, for all of its freedoms and satisfactions, its ancient dignity and wild excitement, is a hard life, and the Lundgrens sometimes wearied of the bush life and the toilsome routines of maintaining a home in isolation. As the children grew up and left Kodiak Island for colleges and jobs in the Lower 48 states, Faith and Ken imagined one day moving south as well, possibly to the Pacific Northwest, knowing, of course, that they were not the first Alaskans to talk of pulling up stakes and moving Outside, just as folks in the Lower 48 talk with dreamy optimism of heading north to the Great Land.

The Lundgrens will have many memories of the life they forged in the rambling house on Dry Spruce Bay, and the memories are inviolable, but the house itself was reduced to ash in 2014, put to the torch by the Afognak Native Corporation in the execution of a legal settlement. Scorched trees are today visible at the edges of the site where the Lundgren house once stood. A generation earlier, the Lundgrens had erred in the placement of their first beachfront dwelling, erred by occupying ground some two hundred feet beyond their property line, on land that had recently been conveyed to the Afognak Native Corporation under terms of the Alaska Native Claims Settlement Act. The Corporation ultimately became aware of the encroachment and in 2012 filed a lawsuit to evict the Lundgrens.

The Lundgren trespass dispute became a cause célèbre in Kodiak. The Native and non-Native communities get along well here, but the Lundgren case reopened old wounds. The statute of limitations (Had Afognak Native Corporation waited too long to sue?) and the question of squatter's rights (Did the Lundgrens have an interest in the real property they had illegally occupied?) were addressed by the attorneys. The Lundgrens denied that their encroachment had been "willful and intentional." Afognak Native Corporation shareholders equate the integrity of their land and its borders with the preservation of their Alutiiq culture. The history of trespass against that culture is indisputable. Did this justify incinerating the Lundgren house before the family had raised the funds to relocate it? In the blogs and social media, this was the argument, and the back-and-forth was heartfelt and sometimes acerbic:

"First the Russians took it, then the US took it, and now the Lundgrens are trying to steal part of what is not theirs. Stop trying to play victims. You are stealing, and the rightful owners ... deserve their land back."

"ANC is behaving in a cold-hearted and mean-spirited manner. Why would they want to do something like this to good honest people? Isn't this similar behavior that they hated when it was done to their ancestors?"

At the website Change.org, activists started a petition: "Please don't destroy the Lundgren Family's homestead of 30 years." Alutiiq friends urged that the family be given more time to salvage their belongings. The dispute had moved into the arena of public opinion, but in point of fact the legal battle was over. In March 2013 the Lundgrens accepted a payment of $10,000 as part of a binding settlement whereby they were given one year to remove from the subject land "any encroachments and personal belongings." A year later, the house was deemed abandoned.

I have been reluctant to discuss the case of *Afognak Native Corporation v. Lundgren*. My discussing it, and the resistance I encountered from both parties when I approached them about doing so, becomes an instance of the problematic theme—and the challenge—of neighbors and neighborliness. Human relationships are part of the ecology of a place, and I discerned in the trespass dispute an overriding symbolic significance. Aya Lundgren, the eldest child, an attorney, expressed her family's pained bewilderment when she questioned what ANC hoped to gain by their action "other than a few feet of land, which will be washed away by the tides in a few short years, and a pile of burned rubble." To the shareholders, on the other hand, the land conveyed to them under the Alaska Native Claims Settlement Act is their most valuable asset, culturally and economically. Consistent with their rights under the final judgment in the case, they cleared the land of the encroachments and restored it to what they had described in their initial complaint as "its original condition."

The Babcocks

One rainy night in September, we looked in on Buster Babcock and his young wife, Libby. The rain was beating on the rubber roof of the tent in which the couple lived while Buster built a log cabin. Inside, the Babcocks had used the last of their cake mix to cook, on a battered Coleman camp stove, what Libby laughingly called "mountain cake." Libby's English was unsophisticated—she was recently from the Philippines—and the appellation "mountain cake" was probably Buster's. Cherry sauce and marshmallows were gooped over this confection, which looked, frankly, terrible, but the Babcocks had done us the neighborly turn of offering it, and so we sat with them in the long tent in the rainfall and ate mountain cake, the children much happier about it than Martina was.

I had been in Fairbanks getting the family ready for our move to Cottonwood when the Babcocks showed up on the peninsula and I heard rumors of them. The parcel of land which the Babcocks were homesteading was in the same survey section as ours. One informant called Buster a "character" and described Libby as "a large-mouthed country girl from the Philippines." Another informant, a skipper who had transported the Babcocks in his boat, described Buster as an "eccentric" and "a failed pioneer with a mail-order bride." A neighbor warned me that Buster would "poor-boy" me, i.e., he would plead poverty in asking favors of me.

I found Buster Babcock to be chatty, energetic, physically fit for a man of sixty-one years, and, in his verbal fluency, repetitive and pompous, what fine folks call a boor. Homesteading was Buster's dream: to build a log cabin with a sod roof was Buster's dream and by God, he was doing it. To come out here where there was nothing at all and to build a log cabin with a sod roof!

As a matter of fact, in little more than three months, Buster, with Libby's help, cut a clearing in the spruce wood and built on it a 15-foot-square cabin of three-sided spruce logs. A janitor and tinker from Anchorage,

Buster earned my respect for his hardscrabble building skills. Making do and making shift were an art with Buster Babcock. Scraping by and cutting corners were his métier. I had never seen a man hew boards out of a log the way Buster did it. He had no milling equipment; he just snapped a chalk line down the length of a spruce log and ripped the boards straight out of it using a Stihl chainsaw with a 36-inch bar and a cutting technique he had learned in the Philippines. "I sat down one day," he recalled, "and watched these Filipinos sharpen their chainsaws with the file perpendicular to the saw teeth, and they cut perfect lumber out of coconut trees using nothing but a chainsaw and their fingers for a tape measure."

So described, the process sounds simple, but the feat of ripping lumber lengthwise out of a log is physically grueling, and when I saw Buster some years later—it was the last time I saw him—he was a ruin, a pig valve in his heart, plagued by arthritis in the hip and hand, and hobbled by a calcified shoulder that he blamed on the cabin-building.

When it was time to fit his new cabin with a door, Buster came to me for plywood. I gave him two sheets of three-eighths-inch plywood in exchange for the firewood and lumber tailings that I took off his property. I had already given him several sections of chimney pipe and a coffee can full of nails. Buster noticed that our raft was inflated, and he asked about a ride to town. "If that man shows up, you know he's going to want something from you," Martina warned me. "As soon as he sees you, he asks for something."

There was some truth in her observation. Bush residents are generous with their help, but they start from an expectation of preparedness, of dignified self-reliance, and Buster Babcock had a strain of unconcern or improvidence that approached shamelessness. He and Libby planned to return to Anchorage in mid-October, but they didn't have a means of getting back to Kodiak, let alone Anchorage. "It would be funny if it wasn't so sad," one neighbor said to another. Buster was genuinely wanting in resources, and people did him favors out of decency, but they couldn't refrain from taking swipes at him. Two men bucketed up some used diesel oil for Buster—strained through a rag, the oil served as bar-and-chain oil for his chainsaw—but even as they did this they quipped, "Maybe we should put sand in the oil. It'll ruin his saw and he'll have to leave sooner."

What people objected to was not Buster's poverty or his need of assistance; it was his knowingly putting Libby and himself into a bush situation where their success and even their survival were in jeopardy if they did *not* receive assistance. Martina had a notion that Buster had brought Libby here from the Philippines as a kind of slave labor to help him in the bush work and serve him in the necessaries and never warned Libby what she was getting into. Martina reported meeting them on the trail one day, and Libby having wished Martina a good morning, Buster turned to Libby and said, "It's afternoon, idiot."

I wasn't there. When Martina reported this jaw-dropper to me, I wondered if she was taking liberties in the manner of the touchy-feely translator who gives you the so-called spirit of the thing rather than the actual words. Instead of "It's afternoon, idiot," the words Buster had spoken might have been "Libby, darling, forgive me for dwelling upon your misapprehension of the time, but please be apprised that we have entered upon the postmeridian hour."

Be that as it may, the next time I chanced to meet the Babcocks, both of them wearing mosquito nets over their faces, I hurried out a greeting of "Good morning" just to get the proper salutation out in the open.

Around this time I heard another Buster-humiliates-Libby-in-public story, this one from our neighbors the Petersons. Speaking of Libby's predecessor, a Filipina who "hadn't worked out" and who had been sent home on the airplane, Buster reportedly told the Petersons in front of Libby—reportedly, mind you: "You should've seen the one before Libby. She was even prettier."

I wasn't there. It's only fair to say that I never witnessed anything that suggested that Buster was exploiting or even denigrating Libby. Either I'm a fool or Buster elevated his behavior in front of me. There's no denying that Libby was ignorant of Alaska, but that's not a reason to blame a man for enjoying her company though he's twice her age and then some. Buster told me that he had explicitly warned Libby in Manila what she was getting into and tried to talk her out of traveling to the United States with him. In my presence, Buster praised Libby for her hard work and said he couldn't have built the cabin without her. "I am so proud of this gal. A man can't be prouder of a woman than I am of Libby. I wouldn't take a stack of gold from here to Anchorage for her," he said, and Libby affirmed how much she liked Kodiak Island and never appeared unhappy or constrained before Buster. Their first priority when they returned to Anchorage was to dine at Libby's favorite restaurant, the Twin Dragon.

Regrettably, men and women aren't infallibly kind to one another. Buster Babcock told me the story of his failed first marriage, and he told and retold the story with verbose and masochistic relish. I won't repeat the details of his wife's betrayal, but in a nutshell she ran off with another man—Buster's brother, as fate would have it. "It was her long-term plan," Buster told me. "She got a taste for expensive things. No, she wouldn't do any of this *camping*," he said with mock horror.

I have left until last the allegation that Buster cheated on the homesteading rules and never intended to live on his homestead for the twenty-five months required by Alaska's homesteading law. Rumor had it that Buster had photographed a discarded propane stove and had submitted the photograph to the state as evidence that he had fulfilled the cookstove requirement. The idea that Buster might fraudulently acquire a parcel of state land and then sell it at a profit provoked understandable resentment among the scattered area residents. We debated it. If you suspect someone of cheating, how much effort should you make to find out? Should you report the fraud? What is the claim of a would-be homesteader who, displaced by a charlatan, never gets a chance at his or her dream? If a system is indifferent to corruption, what should a principled individual's stance be toward the system? The case of Buster Babcock stimulated among us few residents impassioned and wide-ranging discussions of ethics and character. The women expressed a stronger repugnance than the men. Martina, who loathed Buster Babcock, gave me grief for my compassion for him. But I had no cause to condemn the man and I wasn't about to do God's or the government's job by hounding my neighbor for insufficient cause.

There is a natural, justifiable pride in homesteaders who earn a freehold through toil and grit and an investment of time and resources. This pride is the reciprocal of a great humility. The word *sacrifice* is inadequate. A homesteader's heart is in the land and in the project of building a life on it, and what looks to others like a sacrifice—the deprivations, the hardships—is no such thing to the homesteader. Our satisfaction in homesteading did not depend on Buster Babcock, and I begged Martina not to let the question of Buster's dishonesty tarnish her experience at Cottonwood.

 In the ensuing months and years I saw little of Buster and Libby. After his cabin was built, after he had proved what he must prove, Buster looked immensely tired and careworn. He eventually got ownership of the homestead and sold it. I never knew whether Buster cheated for the property or not. Three witnesses must have signed affidavits for him, testifying that he had met his statutory obligation to live on the homestead, but he never asked me to sign for him and I was spared any soul-searching on his account.

I have found that when people settle in proximity to one another, even in as thinly populated a neighborhood as the Kupreanof Peninsula, it can begin to feel crowded, and it may not be long before you witness some of the ills, animosities and moral dilemmas of the society you left behind. But Alaska's bush is so large and little populated that I am seldom thrown involuntarily into the company of others. I do believe there's not a man or woman on earth with whom I couldn't enjoy neighborly relations if he or she lived in a cabin a half mile distant. Neighbors offer a welcome respite from solitude, and I gladly go out of my way to cross paths with another human being and to get word of the world.

OTTER

One drizzly morning a sea otter emerged at our trailhead, galumphed past the cabin, and, heading away from the saltwater, disappeared in the willows. I wish I knew where he was going. With his webbed feet and stout legs, he moved like the monstrous offspring of Quasimodo and a seal. I'm sorry to drag the Frenchman into this, but I can't think of a better way to convey the awkward locomotion of a sea otter on the land.

Maybe he was electromagnetically challenged, a victim of global warming. Maybe he was a beatnik otter following an eccentric beat. A naturalist otter in search of the inland beavers. An explorer otter determined to be the first sea otter to cross the Kupreanof Peninsula on foot. Maybe his people suffered from an obscure mineral or vitamin deficiency and he knew where to get the stuff and would return home a hero.

There were many explanations why a sea otter might venture so far out of his element, but the personnel at the Kodiak offices of the Alaska Department of Fish & Game and the Kodiak National Wildlife Refuge couldn't give me a single one. Educated people, they wouldn't believe what they couldn't explain, and they doubted that a sea otter had hiked a fifth of a mile uphill from the seashore and made an ungainly appearance by my cabin. Had I mistaken a river otter for a sea otter? The creature I had seen, big in body, short in tail and ludicrous in gait, was unmistakably a sea otter.

As a child I read Gavin Maxwell's *Ring of Bright Water* and I have since been a fan of otters, of river otters and sea otters alike. Not everybody is as fond of otters. River otters are known to occupy and befoul the crawlspaces under people's cabins, and I have yet to meet the homeowner who doesn't have a threshold at which warm-hearted affection turns to cold-hearted problem-solving. The river otters are unafraid of saltwater, and if surprised on shore they will dash for the safety of the sea. We unintentionally bayed a river otter on a forty-foot clifftop and she hissed at us and flung herself off the cliff—kerploosh!—in a dramatic gesture worthy of the Greek priestess Hero, who flings herself into the Hellespont after her beloved Leander drowns. Curious, we followed the otter's small footprints and her long, slim body prints to the base of a spruce tree where she had been hollowing a den under the tree roots.

River otters are native to Kodiak Island, and Kodiak lies at the heart of the northern sea otter's range. Sea otters are our neighbors all year long and in every kind of weather. Rafts of them snooze and feed among the kelp beds in the lee of the nearby islets. When we beachcomb it's not unusual that a frisky sea otter follows in the shallows. She treads water, observing us, then she vanishes, and presently her whiskered face pops up elsewhere.

If on land the sea otter is ambulatorily challenged, a terrestrial misfit, at sea she's a sleek, graceful nymph. Her wake, visible from our cabin window, is a single dreamy line in the glassy water. In foul weather she is maddeningly nimble and nonchalant. I might be drowning while she floats on her back paring her nails. Her dense fur keeps her warm and buoyant in the frigid waters. If a wave breaks on her, she casually tosses her head like a surfer shaking the wet hair out of her eyes. During a winter storm I worked to save some equipment that I had been foolish enough to leave on the beach. The snow was falling, the surf breaking, the tide driving high on the beach, and a trio of sea otters watched me scurry about like their midday entertainment.

In winter and summer, in lousy weather and fair, the mothers and pups punt along in a happy domestic embrace. The mother likes to swim on her back, and since her nipples are on her abdomen, her pup lounges there while pulling at the milk. These tender scenes are common, the mothers and pups cuddling and eating and grooming at sea. We once heard an otter keen for hours in terrified grief, we assumed, for her lost pup. The screams were heartrending in their hopelessness. Sea otters are protected by law, by human law, but killer whales and sea lions and salmon sharks answer to a different law.

It's probably a good thing the sea otters have natural predators. Otters consume tons of forage and may impact a shellfish population. Fisherman Mark Thomas blames the smash-and-grab otters for the decline of Kodiak's Dungeness crab. "The otters wiped out the west side of the island and they're moving east and south," Mark tells me. "They catch a crab in their paws or bash it open with a rock and munch the soft meat and move on to the next crab. I always loved sea otters, but in Seward Harbor I watched an otter bring a Tanner crab up from the bottom. He ate what he wanted, threw the parts away, dove down and got another one, and in twenty minutes he ate, like, twenty crab. How's that possible? That's when I knew there was a problem."

Another fisherman friend was attacked by a "water weasel" as he drove it off with an oar. The otter had been stealing salmon from his net. The otter hissed at him, bit the oar and tried to wrestle it away from him.

Sea otters belong to the exclusive club of tool-wielding mammals, and this otter nearly seized the oar and brained my friend with it. I was fishing with my family one day when an otter slung his paw over the edge of our raft, looked in at us and sniffed the bait bucket with such relish that his whiskers loudly rasped on the boat vinyl.

I imagine a coffee table book of old otter faces like those photo albums of wizened Tibetan faces and pensive Mediterranean faces. Our raft nearly collided with one old codger—hard of hearing, maybe—before he shrieked indignantly and slipped underwater. Groups of senior otters with white collars stare at us like faces from a Velázquez portrait. Their grizzled faces are scarred by everything from crab claws to rough sex. According to biologists, the scarred face of an elderly matron may chronicle a lifetime's sexual vigor. It's an excellent thing that sea otters breed all year long. Once almost exterminated, sea otters now thrive in Alaska and we humans have made true progress in our relations with them.

OUTHOUSE

Outhouses aren't amusing or romantic, but a great part of the world relies on them and I won't turn my back on them. All civilization started from a hole in the ground and progressed from there, and outhouses are a necessary stage in the evolution of self-composting, health-monitoring smart toilets.

In Alaska, outhouses are a specialty. Even today they are common, and abandoned outhouses add a rude or picturesque touch to the landscape. The ocean-view outhouse I built at Cottonwood in the summer of 1997 was modeled on a frame outhouse I had seen in the White Mountains north of Fairbanks. I lined the outhouse pit with a ribbing of treated plywood according to specifications I had found in a back issue of *Mother Earth News*. Digging an outhouse pit is sheer drudgery and I never want to do it again. When I worked in wildland firefighting, the worst job you could draw on a deployment was to dig the pit for the shitter (as it was called). These were hastily dug holes, and we weren't asked to impress a romantic partner with them. At Cottonwood I had Martina to consider. I painted the outhouse pink and roofed it with zinc-aluminum to match the main cabin. Later, a brown bear standing on his hind feet tore up the outhouse roof and left it in the shape of a curly fry. Another year, another bear, or maybe the same bear, ripped the outhouse door off its hinges and destroyed it.

Our outhouse stands in a spruce grove a short walk from the cabin, and when the children were young we didn't let them go there alone. There was a real chance of being caught with your pants down by a brown bear. We hung a buoy swing from the spruce branch in front of the outhouse and the children swung there while their mother sat inside reading *Bleak House* or *Crime and Punishment*. Regrettably our young son got habituated

162

to these family outings, and later, in his teen years, he was still inviting us to join him.

As I say, my inspiration during the outhouse construction was Martina, who has no tolerance for a dank, fly-ridden lavatory. I cut a triangular window in the outhouse door and fixed mesh over it to keep the mosquitos out while admitting light and air. In bad weather she could have her ocean view with the door shut. I wanted her to be happy at Cottonwood and not to decline to return on account of the primitive services. I imported a hundred pounds of quicklime to the homestead and periodically sprinkled this white powder into the pit to decontaminate it.

Not to make her out to be a princess, I'll disclose one of Martina's darkest girlhood secrets. I get shivers just thinking about it. As an impoverished five-year-old South Korean girl, little Hyun Ok slipped backwards through the seat hole of an outhouse one day and clung screaming for help for what seemed an eternity until someone came and pulled her out by the leg. There is so much about my wife I understand better now.

Alaskans are comfortable with the word *outhouse,* but other people have other words for it—backhouse, privy, john, latrine and the like. I have also heard compound constructions like *poop coop* and *potty house.* I learned the word *jakes* from the literary master James Joyce. My father dated himself by using the word *bombsight* for any pit-style toilet. We were in a public restroom on a Paris street many years ago, and I clearly remember the strain in his voice and the redness in his face as he explained to me the metaphoric relevance of "bombsight."

One of our summer wildflowers at Cottonwood is the gorgeous and exotic chocolate lily. These chocolate-colored lilies grow in large numbers on the seaside bluffs in midsummer. They stink. If you want to play a practical joke on someone, show them a sweet face, hold forth a bouquet of chocolate lilies, and ask them to try its fragrance. Don't tell them that the chocolate lily's other name is the outhouse lily.

People turn their noses up at the humble outhouse, but sophisticated plumbing isn't always what it's cracked up to be. My fellow homesteaders the Petersons still had their side-by-side two-seater in the backyard, but they got civilized some years ago, installed a shower and toilet, and buried 250 feet of drainpipe between their house and the sea cliffs. During an especially cold winter, when the water backed up in the shower, Richard suspected a frozen drainpipe. Sure enough, bundled up against the north wind, he located a fifteen-foot icicle hanging from the end of the projecting drainpipe. As a first answer he drew his Glock pistol, fired several shots at the icicle and shattered it. Then he tied himself to a tree to keep from falling off the icy cliff, climbed down with a chainsaw, and sawed the frozen drainpipe back by a foot. Brown water spurted onto his head. "Came spitting out like shit from a gargoyle's mouth," he recalled. Roped in place, Richard couldn't flee before 250 feet of brown sludge emptied on his head. When he finally got back to the house he was all crinkly and stiff like an iceman, but at least the lines were clear and he could take a long hot shower.

THE PETERSONS

Y ou could gauge the mildness of the Kodiak spring and the harshness of the preceding winter by the state of Laurel Peterson's garden in May. A good May saw early blue crocuses, bursts of begonias and galaxies of primroses. A bad May saw late crocuses, inches-high daffodils and rhubarb no bigger than a cabbage. "Criminy, last year by this time I was eating it!"

During a particularly brutal winter, Laurel's clematis vine and her bleeding hearts were decimated. Her ornamental golden chain survived, but the leaves of the rhodies were unnaturally curled. Laurel surveyed the devastation like a bereaved queen. She lived for her summer garden, but the summer continued cold, which turned her marigolds blue. For the broccoli seedlings she constructed a windbreak of roof shingles. In her soft British hat and gardening clothes, or, if her angina was acting up, in insulated coveralls, Laurel ran to check the thermometer. "Still forty-eight degrees!"

As young people who come of age in an economic recession are said to languish financially for years afterwards, so the plants that had survived the awful winter and spring were doomed not to prosper that summer. Four lilacs—four—bloomed on her lilac bush. White blossoms finally appeared on the peas, but not until mid-August, which left no time for a harvest. Worm holes riddled the radishes. The reddest thing in the strawberry patch was the rock that Laurel had painted red to deter the thieving birds. In theory, the birds peck at the rock and get a headache, which discourages them from poaching strawberries. Birds are like people, smart enough to learn but easy to fool.

RICHARD AND LAUREL AT THEIR HOMESTEAD, 2001

The desolation of Laurel's garden was in contrast to the fertile oasis I had seen there in better years. I delighted in hiking west through the uncultivated wild and emerging a mile later at the Petersons' seaside homestead. In the blowing wind, finding myself among brilliant poppies and bobbing columbine, among daisy, spurred nasturtium and fragrant lilac, the garden lively with bees and bright colors, the flora overspilling the split-rail fence, I could have been inside a Van Gogh canvas. The wind seized me up and shook me by the insides. Laurel never liked to leave off gardening, because at her age if she stopped it was hard to get going again. "Farming runs in our blood," she said, speaking of the Arndt family's roots in Montana. When Laurel was hospitalized for a heart attack—she was out of state when it happened—Richard, at home in Alaska, didn't dare to send her flowers because he knew it would infuriate her. "I'd like to see that,"

Richard told me. "Hell, no, I won't send her flowers. She'd have a riot." What Laurel needed was to get home to her garden on Kodiak Island.

Richard was antsy on the morning after Laurel's heart attack, and antsy made him talkative. He had never been able to disable Laurel's work ethic, and he blamed himself for not at least disabling her lawnmower. "I come up one day and found her sprawled on her back on the lawn," he recalled. "Another time I seen her dragging a log under each arm while she was popping nitroglycerine pills."

Richard and I spent the day commiserating and missing our wives. We ate bologna sandwiches and dill pickles and we drank Crystal Light. After lunch I settled back in the sofa while Richard reflected on his life. His eyes watered as he recalled losing his friends and his family to his drinking. "Even my folks told me not to come around anymore when I drank," he said. The time was the 1970s, and Richard, holed up in an isolated cabin near Ninilchik, Alaska, was about to end his life. "One day this Indian walks over to my place and asks me if I'm ready to stop playing games and to start living," he said. "It was like it happened out of the mouth of Providence. There was no reason for this Indian to come over and talk to me. I figured I'd better listen to him. The man lived dirt-poor in a school bus down by the crick, as primitive living as you could get, and I lived there two weeks with him. His name was James Cook, and he drives a cab now in Fairbanks."

Richard quit drinking at the time and he never drank since.

Richard Pederson, aka Okie Pederson aka Joe Kilowatt, was a gargantuan man with a chalky nose and questioning, mischievous blue eyes, a forward-leaning posture, sixtyish in years, a white beard to prove it, and on the day in May 1998 when we met, he having hiked over to my homestead cabin, he wore on his head a green John Deere cap with the leaping yellow deer logo and carried a shotgun with a black metal finish, a pistol grip, a folding stock extension and a magazine literally loaded for bear. He was an altogether earthier gentleman than the narrow man of rectitude I had expected to be put ill at ease by, my prejudice having its source in a nuptial photograph I had seen on the wall of their house, a photo in which, beardless and square-jawed, Richard towers stiffly above his bride Laurel, his head and shoulders seeming to fill the room to the ceiling because of the low angle from which the photograph was taken.

Richard suffered from what I call a tall man's complaint, and to hear him tell it, his height was a curse to him. If he suspected a vendor of cheating him, Richard, a Christian and a man who knew what the inside of a jail cell looked like, always gave the vendor the benefit of the doubt. "I can't afford it otherwise," he said. "A tall man like me, I'll get in trouble for it. You can't win. It's a lose-lose situation. 'Why don't you pick on somebody your own size.' If you lick 'em, you're a bully, and if they lick you, they're giant-killers. You go in a bar and all these little guys—I don't know what it is about 'em—they got something to prove, I guess—they look up at you, they say, 'Boy, I bet it takes a big guy to whup you.' 'Yeah,' I say, 'and it don't take him long,' I say, and I walk away from it. You can't win," Richard said, nodding his head self-mockingly. "It's a burden I carry."

In his years at Kodiak Electric Association, Richard had strung power lines all over the Kodiak Island Borough. "Alaska's been good to me," he said. "I found fame and fortune in Alaska. Been here since 1976. Alaska made a rich Okie of me. I got *two* mattresses on my truck now."

He grew up on a hardscrabble Montana ranch and joined the Navy on an altered birth certificate at the age of sixteen. His folks didn't object. It was either the service or reform school. During the Korean War he was stationed mostly in Hawaii. "Never heard a shot fired in anger," he liked to say.[2]

---

2 Richard qualified his remark with the following recollection: "But I had a trigger pulled on me once. I was living on the fringe back then and this woman who carried a derringer in her bra wanted my money. Maybe I shouldn't call her a woman. She pulled the gun on me and pulls the trigger. We were driving up around Oakhurst, California, near where the Hells Angels meet. Dirty Dave in the back seat, he reaches up and breaks her jaw. Yeah, this gal was a biker and Dave was a biker. She knew I didn't like her, and she didn't like me. She was already strung out on amphetamines and whatnot. She knew I had money on me because we were going to do something probably illegal back then. The derringer's in her bra and it's sweaty and rusted and she leans across the seat and points it at my face and pulls the trigger. Nothing happens. I shit my pants. I shit my pants, just—whoosh—lost control. So we pull over. Dirty Dave's broke her jaw already. You know he's in the back seat cause he stinks so bad. He pulls her out of the car and throws her on the ground and kicks her in the ribs, and we left her there. Far as I know, we didn't kill her.
"Dirty Dave, he was quite a character. He's a biker, you know. He'd buy a new pair of Levi's and never wash 'em. He'd get the grease and dirt on 'em and rub it in and they'd get like leather, you know, get to fitting pretty good up here, but they stink. You sitting in a room with him and you knew it.
"This was in the early 1970s, the late '60s. You probably weren't even around. There were the Angels and the Gypsy Jokers, the Presidents and the Rattlers. I worked at PG&E and had a buddy named Tex, the president of the Presidents. The Presidents had a hangout

He earned his high school diploma as a sailor and was discharged shortly after his twentieth birthday.

Out west, Richard tended bar and became a journeyman lineman with Pacific Gas & Electric Company. Linemen are a breed apart, a risk-taking elite, climbing utility poles and handling massive live voltages, and many of them aspired to join the San Francisco Police or the California Highway Patrol. Richard tried to join the CHP but his eyesight wasn't good enough, and by the time the eye standards were relaxed he had a prison record. He knew a lot of the motorcycle cops ("motorsickle," in Richard's parlance) and he used to put whisky in their coffee under the bar in exchange for an unticketed parking spot. On the other side of the law he knew a lot of the bikers, and he'd seen how thin a line divided the types. Many cops were

---

for bikers and their guests, nothing there but some benches and a jukebox chained to the wall. I was there one day drinking beer with Tex when a young guy comes in looking for Mr. Tex and says he wants to be a biker in the Presidents. Now, I got along pretty good with Tex, I rode a bike, but I didn't go for the whole kit and caboodle. Most of the guys were okay, but there were some mean ones. So Tex kind of winks at me and he says to the fellow, 'You want to be in the Presidents, well, first you have to be initiated.'

"'Okay, what should I do?'

"So Tex takes off his boot, and he takes off his dirty sock—and it's dirty, it stinks—and he pours his beer down through the sock so it filters through the sock and into a glass, and Tex tells him, 'You have to drink this beer.'

"So the fella lifts the glass and drinks it up. 'Aaaaahh,' he says. 'Now can I be in the Presidents?'

"And Tex, he wrings his sock out and pulls it back on his foot and puts his boot on. 'No fucking way. I don't want no dumb fucking sonofabitch in the Presidents that's gonna drink beer from my dirty sock, now get the fuck out of here.'

"Those were the days. I wonder what happened to Dirty Dave. If he's in jail or dead somewhere. You ever wonder what happened to people? Older I get, I do. Dave rode around in the barrel in the circus for a while. They had a big barrel like twenty feet across in the ring and the audience looked down and watched Dave ride around inside the barrel. He'd get going round and round and pretty soon he'd be up on the walls of the barrel. Really wasn't nothing to it. The centrifugal force kept him up there. Then he quit that.

"Last time I saw Dirty Dave I was up in Montana working for Montana Power. He give me a call saying he had somewhere to go in the mountains near the Indian reservation and asked if I could give him a ride. So we drank a few beers. Dave had a knapsack full of Benzedrine and he asked me if I wanted some and I said, 'Sure, Dave, I might need it to get me by some time.' So we're driving on the interstate and Dave's feeling tired and he lays the knapsack down on the seat between us and takes a nap.

"Pretty soon we're in the foothills and this truck full of good old boys drives up behind us and I move over to let 'em pass. They slow down in front of us, and I speed up and they speed up, and they keep doing whatever I'm doing, laughing out the window at us—Crazy! Hey man!—and suddenly Dirty Dave's leaning over me sticking his gun out the window at 'em. He woke up and took the gun out of his knapsack and shoved it out the window and when those jokers saw the gun, I'm telling you, big clouds of exhaust blew out the back of the truck and they took off ahead of us and we never saw 'em again or had any trouble. Dirty Dave, he put the gun in his knapsack and went back to sleep. He was quite a character, Dirty Dave, one of the many gentlemen I've known."

undone by drink or corrupted by temptation. "Throughout history, Tanyo, we were never happy, and the good Lord turned us over to what we wanted," Richard instructed me, and he laid his finger alongside his monumental nose—Richard had a way of diluting his wisdom with humor, not to be too tendentious—and said, "What do you think of my nose? How'd you like to have my nose full of nickels? You'd be set!"

When you make a new friend, there is often a learning curve while you get to know each other's idiosyncrasies. I was on the beach one day near my homestead when Richard headed to shore in his skiff and fired at least half a dozen rounds from his pistol. I looked around for a boulder to dive behind. Had my neighbor lost his mind? It turned out that Richard thought I was up at my cabin and was firing to get my attention. For a person on the shore, it's easy to forget that all the waving of his arms and his jumping up and down is invisible to the one at sea confronted by the vast panorama of the shoreline. "Where are you?" he yelled. Richard nosed the *Washington Monument* over the rocks and finally saw me. "This has your wife's name on it," he said, handing me a letter from the mail drop at the local cannery. "I thought you should have it." Then he farted and ventilated his orange survival suit by unzipping it and winging the flap back and forth. "That's the honest beans talking," he said. "Tomorrow's the Sabbath. Come on over for a visit."

In Richard's presence I was frequently reminded of somebody, and I finally figured out who it was. Next day at his homestead, I found him mopping the floor with Simple Green in anticipation of Laurel's return from a stay in town. Richard was wearing blue jeans and a holstered pistol, his long, shapeless belly bared and his white beard grown out from his chin. "Court required me to go to API once, the psychiatric institute in Anchorage," he said, resting on his mop. "I was certified sane."

"That's good to know," I said.

"Dog tracked the floor and I thought I should clean it up. Chirikov was never very affectionate with me, but he saved my ass more than once. Deaf as a post now. We hide pills in his food. In my grandfather's day they would never have spent a penny on dog food. I guess we spoil him. I don't have the heart to turn him out, but he's not supposed to be in here. Laurel has a mind of her own. Women march to a different drummer, don't they?

Give 'em a million bucks in fifties, they'll say why couldn't they have it in twenties." Richard pointed at the couch by the picture window. "I brung the couch from town one day in the skiff and set it there by the window. Laurel and her mom were like two birds, staring at it and criticizing it, cocking their heads this way and that."

Richard had a mildly reddish cast of face, a chalky, bulbous nose, a bend at the shoulders and a mirthful light in his eyes. I looked from his beard to his face to his forehead, where all of the homespun intelligence resided, and I realized who it was that Richard reminded me of. Socrates! Between the Alaskan homesteader and the ancient Athenian philosopher, between Richard Pederson and the marble busts I had seen of Socrates, there was an astonishing physiognomic likeness. Beyond appearances, Richard had a Socratic way of communicating a point, having accumulated so much empirical wisdom in the School of Hard Knocks that he could produce a concrete illustration for any idea or shine a sidelong light on any subject. For example, when we discussed the abuse of power and the psychological mechanisms whereby institutions, governmental, educational and corporate, extend their power over individuals, Richard didn't dogmatize or throw a lot of theoretical gobbledygook at me. Instead, he told me a story and left me to reflect on it. The story begins with a thirsty seventeen-year-old sailor locked up in the Navy brig at Pearl Harbor. The sailor addresses his guard with a request: "Prisoner 83 requests permission to get a drink of water," he says.

"Why are you asking me, 83? Ask the water cooler."

"Alright." So Richard helps himself to a drink of water from the water cooler.

"What are you doing, 83?"

"Had a drink of water."

"Did you ask the water cooler?"

"Yeah."

"What did it say, 83?"

"It said yes."

Bam! The guard slugs Richard in the face with his shotgun. "Water coolers can't talk!"

In retrospect, Richard laughs about it. "The fellow was having fun with me. But let me tell you, when they hit you with the idiot stick, you go down."

We lunched that day on canned chili and soda crackers. I drank a pop while the old paranoid diabetic ex-boozer Socrates, aka Richard Pederson aka Okie Pederson aka Joe Kilowatt, drank Crystal Light. As I mentioned, Richard was armed with a pistol, though he wasn't doing anything more dangerous than mopping dog tracks off the floor. The pistol was a .40-caliber Glock 23 with a 13-shot clip plus a 2-shot magazine butt extension. Richard wore this pistol at home, he wore it in town, he wore it in the skiff, he wore it all day every day, and he had permits to carry the pistol in every state in which it was legal, and in the other states, who's to say?

Richard's minuteman readiness struck me as excessive, but when I thought about it, how is wearing a gun every day less useful than wearing a necktie or a diamond ring? It's not. Richard was a gun nut as there are jewelry nuts and smartphone nuts. He felt good and looked good in a gun, and feeling good and looking good are two of our surviving moral principles in this country. To draw the line at guns is mere prejudice. Considering the popularity of handguns these days, it's fair to say that Richard twenty years ago was in the cultural avant-garde. I learned a lot from Richard, especially about the bush life in Alaska, and we shared many laughs during our talks and our excursions in his skiff, the *Washington Monument,* so named because of the extra-tall steering console that matched his extra-tall frame.

In his devotion to Laurel, Richard redeemed past waywardness, but he now and then liked to get out from under her watchful eye and to squeeze the throttle a bit harder than she liked. "Honey, should we let the kids watch TV on Saturday night? That's an old lineman's joke. Not the kind of joke for mixed company. No, we save the CAT scan joke[3] for that. Yeah, they'll laugh and laugh at that one, but if I tell a vulgar joke, she'll stare at me like a tree full of assholes. Blank. Nothing. 'You've gotten so crude since we moved out here, Richard.'"

---

3   A woman loved her dog so much that she pleaded with the doctor to save it. The doctor passed a cat around the motionless dog in an effort to revive it, but the dog was dead. "Can you at least bury him?" she asked. "Of course," the doctor said. "That will be three hundred fifty dollars," he said. "Three hundred fifty dollars to bury my dog!" "No, fifty dollars for the burial and three hundred for the CAT scan," he said.

His humor was distinctive, not to everybody's taste. He raised his eyebrows like Groucho Marx at inopportune moments when another man might have wrinkled his forehead in studied sympathy. If at lunch Richard thanked the Heavenly Father—"I wonder what part of the world they're starving in today"—before biting into his bologna-cheese sandwich, his cheeks moistened by the steam from his chicken 'n' angel hair soup, this was Richard's way of acknowledging his good fortune in a world too full of misery. His madman's laugh was just a tool in his toolbag. The brunt of his scorn he reserved for those prigs and busybodies whose life mission is to mainstream the differences out of people. "Hell, put me in the White House, I'd be a turd in a punchbowl," he said. "I'm a middle-class, blue-collar redneck, and I have the red neck to prove it. I don't want to live in Kennewickwick with the Kennedys. Can you see me in Washington with Senator Flipflop? No, sir, I'd rather eat turd rolls."[4]

"You've got to understand linemen—they're all crazy," Laurel told me, making allowances for Richard's humor without entirely exempting him from the norms of what was once called decent society. Laurel had met Richard at Kodiak Electric Association, where she worked in management while Richard worked in labor—a relationship, incidentally, which they may have reproduced in marriage. As Laurel remembers their meeting, she one day condescended to eat lunch downstairs with the linemen and noticed Richard choking on his steak. Richard's version is slightly different. During the safety class on CPR and the Heimlich maneuver, Laurel thumped Richard extra hard on his chest and he got back at her by making her blow up Annie, the CPR doll. "Her lips were all puffy from blowing so hard because she wanted a good grade," Richard said. Laurel admitted that she secretly liked the union, the International Brotherhood of Electrical Workers, because whenever the union got a pay raise, so did management.

Richard and Laurel had homesteaded on Kodiak Island's Kupreanof Peninsula since 1990, and until he retired from Kodiak Electric Association, Richard was often away from the homestead on summer jobs. During his absence

---

4   Turd rolls: cream cheese rolled in brown sugar and eaten on Ritz crackers. A strawberry on top makes it a poor man's ice cream sundae. Invented in Montana.

Laurel gardened, hiked with the dogs, picked salmonberries and composed letters to the editor on her new laptop computer. After lunch and again at bedtime she read books. Laurel was no stranger to solitude. Before homesteading, she and Richard had lived five years on the southernmost island in the Kodiak Archipelago, Chirikov Island, where they managed a cattle ranch. Laurel's father and her first husband had been educators in Kodiak, and Laurel maintained ties to people and places all over Alaska, her family having settled here in the 1950s. When I was new to the peninsula, a green homesteader with nothing in my larder but potatoes, dried noodles and bouillon cubes, Laurel gave me fresh vegetables from her garden, and good company, too, since we shared a passion for songbirds and wildflowers. If Richard gave me a mail-order catalog for specialty shot loads, Laurel gave me strawberry plants to transplant from her garden to mine. A woman's politics never mattered to me as much as her strength of will and independence of thought, and if I didn't always agree with Laurel's ferocious conservatism, I always enjoyed her stirring presence.

After my family arrived and we had settled in at Cottonwood, one of the regular features of our homestead life was our weekly social call on the Petersons. Dressed for the weather, we hiked west with the children, and a mile later we removed our boots and jackets in the entry, stomped our feet, passed in by the creaking woodstove and exchanged greetings and gossip. The Petersons had splendid views of the ocean and mountains, and if we saw a brown bear on the slopes, we interrupted our conversation to take turns at the spotting scope. They had coffee for us and treats for the children—a stick of licorice or a soda pop—and there might be vegetable-pepperoni soup or canned pea salad with cheese and pickles.

Homestead building projects, neighbors, a recent boating tragedy, the flora and fauna—our conversations started with local topics and progressed to news and politics: Columbine, the Cox Report and Chinese espionage, sharia law, mass graves, Vaclav Havel, George Orwell, Ayn Rand, terrorism, eschatology, education, union-screwing trade deals, the World Wide Web, technoslavery, civil unrest, genetic and social engineering, sexual shenanigans in the Oval Office, and so on. When I visited Richard and Laurel I often experienced the heady fascination of a vital counterculture. They lived far from society but subscribed to a variety of journals I hadn't known of, and as citizens they were better informed, they were more engaged as participants in our give-and-take democracy, than I with my college degree.

To live in bush Alaska is a challenge for anybody of any age, inconvenient and physically demanding, and the Petersons were not young in years. When Richard received news that his mother lay dying in Montana, the weather was so bad that he couldn't get off the homestead to go to her. "He couldn't get to town," Laurel told me later. "He was so nervous I thought he would have a coronary." Richard finally arrived in Montana in time to hold his mother's hand before she died.

The Petersons spoke more frequently of selling their homestead and moving to the Lower 48 states. In 2001, they listed the homestead for $136,000, inclusive of the machinery. An Alaskan homestead isn't for everybody, and Richard and Laurel didn't put their lives on hold while they waited for a buyer. They replaced the *Washington Monument*'s outboard motor and added other upgrades. Whenever I visited them, when I found Laurel tending her garden or picking wild berries, when I found Richard reading his chainsaw manual for fun or answering the door in his yellow shooting glasses—"Come on in, we'll roll for the jukebox"—I realized how much I'd miss them.

When I hiked to the place in 2002, the furniture, visible through the windows, was sheeted over, and the grounds were overgrown. Mud had engulfed the boat ramp. The new owners would learn what happens to your efforts out here if you stop negotiating with nature. From the back deck, where I had once shelled peas with Laurel and her blind mother, Eve, I contemplated the golden chain tree, and I brooded over Richard's silent anvil on its stump, and I mulled the changes.

By way of a postscript: the new owners, the Carters, proved more than capable of holding their own in the Kodiak bush. Richard and Laurel Peterson found a gardening and shooting paradise in the state of Idaho. When we visited them there in 2015, our conversation was as probing and salty as ever. The driveway of their blue house is lined with petrified wood and other rocks collected during their camping trips in the West. Laurel gardens and hikes, and Richard at the age of seventy-nine is as hale as ever, or nearly so. I noticed he needed an extra second to get up from the lunch booth at Archie's Place in Kendrick. Nothing serious. As he rose from the booth, his shirt momentarily lifted at the waist, and I caught sight of a holstered pistol. Yes, he still packs heat, Richard does, and when he leaves this earth, which won't be but foot first, God knows he'll go out armed and ready.

PRIDE

I was making excellent progress on the cabin. At night I slept on the bare wood floor and breathed the tangy fragrance of plywood and chipboard. I rose before dawn, boiled coffee on the camp stove, admired the ocean view from my new slider, and went to work. The conditions were spartan, the mornings freezing cold, but a glow of accomplishment warmed me. My new cabin roof was as good as the firmament.

Today I unrolled the vinyl flooring and laid it in over the floor deck. Inexpensive and easy to clean, vinyl covers every imperfection. I had chosen a parquet pattern in light wood tones, perfect for a latter-day nobleman. Criticize civilization all you want, but don't hold against humanity an overachievement as ingenious as vinyl.

As I scrambled about the cabin and pressed the vinyl down—so smooth!—it seemed nothing contained me but my threadbare longjohns. I literally leaped with enthusiasm. In the middle of my leap I struck my head on the base of the lantern hanging from a nail in the loft joist above me. The collision sent the lantern crashing to the floor and me reeling and clutching the top of my head. The glass globe of the lantern was cracked and its metal base badly dented. My skull suffered the raising of a spectacular welt that caused my hat to ride an inch higher in the afternoon. All day my head ached, but the lantern, when I replaced its pulverized mantles, emitted light, and I trusted that my brain would come around too. I wasn't too addled to understand what had happened to me. I had finally been given a reason for my head to swell.

QUIET

This return to the root is called Quietness.—Lao Tzu

Whenever I return to the city from the back-country, the hardest adjustment is in the loss of the quiet. This loss, a kind of dream deprivation, begins as a physical stress, an assault on my nervous system by the shock of random, senseless and interminable noise; not just literal noise, the acoustic garbage of traffic, machines and ringing telephones, but also the ambient noise of social media and the endless news cycle, the braying hysteria of the marketplace, the soul-smothering noise that Pope Benedict had in mind when he urged people to relearn human relationship, discernment, contemplation and prayer, to relearn these qualities by relearning the quiet.

The immense quiet of Alaska isn't the same as an absence of sound, not at all. Nor does sound in itself negate the quiet. The hooting of an owl, the soughing of the wind and waves—these sounds are eloquent of nature's quiet. The abiding quiet, not an absolute silence, is the baseline murmur of nature, of the circulating elements, the rhythm of breathing, the tiding of thought, the flow of time around mortal bodies. I sit close-eyed and listen to the wind and water, to the birds calling and bees buzzing, even to the motor of a distant craft dreamily passing by sea or by air. When my sympathy for the quiet has been awakened, I realize that the quiet was never outside of me. The quiet is in me, as the sea is in an inland pond. I stir in its presence. I respond to the quiet

as I was born to respond. I am most alive to the quiet when I am most alive to myself.

How not talk about the quiet? How not invoke the quality that gives a day in the wild so much of its fullness? Quiet, noise, sound, silence—facile dualities, imprecise words opening on a maze of verbal paradox. Sound, silence, figure, ground, left, right, yin, yang, inside, outside, world without end. The quiet of nature, preceding language and surpassing language, is a tension without force or resolution. It's a silence pregnant with potential, but the pregnancy is without term. It's the silence of countless deer as they feed and raise their heads, feed and raise their heads. It's a silence of uncrossed distances, of water molecules at play, of a harmony of blues and shadows. This is the soul of the wilderness, this quiet on the far side of stillness, the water as silent as the shadow of a whale passing beneath its surface.

For some people the quiet of nature is disquieting, a source of despair, of abandonment. For them it's an echo of nothingness, an evocation of the gulf that separates them from God. They hear the silence of vastnesses, of terrifying sublimities, of the uninhabited reaches of space, and, far from comforted, they are oppressed by its inhumanity.

I sometimes reel under the same oppression. I hear the brutality of nature in its screams of predation and suffering. I hear cosmic indifference in the storm that shakes the cabin to its foundations, my family huddled within, the wind and rain beating on the cabin walls. But soon I am outdoors again, where the birdsong peeps out like sunbeams after the storm, and the question of life's significance hardly troubles me. Life is an enchantment compounded of all the day's wonders. That's enough for me. Life's meaning is in its symphony, in the sounds drawn from every quarter, in the supernal hum of the insects mingled with the birdsong in the branches, the chatter of the children and the purl of running waters.

Although I hear the whispers of nature across millions of years of time, my hearing could be much sharper than it is. When my eyesight isn't dominant, at night or in a fog, or when I close my eyes in contemplation, the sounds I hear—the bleat of a fawn, the panting of a brown bear, the splash of a salmon, the fluffing of bird feathers—these sound with a special distinctness. I called at neighbor Laurel Peterson's house one day when her blind mother was visiting. Eve, reliant on her hearing, picked out from our surroundings the song of a chickadee, but Laurel pooh-poohed her mother's claim, declaring with confidence—after all, she lived here!—that we have no chickadees in these parts. I broke the tie in her blind mother's favor by describing my recent encounter with a flock of chestnut-backed chickadees.

On the eve of a deer hunt I will oil the door hinges to keep them from creaking in the morning when I leave the cabin. While climbing the mountain I avoid loud exhalations. I look with my ears, I hear with my eyes. Nature's quiet, its trembling stasis, is palpable on the mountain summit. I am conscious of every footfall. The supple grass of August won't betray me, but the tangled willows and rattling lupine are better avoided. In October I step in the moss and crowberry because these don't hold the frost and won't crunch underfoot.

The stalked deer listens, ears up and alert. The squelch of a wet leather boot. The clink of cartridges in a rifle. Life and death may hinge on a sound. Sound, the management of sound, is part of the subterfuge.

Sometimes nature seems a chaos, a cauldron of noises, an elemental din, a hubbub of breaking waves and blowing winds and screeching seabirds. At other times the country falls mute, utterly, or seems to, slumbering in a timeless oblivion. But the quiet always has a sound if I have the ear for it, now a murmur, now a complex harmony,

> a scurry of voles in the underbrush,
> a flutter of wings,
> the thump of a hare,
> fox sparrows clucking in the red-berried elders,
> the voluminous breathing of whales,
> the swish of an eagle alighting from its perch,
> a rubbing of spruce boughs,
> the whistle and pop of seaweeds at low tide,
> beach stones rattling under the hoofs of a
> frightened deer,
> the mew of a hermit thrush,
> the whoosh of wind in the chimney flue,
> a prattle of porpoises and chatter of gulls,
> the rustle of old leaves,
> the soft, sporadic thudding of spruce cones being
> tossed to the earth by an industrious squirrel,
> the resonant twang of a wind-whipped blade of
> beach rye,
> a shower of rain,
> the overarching Om of the insects,
> and the ocean's great seething and whispering.

RABBIT

Our Kodiak rabbits—hares, actually—aren't native to Kodiak Island. According to the Alaska Department of Fish & Game, snowshoe hares were captured along the Alaska Railroad in the 1930s and resettled on Kodiak to enrich the protein base. The hares we meet today are heirs of these forced relocations of the last century.

Putting aside the ethical questions (never difficult to do), the Kodiak resettlement was a success. We see the rabbits—hares, I mean—at every altitude and in every season. The glimpse is usually a sketchy one because hares are skittish animals with hair-trigger escape instincts. They zip elusively through the lower foliage and show the whites of their enormous, flaring hind feet as they thump the earth in retreat.

Snowshoe hares change color from tawny gray in summer to white during the short days of winter, but the camouflage is imperfect, and sometimes its color betrays the hare. In a warm spell, if the snow melts, a white hare stands exposed. Still, the tabby rabbits of summer and the white rabbits of winter are practically invisible when motionless. I've been three feet from a snowshoe hare in snow and wouldn't have known it was there but for its dark, watchful eye.

In my twenties in Fairbanks I ate some hares and tanned their skins without being clear what distinguishes hares from rabbits. This embarrasses me. At our homestead, young Miranda set me straight. Hares are born furry and open-eyed, not blind and naked like rabbits, and hares don't inhabit underground dens. Miranda associated hares and rabbits with fairies, elves and miniature teacups, and I inflamed her faith in these fine things by saying nothing to corrode it. She and I went hare-watching at the wood's edge after daybreak. We watched the hares flit among the brambles and feed on the spring buds—enormous hares, nervous and upright as they nibbled, eyes and ears always alert. A hare might shift a quarter turn while vigilantly chewing a mouthful of greens, but it never stayed in one spot for long.

Considering its perilous place in the food chain, a hare's caution is well founded. The local predators include fox, eagle and bear. Inevitably a fox and hare go peaceably by, the one hanging from the mouth of the other. A hare with a leg wound dragged across our path one day, a doomed creature who wanted badly to live. How can I forget the tragic look on Miranda's face? But nature's tenderness is balanced by its harshness, and the far side of the moon was no less a part of the moon when it was dark to us.

I once happened on a young eagle in the spruce forest. The eagle clumsily flew among the trees and bruised its wings on the branches. It was the awkwardest show of adolescence I had ever seen in a bird. Back and forth the eagle flew, its wingspan too big for the close growth of the trees. My presence only agitated the bird, and a few steps along

I saw the reason. Two hind legs and a length of backbone strewed the path, and I found a pile of softer parts that included a rabbit's face with its nose chewed off.

The season of spring, before the vegetation thickens, is a good time for watching rabbits. There's a day of license each spring when the rabbits celebrate the season with climactic and feverish abandon. A rabbit alone—a hare, I mean—is a trembling, humorless, fearful creature, but when they flock in the spring, when they go Maying, when love is in the air and the grass and horsetails and fiddleheads sprout, the hares scamper from cover, chase one another, hip-hop in broad daylight and run rings around our feet, life surging so imperatively, so irrepressibly through them that, mighty in their madness, they lose all caution and sweep past us in a headlong frolic, circling and playing, to all appearances having become the fairies the children always wanted them to be, our fellow denizens in a fantastic dream.

RAIN

A one-eyed fisherman told me he had lost his other eye in a blinding rain. We were drinking lagers at the Mecca, true, but who was I to argue? The horizontal rains of Kodiak are infamous. If he had stared too long into the flying darts of a sixty-knot rain, I could believe it.

You have no choice but to get wet on Kodiak Island, where the weather is fluid in both senses of the word: wet and changeful. The changefulness usually involves some permutation of the wetness. The wind adds variety and sting to the rain. You get a respite and then you get wet again.

If it's only sprinkling, you are probably between rain systems. Glory in an Arcadian day when it's there, because fair weather is as fleeting as a ten-minute rainbow. Get your painting done and don't forget the linseed oil. When weather's fair, prepare, prepare!

One May it rained so much that we didn't go outside without dressing the children in lifejackets. For weeks the rain streamed off the cabin roof and blurred the windows. The hills greened, the creeks ran full, and the exposed earth turned to mud. Torrents of water cascaded from the sea cliffs and carved deltas in the beaches. I mired our four-wheeler in a bog that had once been terra firma. I rocked the bike back and forth, grappled with the gears and wedged branches under the tires for leverage, but to no effect. The mud was oozing up through the footguards when I abandoned the bike and ran to the homestead of our neighbors, the Petersons. Richard's two-wheel-drive bike couldn't generate enough traction to extract my bike from the mud, but he brought along a two-ton cable hoist which had enough pulling power to free me.

Kupreanof Peninsula is within a maritime climatic zone with high humidity and frequent clouds. This is how our weather was described in the homesteading handbook issued to us by Alaska's Department of Natural Resources. Expect six feet of rain and six feet of snow a year, they said. They didn't tell us that nothing dries here. When it's forty-two degrees out and everything's saturated, no wonder. I've seen the same water drop tremble on the same rose petal three days in a row. The plants lean into the trail heavy with yesterday's rain and I emerge from a stroll as wet as if I had forded a river.

Not surprisingly, mold thrives here. Green mold, white mold, black mold. Our clothes in the dresser, the wooden dresser itself, a leather boot, a hat brim, the Scrabble box, the lumber under the tarpaulin, bear droppings in the forest, a lifejacket fallen in the grass, sheets of sandpaper—it all molds—everything molds on Kodiak except for metal, and if it's metal, unless you galvanize it, grease it or paint it before sundown, it rusts.

I never found a means of combining the following elements—a one-room wilderness cabin, incessant rainfall outside, myself, two children and their mother—into an uninterrupted kumbaya, a permanent domestic peace. Stare at the drizzle long enough and an outbreak of cabin fever is inevitable. High pressure indoors is no guarantee of atmospheric stability. My preference is for wild rains, high seas, swaying branches and shrieking winds, but if it's a dreary wetness, dull and flat and gray, an inner funk develops, a pluvial angst, a bleakness that reflects the outer funk of the weather, and this irritable gloom, the very mainspring of cabin fever, sabotages every attempt at clear and considerate messaging vis-à-vis your significant other.

Sometimes the only answer is to take a cue from the children and to revel in the rainfall as they do. Wear a Nantucket rainsuit or wear the simple suit you were born in, it makes no difference to a heart at play. Seize your love's hand and run barefoot through the grass together. With hey, ho, the wind and the rain! Is a fortnight's rain to trifle with your happiness?

And why so hard on the rain? Take account of its blessings. The Kodiak Archipelago marks the northern end of the Sitka spruce rainforest. The soul of the temperate rainforest is in its mist and moisture, the dripping verdure of fern and evergreen. Think of the freshness of the rain. Think of its music, its lullaby patter and percussive vitality, the quick shower of drops and the sustained barrage.

I only know a fair day's glory by the gloom of the days on either side of it. The rain brings out the fragrance of the greening cottonwoods. We rely on the rain for our drinking water. After the flood of snowmelt, without rain our creek would shrink and become turbid and sluggish. The next time I catch myself griping about the rain, I'll remember the dry August when our creek turned to red mud.

After days of chill and stupefying rain, of deluge and overcast, the clouds dissipate and the sky is as wondrous blue as the turquoise skies in Italian triptychs of the Middle Ages. A vivid rainbow arches overhead. Embrace it.

SALMONBERRY

Nothing confirms my feeling at home on the planet like the sweet feast that nature spreads before me. The wild berries please my eye, my tongue, my touch, and my sense of rightness, too, since few pleasures are as meaningfully satisfying as to reach out my hand and pluck a ripe wild fruit to nourish me with.

A stranger approached us one summer night in the parking lot of a cheap motel in Anchorage. Shabbily dressed, clearly intoxicated, she was in a bad way, no doubt about it. Martina and I were twenty-four-year-olds with no fixed place in life and scant money between us, but we had spent the day picking salmonberries at Mt. Alyeska in Girdwood, and Martina, who held the harvest bag, offered it to the woman. The transformation in the troubled woman's features was unforgettable. When she saw the wealth of yellow and red berries and understood our meaning, her cheeks broadened and her eyes brightened with affection. Her words were hackneyed, but that beaming smile could not have been faked or purchased, certainly not purchased by whatever cash we might have given her. The woman warmly accepted the gift and hugged Martina, and although she didn't go sober from that dreary parking lot, she went away alive.

The salmonberry is far and away the dominant berry at our Kodiak Island homestead. The watermelon berries are sweet but few; the crowberries are high up the mountain; the devil's club berries and elderberries, though enjoyed by birds and bears, are unpalatable when raw; but the salmonberries! I've spent summer afternoons exploring for the next sumptuous thicket and with flying hands and a chomping, squirting mouth have gorged until my belly couldn't accommodate another berry no matter how enticingly it dangled before me, every berry a sweet recrimination to the jaded palates who say the salmonberry is tasteless.

Tasteless! So crush a cordial from it. Add spirits and sugar. Try telling the children not to eat the salmonberries because they're tasteless. They could never gather a bowlful from the berry patch by our cabin without losing most of them on the way home, emerging from the berry patch with their hands and cheeks stained red and the burgundy drupelets sprinkling their hair.

The Kodiak Alutiiq have found medicinal value in the stems and leaves of the salmonberry. The plant is a vital organism here, its fruit a seasonal staple valued by insect, bird and mammal. I am only one of many who partake. A bear cuts a fat swath through the berry patch, breaking the canes and leaving a pile of gleaming indigo, and I am swift to withdraw if I see a pair of brown ears poking from the brambles.

In a fruitful year we feast on ripe salmonberries by the Fourth of July. For this we must see flower blossoms in early May. In winter the plants are deathly bare until the pink flower buds and the green leaf buds jewel the canes in the spring. The five-pointed flowers exude the subtlest fragrance. Soon, too soon, the petals fall to earth. The berries ripen from green to yellow to red to royal purple. Birds feast beside us. Red mites scramble over the globes. Black beetles worship under scarlet and purple domes. Hornets home in on the dripping nectar. Side by side the generations hang, the green nuts hard as acorns, firm berries mottled yellow and red, plump ruby prizes, and the great sagging darkened fruits, the old majors, unreaped and bearded with mold.

Picking wild fruit is a delight, an act of appetite and joyful gratitude. In a good year we'll feast on salmonberries by the Fourth of July, but I've seen Fourths when the salmonberries weren't nearly ripe and Augusts arrive in which the birds were beside themselves with impatience. Certain years stand out for their reach-out-and-grab-one bumper crops (1997, 2001, 2016, 2019) while other years (1999, 2007, 2017) are standout salmonberry bummers. A harsh winter and late spring mean dead plants, delayed blooms and sparse, stunted berry crops, and from one year to the next there can be more than a month's variation in the berry's calendar.

SEA LION

Lonny K was already on probation for a felony when he was photographed shooting at a sea lion. What had begun as a verbal turf war between Lonny and his neighbors, commercial fishermen on Kodiak Island's west coast, had escalated into violence when Lonny rammed the neighbors' fishing skiff with his own, a 23-foot aluminum skiff driven by a 150-horsepower outboard engine. That's where the felony comes in, because in the eyes of the law a moving boat is a lethal weapon.

As a felon, Lonny shouldn't have been anywhere near a firearm, but there he was, shooting his rifle at a sea lion that was robbing the salmon from his net and tearing holes in the mesh. Lonny's setnet, anchored in place and stretching perpendicular to the beach, was completely vulnerable to the sea lion, but shooting at a sea lion is a federal crime, and the neighbors, the ones Lonny had feuded with, snuck over and photographed him doing it. That's how Lonny came to spend the next part of his life behind bars.

It's hard to say where a life pivots, where a fateful course of events is set in motion. Character is one thing, circumstance is another, and if the one looks inescapable, the other may look freakish or unfair. People who knew Lonny, friends and family, thought it was a mistake to have accepted a five-year felony probation in the first place. "Five years! That's a long time to stay out of trouble." "You better not even have a bullet, Lonny. You're a felon. Don't take your gun to fish camp. They're watching you. They're laying for you."

All this turned out to be true. "In one ear and out the other," his mother, Audrey, said. Sometimes Lonny drank too much, and it wasn't for nothing that he had a reputation for hot-headedness. Even after the photographs emerged, the ones that showed him shooting at a sea lion, the Alaskan prosecutors would have dropped the probation violation if Lonny had been willing to sell his commercial fishing rights. They didn't want him going back to fish camp and stirring up trouble with the neighbors. But the federal authorities had a different agenda. Lonny's crime was shooting at a Steller sea lion, and the feds weren't interested in doing anything but making an example of Lonny K. Lonny's friends saw the federal government as a massive golden sea lion lunging out of the water and shaking a salmon in its jaws.

At the Cook Inlet Pretrial Facility in downtown Anchorage, the new arrivals waited in a hot, windowless cell, a foul-smelling hellhole of a cell. To Lonny the place stank worse than a pack of sea lions. The sweat rolled down his sides and he was left there to stew for a long time. His ordeal had begun.

His mother visited him at the Cook Inlet facility, and she later remembered the indignities with a bitter shudder. She thought she would rather die than be locked up like that. Audrey felt sorry for her son, but he had been given many chances to straighten out. She was old school in this regard, a law-and-order, take-responsibility woman. Lonny had always been a jock, humored and indulged, and the pattern of indulgence had finally caught up with him.

Privately, Audrey believed that a tendency to alcohol abuse ran in the genes, on her late husband's side. But this was no excuse. Lonny was thirty-four years old. He had time to change his ways. Pink-faced, square-jawed, Swedish and German by blood, and with winning blue eyes, Lonny had looks that worked magic on certain women, often women who had a fire-breathing streak of their own. One of these was his girlfriend Florence, a twenty-two-year-old from one of the island villages. Privately, Audrey had doubts about Florence, who liked to "party hearty" and who might not be the best influence on her son. But Audrey didn't want to hex Lonny by giving up on his judgment. If he would leave off drinking, if he would wed Florence or another woman and find room in his heart for God, Lonny could turn his life around.

For his part, Lonny had a single great fear: that his grandmother would learn he was in jail. He was extremely fond of his grandmother, and he begged his mother not to tell the old woman what had happened.

It was January when Lonny began serving time at the Cook Inlet facility, and until his sentencing he was locked up for twenty-four hours a day, except for commissary trips and twice-weekly gym exercise. He was eventually moved to a minimum security wing where his cellmate was a small-time drug offender. In February his sentencing made Kodiak's newspaper, the *Daily Mirror*. The townspeople who didn't already know Lonny's story now read it in the newspaper. Fortunately, his grandmother lived out of state and his secret was safe from her.

For taking pot shots at a sea lion, Lonny was sentenced to eighteen months in prison. He had already served two months; fifty-four days were suspended, leaving him with fourteen months to serve on the federal charges.

In March, Lonny was transferred to a federal prison outside of Alaska. This happened abruptly and without any notice to his family. His sister Janice had sent him a letter with an enclosed religious pamphlet and a picture of Jesus, and the packet was returned to her undelivered, with a note informing her that the material she had sent was "contraband." His family worried about him until they learned that they could write to him at the Federal Detention Center in Seattle. "Be sure to use the correct inmate number," they were told, "or he won't get the mail."

Because the move to Seattle happened so abruptly, only a day after Florence had visited him, Lonny suspected that the authorities had relocated him to deprive him of this last happiness of receiving visits from his girl. He was alone now to ponder his transgressions. But not really alone. At the Federal Detention Center in Seattle, he was surrounded by illegal immigrants and petty drug users. Lonny wasn't sure how to interpret this. Did it say something about the relative gravity of his offense? Did it speak to the efficiency and appetite of the criminal justice system? "There are so many innocent people here," he wrote home in a letter. And indeed it shocked Lonny that ordinary people served sentences for simple drug possession or a border violation. Most of them were good people, and he sometimes thought of them as his roommates, not his cellmates.

By June, Lonny was working six days a week for six hours a day in the prison bakery. The job relieved the tedium of incarceration, and in his spare time he studied the Bible for self-improvement. Fishing was the work he loved most, and this was the first summer in memory that Lonny didn't fish. He normally setnetted for salmon in the summertime, and in the winter he crabbed for king crab in the Bering Sea. Lonny had always said that crabbing was young man's work and he would quit it at the age of thirty, but he was too fond of living on the edge—crabbing in the Bering Sea is a lucrative thrill—and after he turned thirty he kept heading west to the crabbing grounds. Now, in federal custody he fished for nothing.

Back in Kodiak, many of Lonny's colleagues spoke their minds about the heavy-handedness of the government in punishing Lonny. "If the people who make the laws were turned out and had to earn their living fishing, things would come around different."

"You got that right."

"Sea lions yank the salmon right out of my hands. They'll rip out the stomach and leave the rest. Roll around in the net and take what they want and leave the fish heads."

"They get us seine fishermen, too. Swim right into the seine before we close it. They'll toss out thirty or forty salmon and go get 'em. You look in your net and the sea lion got more fish than you did."

Lonny went back to fishing after his release from custody in the spring of the following year. He repaired the bear damage at his neglected fish camp, and during salmon season he deployed a hundred fifty fathoms of moneymaking gillnet. In the winter he crewed a crab boat in the Bering Sea, as before, but the catch of king crab was not what it used to be. The crabbing season was shorter than ever, and when Lonny factored in the weeks of preparation and cleanup, his paycheck of nearly $10,000 was a disappointment.

Florence had gotten pregnant in the fall, and their baby was due in the month of June, around the time the next commercial salmon season opened. Ordinarily Florence would have her baby at the Native hospital in Anchorage, but she decided to stay in Kodiak so that Lonny would not have to choose between the baby's birth and the start of salmon season. If it ever came to a choice, though, she wondered what choice Lonny would make, and she asked him this. Lonny pondered the question and decided it was a toss-up. He played cool about the prospect of becoming a father, but Flo wanted the baby a lot, and this made him happy.

Lonny's court sentence included three years of state probation concurrent with six years of federal probation, and as an ex-convict he needed to pay attention to every rule. Even a fuel seep from his engine filter could land him in trouble, and Lonny couldn't afford trouble. "I've got friends where I'm going," he would say, referring to his nemeses on the fishing grounds. Lonny's supporters, gauging how his experiences had changed him, noticed that he used the word "seem" a lot, as if he didn't quite trust in appearances anymore. "Seems like it'll be a nice day," he said. Or, "He seems like a nice guy."

Not to be caught in a trivial infraction, Lonny used buoy paint to stencil his boat registration number on the bow of his skiff. Enforcement of the boat registration rules was passing from the Coast Guard to the Alaska State Troopers, and a crackdown was expected. As for the sea lions, Lonny refrained from actively repelling them, but it vexed him that people didn't understand the scope of the problem. It wasn't one or two sea lions inconveniencing him; it was twenty of them violating his net. They were predators. He thought about poisoning them, but a bevy of dead sea lions washing up on his beach would look very bad indeed.

Lonny was pleased that he hadn't knuckled under to the authorities and sold his fishing rights, but the truth was that Lonny had wearied of fishing. And this was something he had never believed would happen. The fishing was less productive than it used to be, and Lonny wasn't getting younger. He had long ago dreamed of becoming a high school wrestling coach, but this dream was impossible for a felon. With a baby on the way, Lonny thought about finding work in the North Slope oil fields, and he contemplated an apprenticeship in the trade of heating and air conditioning, but these possibilities lay in the future. Lonny still had a difficult choice to make before the way ahead became clear to him.

The commercial salmon fishing was set to open on the 9th of June, and two days beforehand, Lonny left town and headed to his fish camp to prepare his equipment. Florence, knowing that the baby was close, broke into tears when Lonny told her he was leaving. She begged him to stay in town with her, but Lonny's fishing instinct was so strong at this time of year that he really had no choice. He had to go. It was not an easy decision to make, but he made it.

At three-thirty on the morning after he left, Florence went into labor. From the hospital she called Lonny on the satellite telephone, and Lonny got the news and tried to return to town to be with her, but the weather had changed since he left, with gale winds blowing and dangerously high seas, and Lonny couldn't get closer to Kodiak than the village of Port Lions. Stranded there during the storm, Lonny missed everything, both the baby's delivery and the start of salmon fishing.

"He'll hear about *that* one for the rest of his life," the old salts in Kodiak like to say, and they tell Lonny's story with a laughter born of a lifetime's learning. "He made his decision and it was the *wrong* decision."

This turned out to be the last season of commercial fishing for Lonny K. Today Lonny lives with Flo and their children in the Pacific Northwest, far from the fishing grounds of Kodiak, Alaska.

SQUIRREL

Self-righteous, meddlesome, scratch-your-eyes-out territorial, gloatingly at ease in the tree branches: this is the red squirrel. Zoologically, these furry, fast-moving, bug-eyed shriek-a-minutes are a lot like a neurotic sister. You stroll peacefully through the woods and a squirrel screams at you for it. They double as a bear alarm, and if I'm working outside the cabin, the sudden, inexplicable shrilling of a red squirrel makes me stop what I'm doing and look around.

The red squirrel, though not native to Kodiak Island, is well established here, but longtime locals have assured me that the squirrel is a newcomer to our part of the peninsula. I'm told there were no red squirrels around Port Bailey Cannery until the 1990s. If so, the red squirrel offers a phenomenal example of a pioneering species. I doubt there's a spruce wood on the peninsula that hasn't heard the hearty chatter of a red squirrel. In theory the squirrels migrated to Port Bailey Cannery via a four-wheeler trail from the village of Port Lions, but if I know red squirrels, they didn't just scurry along a four-wheeler trail, *they rode on the bike,* either in the tool box or in a comfortable nest under the seat.

I was outside one day and chanced to look up at the cabin. A red squirrel, craning her neck, was looking down at me from the roof of the arctic entry. She strongly disagreed with the premise that the cabin was mine. She chirred in alarm, a high-pitched, obnoxious whistle of warning, pugnaciously rapped her front paws on the roof's mineral paper, and as I climbed the ladder toward her, she jumped in 180-degree turns and glared at me out of one eye and then the other. *Back off!*

Once a squirrel gets a toehold in your dwelling, she's loath to give it up, and it wasn't enough for me to scoop away her nest, a cozy mass of straw, moss, deer hair, feathers and tarp shreds. I also took care to block off both ends of the access so that she wouldn't return and rebuild. She had built her nest in the hollow space between the eaves of the main cabin and the slightly lower roof of the arctic entry. To block the tunnel I used metal, not wood or plastic, having known squirrels to chew through formidable thicknesses of the weaker materials.

There is no keeping out the marauding side of nature. Years ago, when I first homesteaded here, I cached my food in a spruce tree to put it out of reach of the brown bears. With time, my simple pulley cache evolved into a tree stand on which I stored a lidded tote containing the dry provisions I preferred not to store in the cabin when I was away. One winter, the squirrels ripped the rainproof tarpaulin and gnawed through the hard plastic bottom of the tote. In the tote they built a nest of grass mixed with blue tarp shreds and purple tote shavings. Surprisingly, they didn't go whole hog on my Raisin Bran. Too much sugar maybe. Anyhow, in fortifying against the brown bears I had put out a welcome mat for the squirrels.

Just after mating season I heard peals of laughter coming from behind the cabin. I investigated and found my wife and daughter in stitches over the antics of a red squirrel. The squirrel was frantically cropping the grass with her bared teeth, and by grass I mean the stubby yellow grass of early spring. She tore up a clump of it, turned to us in paranoid fanaticism while she stuffed her cheeks with it, then she tug o' warred with the next clump of grass, pulling and stomping and stammering with the effort, and finally, with yellow tufts of grass sticking from her mouth, she ran away to plug the walls of her den or to line the dray bed. I saw this energetic squirrel a couple of months later in the bloom of motherhood, dragging her youngster along while licking and grooming it.

These neighborhood squirrels have adapted to sharing their spruce grove with us. Our long-handled tools lean on the trees and our ropes hang from the branch spurs. The grove has a dominant tree around which the squirrels center their activities, but they range across the evergreen canopy and harvest the cones of the surrounding trees as well, often leaping from branch to branch and bypassing the ground altogether, though they'll descend to collect the spruce cones they've dropped, and they sprint through the shrubs and greenery that surround the grove—horsetail, salmonberry, willow, alder—to reach their outer burrows and to raid alien territories.

Another inhabitant of this range, the short-tailed weasel, or ermine, is a sleek little carnivore with the arboreal agility of the red squirrel but shyer and less flamboyant than the squirrel. Reticent and often nocturnal, the weasel is a creature seldom seen, though he sometimes peers sweetly at us from our woodpile or from beneath some secluded overhang. The weasel is known to be a lethal predator who will make a meal of a juvenile squirrel if he can get one.

If you're a student of obsessive-compulsive behavior, red squirrels will fascinate you. No telling the hours they spend in hoarding spruce cones and shelling seeds. Morning and evening, perched high in a spruce tree or seated on a low guard branch, the squirrel gnaws and eats and builds its stores for the winter. The characteristic sound of these labors is a continual fall of spruce cones and a light sprinkling of twigs and other debris.

A compact squirrel with wraparound almond eyes occupied a branch three feet away from me. The season was midsummer, but the squirrel worked with the urgency of autumn. His first spruce cone was a brown cob with a few scales left at either end of it. The squirrel held it horizontally in his paws and stripped out the last kernels like a man devouring an ear of corn. I later retrieved the cob and found it wet with squirrel spit. The second spruce cone, purplish topaz in color, the squirrel gripped vertically between his paws, and as he chewed it, the cone shreds rained around him. At one point, distracted by an itch in his side, the squirrel flipped forward with his front paws on the tree branch, and, the cone dangling from his mouth, he scratched his side with his back right foot. You had to watch closely to see it happen. In the blink of an eye he was upright again and chewing on the spruce cone.

SHORT-TAILED WEASEL

These homestead squirrels grudgingly accept us, but if we're away from Cottonwood, hiking through strange country, the squirrels either withdraw into silence or they dart through tunnels and over tree branches to harass us and escort us from their domain. We know we're in the presence of some great squirrel lord if we find a litter of stripped-out spruce cones. Especially after snowmelt we see these depleted granaries, these vast, sodden middens of red debris—cone scales, cores, bracts, seed wings and every kind of spruce chaff heaped against the spruce trunks.

With the coming of spring the squirrels mate again, and they spruce up their nests and await the next generation of squirrels and of spruce cones. Their lifespan isn't long, but the squirrels live their allotted times with pious energy, and I've done them an injustice if I've made them out to be merely high-strung and unreflective. Who's to say the squirrels don't wonder? Early one morning I saw a squirrel silhouetted on a branch, motionless, a spruce cone in its paws and its bushy tail drawn up in a question mark, and in the long, gray silence the squirrel seemed to have moved beyond the settled matter of the spruce cone in hand and to be meditating greater causes.

THOREAU

A seaplane pilot asked me, as he made a note in his flight log, what I called the homestead where he had picked me up. "Cottonwood," I said, gazing down from the window. We were just then flying over some buoys that tipped west in the current, all of them leaning in the same direction, but I noticed an anchored boat trailing strongly to the east, and I shifted in my seat and looked back at it. Its defiance of physics was only apparent—the boat was anchored in an eddy—but here was a memorable symbol of difference, of standing against the tide, and a line from Thoreau came to me: *Why should we knock under and go with the stream?*

It was a long time, years, since I had given more than a passing thought to Thoreau. I had by now acquired the title to my homestead, and the land, though taxed for the public revenue, was no longer a public holding. I had learned many things since I first came to Cottonwood. Where I had once felt diminished by a sense that life had somehow deceived me, these days I felt thoroughly undeceived. I was long past believing that my worth and capacity as an individual were in any hands but my own. I no longer turned to Thoreau as I once had, but early in my homesteading Thoreau had been an inspiration to me. "In a glib, gilded age," he assured me, "a time of frank cupidity and false speech, finding yourself at odds with so much and so many, you are right to make a little hideaway for yourself. Perhaps you'll escape some of the damage." Another time, when I had protested to Thoreau the unwisdom, the impossibility, of rejecting society, he was patient in his reply. "My object was never society, you see, it was the premise, rarely examined, that society precedes the individual."

When you find yourself out of step with the march of the times, as I did in the 1990s, when Wall Street and Silicon Valley carried the drums and the horns, then having in your corner a friend like Henry David Thoreau counts for something. By moving to Alaska in the 1980s, when nuclear winter was the apocalypse du jour, the sword of Damocles hanging over us, I had already traveled far in my search for what was essential or meaningful in life, for what spoke truth to me, for whatever had been missed—I was sure much had been missed—by my college education, and I remained skeptical of the dominant paradigm held out to me. In the triumphalism of the New World Order, spawned by the merger of high finance and high technology, intelligent people articulated the belief—a faith, really—that history had outgrown itself, had in effect ended, and we were witnessing the birth of a qualitatively different humanity, the dawn of an age of global superproductivity, scientific panacea, beneficent corporatism and so on. It was a mishmash of high-sounding self-delusion. You would think electric lights, telephones, microwave ovens and nuclear energy had never been invented. The computer and internet are marvelous tools, and I love a useful tool as much as anyone does, but it isn't my way to rush after a novelty without wondering what its worth is beyond the ballyhoo and what its costs might be beyond the price tag.

With Thoreau the individual conscience is the starting point, and this is what makes him so radical. It's not because he likes to ramble. It's fashionable these days, in fashionable circles, to denounce Thoreau in excitable terms, a sure sign that he is subverting the prejudices and complacencies of a new establishment. Thoreau is, as a writer, edgier, far more "dangerous," than most of the writers packaged and sold to us as such. How the notion of pulling one's weight is distinct from the notion of pulling the weight others ask one to pull "for the good of all"—this is Thoreau's specialty. The two pulls may coincide, but then again they may not, and the individual, the one perceptive enough to know the difference, decides.

If the community asks me to stay indoors, what if I shrug my shoulders and go for a bike ride? Do I want to live like this? What do I need and what do I want? An apartment in the city with reliable hot water but not much more than that? In exchange for what? An employment that occupies my waking hours but numbs my soul? We are social creatures, yes, but so are sardines: Were they made to be packed in a can? Which will I regret more, to offend by my speech or to abide the offense of being directed to hold my tongue? True, the world's no better off because a solitary man and woman live deliberately and please themselves by their choices, but is the world better off because they live in secret misery for fourscore years and go to their graves in pious silence?

It is alright to ask, Thoreau says, and if the answer is unpopular, that's alright too. Hector St. John de Crèvecoeur, Thoreau's forerunner in this, examines the conditions under which the natural man and woman, the human animal inside of us, gets the better of the loyal, cooperative civilian, and this is the shifting moral frontier explored by Thoreau. When we ponder our place as individuals in society, the validity of our opting out or withholding our assent, and the potency of conscience, we are considering questions that occupied Thoreau, too.

Asking questions isn't always easy. It's easy enough when the questions are approved by authority, when so-called transgressive questions, for instance, are trumpeted at the highest institutional levels and the answers preapproved. This reminds me of the US Forest Service posting I once encountered in Alaska: *Feel free to wander around, but please keep to the designated path.* It's riskier to ask the questions that probe at authority's unstated assumptions. The work of Socrates and Jesus is never done, because in every time and place authority reinvents itself, never without insidiousness. The inclination of the few to control the behavior of the many isn't peculiar to any political system. The government of the many by the few is a manifestation of human nature, but what begins with some justification in human necessity always ends, historically, in excess and abuse, and in spite of the promise and faded fanfare of the new millennium, I see nothing that persuades me that the arc of power will this time be different, or if it is different, that it won't be for the worse.

Thoreau is, more than a moralist and rebel, a great consoler. In our extrovert culture, one in which being Muslim is the only quality more suspect than being a "loner" who "keeps to himself," in this binary world of team players and proto-terrorists, Thoreau is a champion of the introvert, of the realm of value found inside of us, the world of solitude and silence, of doubt and introspection, of simplicity and sworn integrity. Thoreau founds his inwardness not in clouds of abstraction but on earthy footings. By identifying it with the wilderness, he infuses it with the strength and resilience of root and branch, and by doing this, by giving it nature's sanction, he makes it virtually unassailable.

This is how I understand Thoreau, who never offers comfort without throwing down a challenge:

Your destiny is born in difference, in consciousness, in conviction, in the courage of decision and action. What alienates you, what repels your soul, you naturally don't feel obliged to or answerable for. You seek other choices, and what you find, as you feel your way toward self-acceptance and wholeness, may lie far off the common path. Go with it. Go with God at your back and your humanity clearly in sight before you.

As a young man of his day, curled up in his safe New England inglenook, Thoreau may have suffered a personal crisis, caught between his belatedness—New England was fenced and settled—and his being left behind by the venturesome youths he saw striking west across the continent. In the west, California beckoned, and Cambridge and Concord may have seemed precious by comparison. The young Brahmin Francis Parkman was making his celebrated journey up the Oregon Trail while Thoreau was still holed up at Walden Pond. The Walden years predate the passage of Abraham Lincoln's Homestead Act, but homesteading had long been in the public consciousness, and Americans had for decades been streaming west, building their cabins on the shores of unsung ponds, asserting their freedoms and declaring their independence of received wisdom. Most of them didn't have a friend and patron like Ralph Waldo Emerson to let them squat on his property and conduct an experiment in living, but even if they had, they weren't likely to have had Thoreau's literary gifts. *Walden* stands as a triumph, a paragon of the kind of writing that loves nature for itself and not just as a backdrop for a pilgrim-narrator's awakening or an adventurer's exploits, and while it may be a stretch to say that I wouldn't have written of homesteading in Alaska without the precedent Thoreau sets in *Walden*, it would be difficult for me to overstate my regard for him.

Thoreau stirs aspirations to freedom and dignity, fundamental human aspirations which his abusers in the twenty-first century consider so hopelessly out of reach as to be counterrevolutionary. It is the mode of these latter-day Pecksniffs to pick through the words and biographies of dead writers and to have their way with their reputations. Fencing with the dead! Thoreau will withstand the handicap. My response to Thoreau is of course my own, that of a solitary reader, of one individual to the superb prose and singular intelligence of another.

In college I read the *Poetry & Repression* of Harold Bloom, and I have it here beside me, a calendar bookmark for 1982 protruding from its pages. Concerning Mr. Bloom's argument, here and elsewhere, that authors more or less consciously struggle to assert themselves against the literary influences of strong forebears, I suppose at some level I must be grappling with Thoreau—one is never sure about these things—but two centuries after Thoreau's birth, my situation seems to me sufficiently my own, or different enough from his, that I feel I'm rather collaborating in a common cause than reeling from a head-on Oedipal collision.

Humanity faces staggering challenges, and in a crowded and clamorous world the problem of how not to lose our individual dignity is one of them, and to my way of thinking not the least of them, not less vital or global in its ramifications than the more familiar crisis of physical disease. In a mass-market, big-data, artificial-intelligence world, the reflex will be to ridicule what I've said, to persist in the deconstruction of the individual and in the denial of his and her sanctity, to continue in the erosion of privacy and of the prerogatives of selfhood, and, disparaging the self's claims to sovereignty, to ride roughshod over his and her natural liberties; but the costs to us of the impoverishment and disenfranchisement of the individual human animal is high beyond calculation, and I fear that when billions of stifled souls simultaneously erupt, the planet will warm much faster than what the computer models had graphed.

But I had forgotten: we've agreed to do without souls. In the age of micro and nano, we are hollow all, our skins literally permeable, our bodily boundaries breached by our neighbor's wireless technology, our interior spaces cluttered by digital ephemera, our senses gone scratchy, our depths made shallow, and our minds debased by subjection to the mindless electronic leviathan. The time will come when the old model of personhood with its simple integrity, its grounded solidity and physical boundaries, with the privacy we once expected, with the self-sufficiency required of us in the days before telecommunications, the time will come when this model of the individual will reek of archaism. The freedom and privacy which I have known in the Alaskan wild are already inconceivable to men and women of the city and suburbs. How unendurably out of reach, how threateningly foreign they will seem in a few short generations. Imagine going off to a wild country and making a home for oneself—to do as people have done since the beginnings of history, to carve a little place for oneself in the wild—what an obsolete luxury, an impossible indulgence! We ought to have moved beyond such selfishness. With all the human rights you've been given, friend, you should be content with your circumstances; now get along and do be quiet with your sanctimony about the individual.

The problem of the individual in society originates in the complexities of our nature and isn't a problem with a solution. The problem is with us for as long as people wonder to what purpose they live their lives. To dismiss it is to live in blindness. To neglect it is to fail to reckon with the consequences of our reaching the point in our success when it is no longer possible to escape into geography, to go forth after freedom and a better life: when there is nowhere else to go. There is nowhere else *on earth* to go. We will live with the ravages of reductionism as we live with disease, but it isn't clear to me that an extreme abridgement of our natural freedoms is the inevitable price of progress, or that the costs of that abridgement and of the accompanying demoralization won't in the future become so unacceptable that we'll be forced to question the value and desirability of the so-called progress that comes at so intolerable a price.

The *Salt Lake*, a rusty Panamanian vessel flying a US flag and bound for the Far East with its hold full of salmon, lies at anchor in Dry Spruce Bay. Crossing below in my raft, I am yelled at and urged along by a seaman gesturing at me from the deck, and when I look up at the prow of that massive ship, I feel the menace of it, of the big for the small, the machine for the flesh and blood, the force of size and organization for the modesty of the solitary self. Later, ashore, I meet some of the crew and am glad for the exchange of handshakes, but I can't quite shake off, I can't quite get out from under, the shadow of that looming ship. Isn't it likewise for the individual? The rusting factory trawler or catcher-processor called society is abuzz with its pressing interests, but the watch on deck worries about the solitary boatman who goes his way, crossing below as he tends to his affairs. In these same waters I once found an abandoned bidarka, swamped and crewless, but I never learned how it came to be floating there in that condition.

TIDE & SEA

O ne of the worst things I have done before returning to Cottonwood was to forget to pick up a tidebook in town. These pocket-size booklets, available for the taking at the sport shop and the hardware store, will tell you what time of day and by how many feet the tide will rise and fall. We keep a tidebook on the windowsill and consult it with an astrological zeal. Before we boat or fish or beachcomb, we check the tidebook. I like a tidebook that indicates the lunar phases, because I like to be reminded of the connection between the sea's tiding and the moon and sun above, between my life at sea level and the greater solar system. These days, to save paper, we print the relevant pages of a tide table beforehand and bring them with us.

When we first came to Cottonwood as a family, we arrived on a flood tide with several tons of gear and provisions. It was a spring tide in late summer, an especially high tide, and Captain Ross anchored his boat close to shore while we offloaded. High water allows a boat or seaplane to float over the rocks of the intertidal zone and to draw up at the head of our beach, a convenience that saved us a lot of hard labor, but the same forces—spring tides, a full moon—promised an even higher tide in twelve hours, and we had our hands full to ensure that all of our cargo was out of reach of the tidewater.

Absent a tidebook, we learned to anticipate the tides by observing them. We planted markers to study how high on the beach an object needed to be to really be safe from repossession by the ocean. If we became complacent, if we forgot how the tidal effect varies with the shape of the beach and the wind direction and wind speed, we lost things: tarp, rope, fuel mix, plywood and clothing are some of the items we have forfeited over the years. I once received a radio call from Bud and Cherie Carter, neighbors to the west of us. They reported seeing an object float by their window that resembled a human body wrapped in a blue tarpaulin. This sounded suspiciously like my inflatable boat when I have rolled it in a tarpaulin for storage. I recovered the boat, mortified by my failure to allow for the tidal effect of the gale winds that had been blowing. The tide taketh and giveth away, and over the years we have found many gifts washed ashore—antique bottles, a backpack, a jumbo cutting board, useful tools and buckets, and, surreally, a spilled shipload of miniature footballs and basketballs.

Among the sea's most useful gifts are driftlogs and dimension lumber. A pallet or a sturdy plank wins the homesteader's heart. When I found a weathered twelve-by-twelve on a nearby beach, I hefted the dank, heavy block of wood onto my shoulder and carried it home, wondering what seafaring vessel or foreign port or lost Atlantis it came from. In the economy of Cottonwood this block of wood, worked by human hands, set adrift by fortune, delivered to us on the Alaska Current, and destined to become part of a bridge or a bench or foundation, was a treasure.

The State of Alaska, when it opened this seacoast to homesteading, made no promises about its hospitableness. I was warned of the tsunami risk. Still, I had no understanding of the extreme tides or how they would impact our lives here. High tides of ten to twenty feet are routine in Kupreanof Strait, and the monthly spring tide brings ranges of twenty-five to thirty feet. Our beach is completely exposed on the north, rocky in its middle and lower reaches, and backed by rocky cliffs. We have no natural moorage. Winter storm surges are severe. In summer there's a narrow band at the top of the beach where it's safe to leave a raft (safe from the tides, not from the brown bears), but we tie it to a log anyway, and if the tide climbs upwards of nineteen feet, especially in a north wind, we winch the boat off the beach or disassemble it.

In my early months of homesteading I learned by trial and mostly error. Careless in launching or landing the boat at low tide, I put holes in it. It is wiser to exploit a high tide, but the highs and lows being separated by about six hours, I normally contended with a low tide at either end of my outing. I experimented with weights and lines, devising a rigging whereby the boat would ride at anchor and I could haul it ashore when needed. The boat ended up beached and swamped, the lines tangled in kelp and the keel scratched by barnacles and rocks.

Dick Ross, captain of the *Schatzie Girl*, sat me down in town one day and educated me. This man worked in the harbormaster's office in Kodiak and had the nautical experience of a Neptune. What I wanted was the convenience of a summertime running line that would allow me to keep my raft in the water and out of reach of the brown bears. Dick Ross designed the very thing. We drank refreshments in his living room while he tied knots and splices and explained to me the rigging: an anchoring loop on shore; an endless loop of ⅜ -inch, 3-strand nylon extending to sea; a sheet bend joining them; an all-important blood knot; a modified bowline knot to which the boat line would clip; a metal ring; a crab float; a stout spliced line 2 fathoms long; a length of ¾-inch chain with 51,000 pounds of breaking strength; a shackle with a 1½-inch stainless steel cotter pin; a 25-pound anchor; and whatever else. It was beautiful. Elegant. Simple. And it came with a master seaman's stamp of approval. I still dream about it.

Only problem was, it didn't work. At low low tide, I set my anchor on the sea floor and watched the water flood in and lift the bright crab float. From shore I lined my silver raft out on its endless loop and proudly gazed at it. The running line was done. I gave the blood knot a reassuring tug and retired to my cabin, confident that in the morning I would draw the raft to me like a rider summoning his steed. I had a strange dream that night of a camel lying dead and bloated in the desert. Stranger still, this was no dream but a prevision of my boat lying catawampus on the beach next morning.

The anchor had dragged one way, the boat had pulled the other way, and masses of kelp had turned my endless loop into an endless headache. The boat had taken buckets of saltwater. Northwest winds of ten to fifteen knots had been blowing, not unusual here. I finally understood why my neighbors the Petersons, whose heavy-duty running line was anchored in bedrock, didn't trust their skiff to it for more than a few hours but instead kept their skiff ashore and launched it with a tractor. I resolved to appreciate my inflatable boat for what it was, a glorified raft, and to make the most of its simplicity and portability. Using a hand winch and a series of fender floats, I developed a method of getting my boat in and out of the water without piercing it on the rocks and barnacles at low tide.

To the twenty-first century landsman, a preoccupation with the tides smacks of quaint seamanship, anachronistic lore from the days of the clipper ships. Not so for Alaska's fishermen, whose wild-caught harvest of seafood feeds the landsman. For a fisherman, the interaction of the tides and the salmon runs—tidal currents affect net behavior and salmon behavior—is consequential and real. There aren't many residents of Kodiak Island whose fortunes aren't in one way or another touched by tide and sea. Mariners lose their lives every year in these waters. Mercurial weather, freezing temperatures, high seas, squalls, fogs, gales, powerful tidal streams, hazardous rocks—these are some of the dangers.

Complicating the waters of the Kodiak Archipelago is a labyrinth of channels, bays, fjords and straits through which the tides don't ebb and flow harmoniously. Whale Passage is an example. The meeting of waters and currents at the east end of Whale Pass creates violent rips and whirlpools that hamper a boat's navigation. Standing rocks add to the peril. Here the wreck of the *Selief*, grounded on Shag Rock many years ago, lies abandoned, a warning to all who enter the pass. I don't travel Whale Pass in the raft; too many people have warned me against it. But if I absolutely must, I have learned to do it in slack water or with the tide at my back. To buck the tide in an inflatable is like climbing a river's rapids. I once rode in the fishing boat of Mike Resoff during the spring tides, and because we were late in getting to Whale Pass, the current met us head-on in a torrent of eddies and whitewater rips. At times the *Neva*, straining at high throttle, stood still, or we progressed by inches, Mike fighting the whirlpools for control of his boat. Mark Thomas, of the *Valhalla*, lost his steering in Whale Pass and calls it a miracle that he didn't go to pieces on the rocks. By manipulating his forward and reverse gears he was able to ride the currents to a safe anchorage. I once heard the skipper of a commercial fish tender, seeing what lay ahead in Whale Pass, become gloomy, telling his fellow skipper on the radio that he was making no headway.

CATCH OF THE DAY, A PACIFIC HALIBUT, 2002

"Keep the north side of Whale Island," he was advised. "Hug the north beach there. Catch the back eddies and take a few tree branches along with you."

"I could use some coffee with bee pollen right now—a shot of adrenaline."

"Hug it close. Makes you not want to leave your seat. You'll stick on the vinyl like an octopus on a piece of glass. If you get a big swirl it'll put your bow on the beach in a hurry."

"A tide like this, it's pretty hard to make it in a five-knot boat."

"We once took four hours to get through there. Half mile an hour. A haystack of gear in a big old minus tide. Didn't want to turn around, we were afraid we'd roll over."

"If I didn't have all this fish I'd anchor up in a cove."

"I've seen boats going backwards in there."

"Tide's moving five knots easy, but I'm not at the worst part yet."

"Just hold steady on the north, it'll flatten out for you. If the worst happens, just swing your bow over and go downhill with it, over."

TIDEPOOL

Starfish, urchin, oyster, triton,
    Mussel, limpet, scallop, chiton,
Periwinkle, hermit crab, fingerling, tube worm,
    Barnacle, sea star, gastropod, echinoderm,
Sand hopper, sand dollar, moonshell, sea jelly,
    Isopod and hydroid: spongy, runny, smelly:
China cap, cockleshell, octopus and eel,
    Crawling and slithering, all scouring for a meal,
Sea snail, bitty shrimp, slug, clam and squirt,
    Nudibranch, anemone, all mixed with rocks and dirt,
Eggy and slimy and gooey and briny,
    Mottled and rubbery and slippery and shiny,
Glistening and lurid, dank, noisome, viny,
    Wholesome if hideous, sapid if spiny,
Gasping and munching and lying in wait,
    Oozing and crunching and keen to propagate,
Wriggling and squirming, floating free or holding fast,
    Mouths, arms and tentacles stalk their next repast,
Scuttling and prowling, springing, snapping, waving,
    Preying and prying, I won't say misbehaving,
Wheeling and wafting and popping and dying,
    Teeming and breathing and God knows multiplying,
Spitting, sucking, splashing, all searching for a treat,
    And thanks to all the plankton, there's lots of stuff to eat.

I cannot say who made it,
But I'll say I'm fascinated,
The bubbling foam and crackling scum
Excite my dull sensorium,
The colors heady, all compounding,
Iridescent and astounding,
Thickly layered, amber, green,
Dazzling orange and tourmaline,
Striped and dappled, pearly, dusky,
Pink, maroon, marine and musky,
These dwellers of the ocean shore,
Some herbivore, some carnivore,
In balmy or in brutal weather
Subsist between the tides together,
The life so vivid, protean, hectic,
Bright and fertile, pyrotechnic:
It's delicious, a delirium,
A feast, a strange mysterium,
And I find it quite tremendous
Though I cannot comprehend us.
Welcome to the tidepool
At the edge of the sea:
It's like looking in a mirror
And seeing you and me.

TOOLS & MACHINES

I wrote up a list of must-have homestead tools—

line
tarps
hardware (fasteners, hinges, hooks)
hand tools (hammer, screwdrivers, wrenches, saws)
level & square
shovel
power drill & circular saw
chainsaw
four-wheeler with winch
water pump
foot pump
chisel
bacitracin
knife
duct tape
electric generator
shotgun
pen or pencil
matches

—but I wasn't satisfied with it. I tinkered with the list, put it away and tinkered some more. Should it include X? What about Y? What makes a tool? Why is bacitracin on the list?

"Because bacitracin is a manmade substance instrumental in preventing infection when I have burned or cut myself with one of the other tools."

If your list includes an ointment like bacitracin, shouldn't it include the grease and lubricants that are instrumental in operating and preventing corrosion of the machines and tools you find so essential?

"I suppose we could include oil; sure, why not? I haven't listed everything. When I say 'winch,' I don't list every hoist, pulley and come-along that comes along."

You've included as must-have tools several machines that burn gasoline. Shouldn't gasoline be on the list?

"I never thought of gasoline as a tool."

Isn't it manmade and instrumental?

"I see your point."

Which is?

"That refined gasoline, being manmade and instrumental in running my machines, is properly seen as a tool. But gasoline is a liquid. It has no shape or handle. It doesn't *look* like a tool."

Tell me this. If you needed to drive a nail but had misplaced your hammer, would you use a rock to drive the nail?

"If it does the trick, sure."

And yet the rock is not manmade.

"Not exactly, no."

Not exactly?

"Not at all."

But used as a hammer, the rock is nevertheless a tool.

"Used as a hammer, yes, it's then a hammer. I hammer the nail with the rock. I grant you that a tool doesn't *have* to be manmade."

After the rock is used as a hammer, does it remain a hammer?

"I wouldn't put it down by the real hammer, no. It's a rock."

So the rock is a tool only while it is used as one.

"It's always a *potential* tool. I can always hammer with it."

But it ceases to be a hammer after it has functioned as a hammer.

"Huh?"

(*Twenty minutes later*) You speak of construction and destruction. Does the instrumentality of the hammer lie in the delivery of the blow itself or in the use to which the blow is put? Say, for instance, the hammer is used as a tool of coercion.

"In interrogation, no doubt! You are a frustrating interlocutor."

(*Three hours later*) Please tell me this. When you fish in the sea, would you tie a hammer to the end of your fishing line and drop it to the sea bed as a weight against a strong current?

"What an absurd thought! I would in principle, yes—if I had no other sinker."

Clearly, at the bottom of the sea the hammer isn't used to deliver a blow.

"Except to the fish."

Ah, yes, very good. But no concussive force is being applied.

"I see where you're going, friend. You'll ask me if the hammer is still a hammer or only a fishing weight."

(*Next day*) Thank you for explaining that. Then it would be fair to say that in using the hammer as a fishing weight, we are using it as a tool but not as a hammer.

"That's right, we're improvising."

So its usefulness as a tool is not limited by its instrumentality as a hammer. A tool is any object, often an item of human manufacture, used to leverage natural forces and to effect a change in our environment.

"I wouldn't say *our* environment. When otters and chimps use tools, they're concerned with *their* environment, not ours."

Ah, quite right. Shall we say *the* environment?

"Fine. Like I said, everyone knows what a tool is."

A cold chisel is handy for punching out the end of a metal barrel, but tin snips and wire strippers are no less handy when I need them. My list of must-have tools doesn't include a ladder—I can always construct one of spruce poles if I need one—but practically speaking, a ladder is essential. A ladder stands at the junction of convenience and necessity: too useful to be omitted. If I have a bow saw, a crosscut saw and a hacksaw, why do

I need a power saw? To make life easier, obviously—to cut down on the drudgery. That's the point of tools.

Every new tool or machine begets a new list of must-haves. If I have a four-wheeler, I need a bicycle pump for getting air into the tires. You don't expect me to put my lips to the tire stems and to blow, do you? If the chainsaw is a must-have tool, what about the spark plug, the spark plug wrench, the cutting chain and the round file for sharpening the saw teeth? What good is a shotgun without shells, a caulk gun without caulk, or a screw gun without screws and bits? As good as a flashlight without bulb and batteries.

At Cottonwood, I have tools and spare parts and a scrap heap for backup, but I never have all the tools I need. Unable to get to a hardware store, I make shift. Improvisation is the homestead way. I scrounge the scrap heap, see what I've got, do what I can, wire it together, and if all else fails, there's always duct tape.

Humans aren't the only tool-using animal, but we're the handiest. It doesn't take a fanatical futurist to appreciate the energy and ingenuity of our big-brained, tool-loving species. A rustic friend of mine built a wilderness cabin using only hand tools—no power tools—and I respected him enormously for his discipline. I noticed, though, that when it came time to roof his cabin, he used a sheet metal alloy manufactured by industrial machines. We all draw the line somewhere between what we consider natural and artificial, necessary and extravagant, modest and wasteful. There is no "natural" man or woman who is not a tool user, and the line drawn at power tools or digital tools is a line drawn in shifting sand. Every drawn line is a line to be surpassed. My rustic friend with his adze and his drawknife was a traitor to the Stone Age.

It's a commonplace that tools are a mixed blessing. They make our lives easier but they also pollute our surroundings and endanger us in ways we didn't expect. We have only just awakened, for example, to the treachery of our cybertools. Compared with these, how simple is the old chainsaw. For clearing brush, blazing trails, felling trees, cutting firewood, building with logs, for all of this and more, the chainsaw is a go-to friend, and the gasoline it burns, for the amount of work it does, is minuscule. It's a marvelous machine with an undeserved reputation for villainy. Still, the beauty of the chainsaw, its effectiveness in accomplishing what's asked of it, is frightening. I am a Lilliputian compared with a Sitka spruce tree, but don't underestimate a Lilliputian with a Stihl or a Husky in his hands. He'll carve a giant with expedition. If a single homesteader spends a productive day felling and sectioning a spruce tree, think what ten avaricious brigands will do with half a dozen chainsaws and a bulldozer in the Amazon rainforest. It's frightening. The variability of human nature is reflected in the variable uses to which we put our tools.

My purple thumbnail attests that a badly wielded tool hurts the wielder—another commonplace. I notice, though, that we humans haven't been quick to renounce the tools of death and destruction invented by the likes of Da Vinci, Nobel and Einstein. It wouldn't do for me to pose as a crusader against the machines that have enabled me and my family to live an independent life at Cottonwood: the water pump, outboard motor, chainsaw, four-wheeler: machines that at my command perform labors that in the past would have seemed miracles. I prize these machines for the empirical smarts and creative will reflected in their engineering. The four-wheeler has been a Hercules on the homestead, a transport and a workhorse. During the cabin-building we used the four-wheeler to hoist the roof panels into place, just as pioneers used horses to raise felled logs onto cabin walls.

The flaw in tool-using man, if it is a flaw, runs deep in us, as deep as our origins. Our machines take us places that once were unreachable, places underground and overhead and inside our bodies, places long ago and out of sight and all but unimaginable. The facts of the cosmos may not be flattering to our species, but we have time and space yet in which to defy space and time, and for now I lay odds that our tools will solve more problems than they create.

The truth is I am sparing in the tools and machines I bring to Cottonwood. One reason is economy. The other reason: I know my limits. I prefer less gadgetry to more, and I value simplicity. I'm rather stupid about machines. Machines confer power, but they also drain it and demand attention. It's too easy to become burdened by the machine that was supposed to liberate you. Take the John Deere 350-B front loader of my homestead neighbor Richard Pederson. Richard used the "crawler" to maintain the earthen boat ramp that he and his wife Laurel depended on. With the front bucket he cleared away the mud that periodically inundated the boat ramp. Every time the mud rolled down, Richard fired up the crawler. Mud. Crawler. Mud. Crawler. Adding a Sisyphean accent was the crawler's susceptibility to breakdown. He had no sooner repaired the machine than something else went wrong with it. One minute he was digging a garbage pit with the backhoe, next minute he was broken down and needed a drive shaft. That's how a complex machine like a John Deere crawler loader turns into a ball and chain. The devil obliges you to service the very tractor that buries you in brimstone.

But if the crawler was a ball and chain, it was a damned useful one. For a multipurpose machine, it was hard to beat. It enabled a couple in their sixties like Richard and Laurel to live in the Alaskan outback in the freedom and dignity they demanded. With the front bucket and backhoe, Richard did things in an hour that I couldn't do bare-handed in a week, if at all. He lifted with it, leveled with it, pulled with it, pushed with it, crushed with it, buried with it, carried with it, dug with it, trenched with it and more.

I marveled at this gifted machine, but I didn't envy them it. What a headache! In the isolation of the Alaskan bush, a minor breakdown can be horribly discouraging. You can't just reach for the telephone or the car keys. It took me four months to communicate with Northern Power Sports in Fairbanks about warranty coverage for my four-wheeler's defective fuel petcock and to get a replacement petcock in the mail. Installing the thing took me half an hour. When I visited Richard Pederson and found him in a cussing mood, it was usually because of a mechanical breakdown. He was particularly touchy one day when all of his machines seemed to have turned against him. He was out behind the workshop, cussing at five grease guns that he had laid out on the side of a giant cable spool. "None of them works proper," he yelled. "It's junk. That's all I got here. I come to realize it. Junk!"

Richard adjusted a valve on one of the grease guns, armed me with it, took a grease gun for himself, and we walked over to the yellow John Deere crawler, where it sat stranded in the mud at the top of the boat ramp. On the way Richard explained to me how one of the crawler's steel tracks had slipped off its rollers and how he had remounted it. "Christ almighty," he said, "I thank the good Lord it happened up here and not on the beach or I'd have lost the crawler."

We squatted by the hydraulic track tensioner on the left side of the machine and I raised the grease gun.

"How's it fit?" Richard asked.

"Fitting's good," I said, but as soon as I squeezed the trigger of the grease gun, a noodle of amber grease squirted out under the cylinder ram.

"What the hell is that?" he said.

I switched to the other grease gun and again injected grease through the fitting, trying to pump up the hydraulic pressure, but again the grease squirted out below.

"There's a hole down here in the cylinder," Richard said, peering closely at what he had discovered. A large man, Richard groveled on his shoulder in the mud. "Can't tell if it's a rust hole or a bolt hole," he said. "Have to get my little mirror and look underneath. If I get my hair dirty, Laurel won't like that."

We stood up, brushed the dirt off our clothes and headed to the house for coffee. Those foot-wide crawler tracks were of heavy steel. Richard had used his four-wheeler, together with a bottle jack and a come-along, to lift the fallen track into place on the top rollers and to reengage the drive sprockets. The track needed to be retensioned, but with the grease leaking from the hole in the hydraulic cylinder, there wasn't enough internal pressure to keep the ram fully extended, and the track would likely slip off again when Richard turned the crawler.

His first impulse was to weld the hole shut, but the story got more complicated. In slackening the tension prior to remounting the fallen track, Richard had removed from the cylinder a bolt which he was not supposed to have removed but only loosened. This misstep caused the loss of a specialty ball bearing that had sealed the relief hole and prevented the grease from leaking out. The ball bearing was long gone, buried in grease like a blueberry in bear crap. Even with the bolt in place, the cylinder would leak grease until a new ball bearing was seated on the relief hole. Richard decided to order one of the "danged pellets" by mail and to maneuver it into position through the bolt hole, maybe by first magnetizing the bolt.

What a pain in the chassis!

Once or twice Richard got so fed up with the crawler that he threatened to drive it onto the beach at low tide and leave it there. But he faithfully maintained the John Deere crawler until he and Laurel sold it with the homestead. They didn't regret owning the crawler, they only regretted not buying a new one instead of a used one. Considering the costs of repairs over the years—they had flown a mechanic to the homestead to replace the clutches—the cheaper and wiser course would have been to start with a brand new crawler. "It's a good lesson to learn while you're young," Richard told me. "Buy new if you can. Buyer beware. I think there's a Latin word for that."

UNITED SALMON
ASSOCIATION

Thom Wischer can't help associating the early days of the United Salmon Association with his having to kill a brown bear. The Wischers had commercially fished in Kupreanof Strait for more than twenty years and never had a problem with brown bears until 1997, the year the United Salmon Association formed and the fishermen went on strike. Thom had gone to town that day to learn what he could about the new fishing union and nobody stayed behind at the family's house and fish camp near Eagle Rock. When Thom got home, there was so much molasses and flour and macaroni on the floor, it had to be scraped up with a shovel. Later that summer the bear returned, aggressively, and Thom shot it. "Didn't want to do it, but it needed doing," he said. He could have applied the same words to the new fishing union.

"The processors finally pushed the fishermen too far," Thom explained to me later when he had taken a leadership role in the union. "Coming together and striking was new for a lot of these folks. A lot of them may have been anti-union in their way, before. These are hardy and independent people. Used to be that the buyers said, 'This is what we're paying,' and the fishermen made a living at it and accepted it and it was done with handshakes. There's real bitterness now."

Salmon Harvesters Unite was the bold heading of the USA notice that appeared in the 1998 Salmon Edition of the *Fair Market Report*, a seafood industry newsletter issued by the Kodiak-based Fair Market Coalition. The newsletter described the USA as a "statewide marketing association," but make no mistake, the USA was a labor union, an organization of working people committed, certainly, to expanding the markets for wild Alaska

224

salmon and improving the product's quality, but above all committed to securing fair-pay arrangements for the fishermen, fair and stable prices agreed to by the buyers in preseason contracts.

In the first years, the union functioned as the fishermen had hoped. USA spoke with authority, and there was enough unity among the members that the threat of a strike gave the buyers a real pause. Kodiak fishermen fish with two main gear types: the seine, which is a mobile, boat-based net, and the setnet, a stationary, beach-based net. It was difficult to get the setnetters on board with a strike because the setnetters, whose nets are fixed in place, have only one chance at catching salmon and making a season. But USA united the gear groups in a common cause. "We had four years of successful preseason contracts," Thom told me. "The fishermen's pay was based on the first wholesale price with a sliding scale. If the wholesale price increased, that's the amount paid to the processors, then the fishermen shared in the profits." To accomplish this, USA lobbied for and successfully instituted the Alaska Salmon Price Report within the Alaska Department of Revenue. The Price Report, published three times a year, tracks the wholesale prices paid to the processors for each of the salmon species and product forms (e.g., frozen fillets).

As the fleet headed out of port in early June 2001, USA announced that a price of 65 cents per pound of red (sockeye) salmon had been reached. This was historically a low price, but at least the fishermen had a contract. A contract let them better manage their accounts. Later, in July, the price of pink salmon was at issue. USA called on its members to keep their nets dry. Again the strike threat had teeth. The fishermen won a guaranteed 9 cents per pound of pink salmon, with 3 cents extra for chilled fish and a bonus for dock delivery to the processor. This was a rock-bottom price, so bad that the fishermen had to wonder if they had won anything, but at least they had a contract, a binding agreement they could rely on. Without a contract they were at the mercy of the company buyers, who sometimes offered a price before delivery and changed it when the fish were dockside, grading the salmon according to a bewildering system that always seemed to work to the disadvantage of the fishermen.

The following year, in 2002, the tensions between the buyers and harvesters came to a head. The 40 cents being offered for a pound of red salmon was 25 cents less than last year's price. The fishermen stood down. Red salmon was normally their money fish. They understood that the canneries were being forced to cut costs, to modernize and compete in a global marketplace, but 40 cents a pound was an insult.

The fishermen no longer trusted the processors. USA negotiators had learned a thing or two about organization during the startup years of the union, but it would be naive to suppose that the companies like Wards Cove, Ocean Beauty and Peter Pan hadn't learned a few things too. The buyers understood the peculiar stresses under which Alaska's salmon fishermen labor. A well-positioned fisherman could switch to a different product like cod, halibut or crab, but many fishermen in Kodiak, Bristol Bay, Prince William Sound and Southeast Alaska depend for their livelihoods on the summer salmon fishery. Fluctuating wild salmon runs, unstable and declining prices, competition from farmed salmon and from exporters like Chile and Russia—these circumstances pressured the companies and fishermen alike.

By June 20, the fishermen still hadn't received adequate price offers for red salmon. Against the midsummer backdrop of mistrust and negotiation, of strike threats and counterthreats, there was plenty of radio chatter among the fishermen. The radio back-and-forth reflected not only the conflict between the companies and the fishermen but also the strains within the fishing community. Fishermen tend to talk about the weather, tides, boats, family and so on, approaching through eddies of small talk the gist of what's on their minds. The following, an exchange between two seine fishermen, has been lifted from a longer, more roundabout conversation.

> I think I'll go home and do some home improvements till I can get excited about fishing.
>
> You heard if they've accepted anything in town?
>
> They're not signing. I don't know if they'd sign if we got them to offer what they offered before. Ocean Beauty will definitely have tenders on the grounds. They're posting some pretty ugly threats on the boards.

What are they gonna do?

I don't know what the fleet wants to do, but our team in town is frazzled. They're worn out trying to get something accepted.

Gotta hang tough, I guess.

Jeez, the boys are thinking you can't get by on much less. It's a matter of will at this point, of steeling ourselves. Canneries are gonna test us, they want the USA to dissolve.

We've all got families, gotta make a living, gotta eat this winter.

That's right. That's it.

You'd think Wards Cove'd know what we're looking at.

From what I'm hearing, there's a few guys with a different agenda. They wanna kill fish and they're thinking they'll do it on volume if the rest of us don't fish. But I think the majority want to regroup. We want the canneries to come to the table and tell us why they can't pay what we need them to pay.

If they get the tenders on the grounds, it's gonna be hard for some of the guys.

That's for sure. Like I say, our people have worked their hearts out. Some individuals are gonna probably wanna fish. It's a matter of how long we wanna sit, it's gonna be individuals' calls, but if they do, USA will probably fall to the wayside.

You're taking it easy, then?

It'll be pretty skinny for a while. I'd like to get my hundred-ton license, maybe take people to look at whales.

That might be the way. It's getting pretty tough to make it on the prices they offer. When the volume shows up, they put you on a limit, so they get you either way.

Yeah, you can't make it up on volume anymore. The canneries don't want salmon like they used to.

Have to hang in there and see what happens, I guess.

I'm not too worried about it. Hell, I own my boat and I own my skiff, and like they say, the ocean and land will provide.

These were representative voices. The speakers may have been deliberately broadcasting their views. Everything said on marine radio is said in the knowledge that others may be listening. When two fishermen conversing on channel 6 decide to "go up a couple," they're not under any illusion that they won't have company on channel 8. This is social life at sea. In the high-stakes summer of 2002, the VHF radio gave the scattered fishing community a way to air their sentiments.

And their differences. Dueling personalities emerged. The all-important tenders, who service the fishermen by transferring their catches of fish, were caught in the middle of the labor dispute, working for the buyers but friendly and collegial with the fishermen. Everybody wanted to work—the issue was at what price. In the following exchange, the strain, the "bad vibe," between the tender and the fisherman was audible in the intonations of their voices.

> Anything finding your net over there? You fishing yet?
> Negative.
> You're on tomorrow's list. Need to clean you up.
> Might be fishing tomorrow. I'll let you know.
> I need to be here early for your first pick.
> Well, if I do set out, it'll be at slack low water tomorrow morning. Won't pick for a couple hours after that.

More sympathetic is the following exchange between a plainspoken tenderman and a fisherman. The context is important. USA had now negotiated a contract with a single buyer, True World Foods. USA fishermen were obligated to deliver fish only to processors who had signed a contract, and since no other processors had signed, all the fish went to True World Foods. As a result, any tender working for True World Foods got very busy very fast.

> We're chockablock. Started taking fish and they kept coming.
> Had our last delivery and put her in high northbound, over.
> Doesn't sound like the bigger canneries want to settle.

We're hoping everybody gets a chance to get to a tender, but unfortunately we haven't heard from the major processors. They're missing out on some nice fish.

It doesn't make any sense. I can't believe they can't sell 'em for more than what they're saying. If we don't find any fish here, we'll probably pack up and move on.

We had forty or sixty boats at Igvak down at the mainland, Kilokak Rocks area, decent amount of fish we tendered, but nothing to set any fires. Some guys got a thousand pounds, some guys got ten thousand, but at 60 cents, that's only $6,000, which is nothing to set the world on fire.

Bad fishing at a bad price—it's a bad combination for us. We're not making much money. The farther from town, the better you do, but it's harder. We're just treading water.

Time to play cribbage. We'll be standing by on the company channel. See how it goes. It's not the best price, but by gorry it's something. At least we're working instead of sitting on our thumbs.

That weekend, word went out about a USA general meeting scheduled for Tuesday, June 25. This was to be a fleet-wide meeting to discuss "a major decision regarding the future of the season." All boats were urged to send a representative to town. Tensions between the buyers and harvesters were at a breaking point. The union membership was divided. Their only buyer, True World Foods, had bought all the fish it could accommodate and was unable to process more. Tender space was scarce. USA worked feverishly to recruit more tenders, but salmon boats were stacked twenty deep at the mainland and fish had reportedly spoiled for lack of pickup. The dominant processing companies, the "majors," held out against a contract but sent their tenders onto the grounds in a bid to divide the fishermen. Weak red salmon runs in Bristol Bay and early pink salmon runs elsewhere exacerbated the strains. At every level the Alaska seafood industry was in distress, and the impending USA meeting became the focus.

Monday was gray and drizzly, and from my window on Kupreanof Strait I watched the skiffs and seiners travel east toward town. All day, the fishing boats headed to port. Radio communications were grave and expectant:

> We're pulling our net. See you tomorrow.
> Roger that. Learn more tomorrow than we probably want to.
> Need you for mediation. You'll set everyone straight.
> Lots of viewpoints. Haven't figured it all out yet.
> It's been an interesting summer.
> I just hope whatever we decide, everyone can abide by it.

On Tuesday, wet and cloudy again, I ride to Anton Larsen Bay in the skiff of a fisherman neighbor, Mike Resoff. In Kodiak I meet up with another fisherman, Adam Wischer, Thom Wischer's son. Adam, tall and deep-voiced, a former high school cross-country runner, attends college in Idaho in winter and setnets in Kodiak in the summertime. His father now leads the union and Adam is conversant on the issues. As we drive downtown in the rain—we stop at the USA caddyshack to pick up some papers that need delivering ahead of the 6 p.m. meeting—Adam outlines how things stand with him and the other fishermen going into tonight's decision:

The first run of red salmon, the "front end" of the run, is over, and next month, July, will be big for both red salmon and pink salmon. True World Foods, the cannery owned by Sun Myung Moon's Unification Church, has been paying the fishermen 59 cents per pound of red salmon. The other buyers, including Adam's usual buyer, Western Alaska, have offered 53 cents for reds. As for the "humpies" (pink salmon), Western Alaska is paying 7 cents a pound. Adam pronounces the words "seven cents" in an understated drawl. He has been netting a surplus of humpies at his site on the south shore of Raspberry Island, a number well in excess of his June average, a situation that highlights a major dilemma for the salmon fishermen. When the fish really run, it's hard to hold out for price. A single processor, True World Foods, was able to handle the island-wide catch of early red salmon, and USA facilitated this by hiring tenders to service the fleet. But True World Foods was out of processing capacity. "They've maxed out," Adam tells me. "When the pink salmon run, there's no way True World can handle all the fish." For this reason Adam believes the fishermen will accept the offer put on the table by the major processors: 53 cents for a pound of red salmon. The strike has taken a toll on the fishing community, and with so much bitterness in the air, there is little chance of holding out longer against the buyers. The fleet has shown a remarkable solidarity, but unfortunately some of the seine fishermen broke ranks after the mainland Cape Igvak section opened to fishing and the USA tenders were overwhelmed by the volume of salmon being caught. Likewise a few of the setnetters—"scabs," Adam calls them—have proved unwilling to withhold their product. One large setnet operation in particular, rumored to have harvested a massive poundage of salmon in June, the only fishermen making money—"they're all scabs," Adam says.

THOM AND KATHY WISCHER, 2014

Some of this scab harvest, processed by Wards Cove Packing Company and being the earliest salmon to reach the Japanese market, will command a high price, but not high enough, according to Thom Wischer at the USA meeting that night, to negate the advantage True World Foods has had in beating the other companies to the wholesale market at a strong profit. Thom Wischer, though not a large man, has a solid physical presence, with the powerful hands, arms and shoulders, the vigor and outdoorsman's color of a veteran fisherman. He is also a schoolteacher and sometime principal, which helps to explain his easy matter-of-factness in addressing the assembled fishermen. "We've enabled True World Foods to beat the other processors with a million plus pounds of number one reds," Thom says. "Our biggest power is to withhold product from the majors, and we've done that. We've withheld more than a million and a half pounds of product, and we thought we could get more movement from the majors by doing this, but we haven't. And that's what we're here to talk about tonight."

Fishermen's Hall, in the blue-roofed Harbormaster building on Kodiak's waterfront, is crowded with USA members and supporters. The four rows of seats are filled and the rest of us stand around the back and sides. The villages of Old Harbor and Port Lions are participating by speaker phone. The tables in front are for the USA board and negotiators. Folding chairs carry the stenciled initials of the United Fishermen's Marketing Association. The atmosphere is serious but informal, fishermen sipping coffee and talking quietly during the lull. A dog pokes around and gets its chin scratched. There's a "Don't Beef, Eat Fish" poster on the wall. Beards; weathered faces; a minority of women, one of whom goes to the front blackboard and writes:

At the end of the season there's going to be A List, B List, and Shitlist.

She returns to her seat, and her prophecy stays there on the blackboard behind Thom Wischer. Thom, after having begun with general remarks and addressed logistical complaints involving the tenders *Buccaneer* and *Rebel*, and before he proceeds to the business at hand, looks around at the attendees and asks if anyone has any comments.

A fisherman hesitantly stands and introduces himself. "I was one of those who lost sight of what the USA was about," he says. In the same shaky voice, the fisherman goes on to apologize to the membership for selling his fish out of contract. "I sold my fish to Ocean Beauty and I only later realized what I'd done. I hope you can find it in your hearts to forgive me."

The remorseful fisherman turns out at the door and leaves the meeting. A woman goes after him and brings him back in. The hall has been dead quiet. Thom gruffly clears his throat and says he wants to update everyone on the status of the negotiations. He reminds people to treat one another respectfully in exchanging their opinions.

"We asked the buyers to give us their best offer, to go back to Seattle or Japan or wherever they need to go, and based on their economics, to give us their bottom line. So they did that. And they came back and it wasn't satisfactory to us. We told them we need time to get to the fishermen on the grounds, and some of the buyers didn't like that. They spun out of the room, they said their offers are off the table, the offers will burn up at 6 p.m. So we at USA, we told them, we need to know, is this good or not, yes or no, because we need to talk to our people. And we decided we'd better get the fleet in here instead of the fishermen out on the grounds talking to one another on the TracFone or the radio. So this is how it is. True World Foods is plugged full. Guys are wanting to go back to their buyers. We're going to consider the offers as they stand. It's at this point that I need to ask the nonmembers to leave. No hard feelings."

USA dues, by the way, were $300 a year.

I learned from Mike Resoff on the following day, Wednesday, that the mood in the hall never heated up past that. People were pleased with the job the negotiators had done, but fishermen need to sell fish, and that's how they voted. The base pay, also known as the posted price or grounds price, was to be 53 cents per pound of red salmon, with bonuses for chilled fish and for dock delivery to the processor.

From my cabin window I watched the boats heading west again to the fishing grounds. On Thursday, when the commercial fishing resumed, the weather was wet and dreary, with a northeast wind blowing and two- to three-foot curlers on the water. If only a fisherman had nothing to grump about but the lousy weather.

Damage is going to be long term from this fiasco.

It doesn't have to be that way.

Hard to talk your way out of this one, man. You're just finding a way to rationalize it.

Had to sell my stuff where I could.

You sold us out is what you did.

I delivered my product where I could get the best treatment for it.

That wouldn't've happened if it wasn't for your company and the others.

The word's already out—Kodiak's got garbage for fish.

Go fuck yourself.

I'll go somewhere else if that's the way it's gonna be.

Good idea.

There were rifts after the strike, bitter rifts, and some of the hostility was aired on the VHF radio. Names were named, and what we heard wasn't always pretty.

The so-and-sos don't give a crap about anyone but themselves.

We've all got a memory like an elephant at this point.

But, by and large, the USA fishermen moved on because they didn't have many options. The age-old drama of work and fair pay had staged a scene in Kodiak, Alaska, and for the time being it was played out. The fishermen fished and the tenders—the *Lucky Lady*, the *Rebel*—took on the tons of fresh salmon that eventually, sold as wild Alaska salmon, found its way into the markets and onto the tables of North America and the world.

Thom Wischer's assessment, when we talked a year later at his fish camp near Eagle Rock, was that the events of 2002 had clipped the wings of the fledgling union. "Their spirit's broken for now," he told me. "Lo and behold, all the processors are offering the same 'best' price again this year. It'll be a while before the members have another strike in them. It was only about a dozen fishermen who broke ranks and delivered out of contract to their buyers, but it was enough. Our leverage over the processors was essentially destroyed, and when we came in to negotiate this year, they said they didn't need to deal with us because their guys would deliver to them anyway."

A few salmon jumped offshore as we talked, and the Wischer skiffs lay at their running lines. Spherical orange floats bobbed on the water. "We've got our work cut out for us. USA needs to focus more energy on direct marketing. The salmon wholesale for more than quadruple what we earn on them. We can close that gap if we cut out some of the middlemen. This is the new world we're in."

Hard-nosed as always, Thom maintained these opinions in the years ahead. He's a tight-lipped man, but when he knows you, he'll speak his mind and tell some yarns. Thom and Kathy had met as undergraduates at Western Michigan University and they taught school in Detroit in the early 1970s. They moved to Kodiak Island after they vacationed here and fell in love with the place. Adam and Lynsey, their grown children, now carry on the fishing.

"The fleet's beaten down," Thom told me in 2005. "They've had no contract since '02. Wild salmon sales were up 94 percent last year, but the harvester-fisherman is still at 53 cents and not sharing in the profits. The guys can't muster the solidarity to wield the only club they have, which is not to fish, to strike. The processors never let things get quite bad enough. Ex-vessel prices, local tax revenue, the fairness argument—nothing works for us because we're the small fry, and the people in charge, the powers that be, they favor the big fish, the processors and the companies."

From what I hear, there's nothing to be out in a twenty-knotter for. It's looking pretty strenuous out there. Not something to poke around in.

Westerly outlook this side, fifteen and not strong. Getting ready to fish here.

Go nail 'em. Big fish stories over the closure.

I'll need to catch quite a few humpies to get me excited at that price. I'd just as soon be lying on the bottom chumming in some codfish.

Just have to keep the nets wet, I guess. Keep the faith.

This faith, the fisherman's faith in the cyclicality of the salmon runs and of the market prices, if not in the fair-mindedness of the company buyers, was rewarded in the ensuing decade as the price the fishermen received for their wild-caught Alaska salmon doubled and then tripled. But Thom Wischer isn't impressed. He cites numbers from the recent Alaska Salmon Price Report to demonstrate the outsize gap between the commercial value of the salmon and what the fishermen get paid for it. Fairness is a big word, but Thom Wischer knows it when he doesn't see it. "After the summer of 2002," he reflects, "USA went quietly into the night, and today things are just the same as they were before and the fishermen don't receive a fair share of what they harvest."

VALHALLA

Valhalla, the legendary Hall of the Dead Heroes ruled by the god Odin, is a noble name for a fishing boat, and at first I questioned the humility of the fisherman who named his boat *Valhalla*. But there's a heroism in the figure of a sea captain, and on reflection I decided the name Valhalla wasn't unsuitable for a crab boat. Think of a Dungeness crab as the soul of a dead warrior. Then the master of the *Valhalla*, who gathers these armored legions under one roof and relies on them for sustenance, is akin to the great god Odin.

Mark Thomas, bearded, fair, strong and gentle, was not unworthy of the comparison, but he would have disagreed. When I asked Mark why he had named his boat *Valhalla*, he revealed himself to be a prince of humility. He smiled, gazed at the wooden boat lying at anchor—we stood on the beach at Cottonwood—and I assumed that he would oblige me with a stirring account, something at once personal and mythological, the sort of tale with which the residents of Valhalla regale one another before the flames of the Great Hearth. Maybe Mark's ancestors were Scandinavian and he identified with the Norse gods. Maybe he was inspired by the ideal of a noble afterlife. Maybe Valhalla stood for Kodiak Island itself, an ultima Thule guarded by bears and eagles and fortified by towering evergreens.

Mark Thomas had left California in 1982 at the age of twenty and embarked on a commercial fisherman's life in the North. In Alaska he had the good fortune to meet the woman who became his wife, Myla, now the mother of his two children. Myla had lately been suffering from dizzy spells and fainting fits, and Mark worried about her. It was through Myla that I had met Mark. She worked at Safeway and at the post office in town, and she and I had struck up a conversational acquaintance. At the beginning of July I came to town to buy ten sheets of plywood, and Myla suggested that her husband, Mark, soon to put to sea in the *Valhalla,* might give me a lift back to my homestead.

Mark, when we met, readily agreed, and we arranged it. His Dungeness crabbing route took him past Cottonwood on his way around the north end of the island. Unfortunately I had slipped into town between low-pressure systems, and Mark postponed our departure because of gale warnings in Shelikof Strait. I got out of town for the price of a seat fare on a floatplane, but I had to leave my plywood aboard the black-hulled *Valhalla.*

A couple of days passed with no sight of the *Valhalla* from my crow's nest at Cottonwood, and I had retired to my cabin for the evening, resigned to the likelihood that I wouldn't see my plywood any time soon, when a black-hulled fishing boat chugged into view in Kupreanof Strait, and in my binoculars I read the name *Valhalla* on the vessel's bow. The boat turned hard to port and came shoreward.

By the time I had descended to the beach, Mark had faced the *Valhalla* into the flood tide and dropped anchor. He was on the afterdeck inflating a sorry-looking raft with a foot pump. He eased the raft off the stern of the *Valhalla,* loaded it with my ten sheets of plywood and rowed to shore. He and I carried the plywood to the head of the beach.

Dungeness crab was at one time Mark's bread and butter, but Alaska's Dungeness crab harvest had declined since the boom of the early 1980s, and these days only seven or eight boats fished for Dungeness crab out of Kodiak. Last year was a good year because of a crab shortfall down the West Coast, but even last year the dockside price for the crab was only $2.50 a pound. Dungeness crab inhabit shallow waters and fall easy prey to the sea otters, and in Mark's opinion the otters have ravaged the crab fishery. Mark lowers his pots—each circular crab pot weighs eighty pounds—into the bays and inside waters, and working the pots alone he is free to rely on his judgment and experience. He baits the pots and lets them soak for two days or two weeks before he pulls them and checks them. He might have five keepers in one pot and none in the next, but it's always in his interest to throw the females and the young crabs back in the water.

I invite Mark to stay for dinner, but he has a couple of hundred pounds of bait herring in the hold and wants to press on while Shelikof Strait is calm. He has 250 crab pots cached on lagoons on the west side of the island and plans to travel into the night to reach the Dungeness grounds. In food and fuel and bait, Mark has $600 invested in the trip, and he hopes it pays off in crab. For doing me the favor of transporting my plywood he won't accept a dime in thanks.

I have a lot of respect for Mark, for his pride and his struggles and his love for his family. Myla's health has been a concern, and if I know anything about health concerns, money concerns aren't far off. Why does he keep fishing for Dungeness crab? The Dungeness season is a long one without much cutthroat competition, and he likes that. And he is invested in the crab pots and the know-how. He always hopes the crab numbers will pick up again, but with the otter population out of control, he is less optimistic.

Before he leaves, there is still a question I want to ask Mark. What inspired him to name his fishing boat for the mythical heavenly fortress Valhalla?

Mark smiles when I ask, and he looks out at the old boat lying at anchor. As I say, I was prepared for a revealing answer, a rollicking tale of seagoing glory, or something more spiritual, something touching on the ascent to paradise. In any case, I expected only honesty from Mark Thomas, and the truth was that he had bought the *Valhalla* from another fisherman and it would have cost him $300 in government fees to rename the boat. This was an expense he had decided to forgo until the crab harvest turned up and he could better afford it.

"Makes perfect sense," I said.

It was nine o'clock in the evening when we shook hands and wished each other well. Mark paddled out in the raft and raised anchor, and the *Valhalla* was soon under way, chugging into the strait and on around the head of the island to the Dungeness grounds.

VIGNETTE: AUGUST 5, 2011

The seaplane touches down in the choppy water and lifts off at once without us, the pilot unnerved by the exposed rocks of low tide and the dark blue of the roughening sea. We wait at the waterline to see if he'll circle back for us, but he flies on. Other pilots would have stuck the landing—the conditions are marginal—but he made his call and there's nothing to be done about it.

We carry our duffel bags and fish boxes back above the tideline. The hours of waiting go rather quickly. You learn a kind of patience in the bush. The kids play cards and read aloud to each other while Martina throws crackers to the bold little fox named Goldenrod. I never liked the idea of feeding the wild animals, let alone christening them, but we're all grown up now and I don't tell anyone what to do.

The west wind strengthens and the water whitecaps all the way to Outlet Cape. I wander up the beach into the wind, enjoying its cool briskness on my face. On Raspberry Island, across the strait from us, the vegetation gives a visible texture to the sunlit slopes. The landscape is dynamic, every part of it in motion—waves, tree branches, grass blades, sea otters, wildflowers, clouds—plush and vibrant and full of miraculous color.

A bald eagle floats in the sky above Cottonwood, and the seagulls come and go. The children's faces, when I lie back on the beach and look up at them, are framed by the blue sky. She's eighteen years old now and he is fourteen and they will soon have other places to go in the summer. That's all right. I had places to go when I was their age. Parents give their kids religion hoping they will come back to it someday. Sometimes they do and sometimes they don't. He was a year old when he first came to

Cottonwood. She is eighteen and in college and he is fourteen and taller than I am now. A week from yesterday, I'll be fifty years old. I sit up and accept a peanut butter and jelly sandwich, and we eat our lunches on the beach by the freshwater pool where the creek splashes down from the cliffs. Swaying wildflowers brighten the banks. In this wind we may not get picked up at all. The cabin is boarded up and bearproofed, and I would rather not have to undo the work just to spend another night on hold.

I walk the handheld radio up the beach until I receive a NOAA weather forecast on VHF channel 4. A switch to low variable winds after midnight, followed by rain with resurgent southwest winds. Could be worse, could be better. The waves wash in and out and the sea foam lingers on the beach at my feet. The stranded sea foam always reminds me of the milk left on a child's mouth after it drinks. I turn the radio off and look around at them. My son sprawls in the pebbles with a flannel shirt over his face, drowsing in the sunlight. His sister and mother sit side by side talking. Above them, above the sea cliffs, the cabin's green roof shows among the spruce trees, and higher still, beyond the cabin, the emerald slopes converge and the mountain ridge transects the sky.

The other day we climbed the mountain and picnicked at our old spot on the summit, and everything seemed the same as always, with the same preferences and the same laughs, but things aren't the same. The strawberries and rhubarb come up every summer, but I don't weed them as I once did, and the garden is going wild. The tools have broken. After fifteen years, everything is fifteen years older than before.

I kneel by one of the waxed fish boxes and reach inside to feel the salmon. Through the gallon bags, the fish feels cold and firm. Throughout the afternoon I move the fish boxes to keep them shaded. A doe and yearling wander up the beach and stare at us, and the bold little fox named Goldenrod returns in the late afternoon to pry more crackers out of us. The songbirds flitting in the wind remind me of the origami tulips Miranda used to make. What happens to all of the things the kids make over the years? You save some of it, you throw some away, and most of it disappears with the days.

KODIAK TOWN, 2014

We read or beachcomb or watch the ocean and reflect. Miranda and Kody chatter and sometimes break into carefree laughter, and Martina and I exchange smiles when this happens. I don't expect any of them to feel about this place as I do. I've watched the spruce saplings grow alongside the children. The homestead can't mean for them what it has for me, but they know what it is to care about something, and if I can tell them what I've seen and say it clearly enough, they'll understand how much it mattered.

After seven o'clock in the evening a floatplane makes a broad turn over Cottonwood and descends to the water. We carry our fish boxes and duffel bags down to the water to meet the pilot. I am surprised he landed. The sea is rough and he won't like these waves.

"You're going to get wet if you want to get out of here, there's no two ways about it," the pilot yells, ducking under the plane's wing and jumping off the float.

I help him to nose the plane around, and I have no sooner grasped the wingtip rope than I am lifted off my feet, the plane rolling on the waves. My family pass the cargo to me and I relay it to the pilot, but the floats are taking a beating on the rocks and we don't get much done before we have to push the plane off the beach. We finish loading, then the pilot hurries forward to the throttle and drives the plane off the beach again.

My hip boots are full of water, and Martina and the kids have only rain boots. They slog toward me in the surf and one by one climb onto the float and into the rocking plane. I sit up front by the pilot and put my headset on while he speeds across the water. After ten hours on the beach, we are relieved to be airborne. It's a bumpy takeoff, one we won't soon forget.

Martina squeezes my shoulder as I look out the window at the cabin. We circle the homestead and leave Cottonwood behind. The pilot flies us east over the coastline and he cuts inland through the passes toward Kodiak town. The engine is loud and we don't speak over it, but I know how excited the kids are to get back to town, and before we arrive I turn in my seat and smile at them.

WILDFLOWERS

But of course we were flower children, heeding the call to freedom and delight, stopping to savor what pleased us: this is how we lived, away from the madness of the world, rejoicing in our love and asking nothing more, from the shore to the field to the mountaintop rejoicing, in the upland meadows and mossy bottoms, in the grassy pockets and rocky clefts, rejoicing in the wildflowers whose color and fragrance filled the air of what seemed to us an immense chapel without ceiling and without walls.

It was a kind of madness, I see, not of self-delusion but of youthful rapture, the madness of spring, of eros and of love: the madness of wildflowers.

None of us alters the terms of existence, but heaven-on-earth was for me more accessible and more tangible in those wildflower meadows than in the profoundest cogitations of the wisest ecclesiastical and political authorities. Books piled high never elevated a body to heaven, and not one of history's revolutionists or accomplished Machiavels ever brought heaven a rung closer to earth.

Eros, assuming a human form, comes, I think, barefooted or sandaled in a robe of wildflowers loosely open at the front, belted with plaited fibers and piped around with blossoms, a smudge of pollen on the cheek, catkin dust in the hair, and at the ear an airy escort of bees and butterflies.

The celebrity mammals get the lion's share of attention in Alaska, the bear and wolf and moose, but an overlooked emblem of the wild, of the fertility and animating energy of nature, the source of so much of nature's exquisiteness, is the wildflower. What I get from a wildflower that I don't get from a cultivated flower is something more than a childish surprise;

it's the sense of the earth as a procreative force preceding and superior to me, independent of me and my designs. Show me a geranium in a planter in Montreux or Malibu and I'm jaded. Oh, I like it enough, the bright colors impress me, but are they real? But put me before a wild geranium on a Kodiak clifftop, the veined and violet petals starting softly up from the grass and moss, and my knees shake.

My gratitude among the spring wildflowers is the twin of wonder. The wildflower *is* the spring, the rebirth, the second chance, the reprieve of the condemned, the paschal mercy, the pell-mell dash into sunlight, the festal awakening, the warm-bellied embrace, the desperation of desire become the inspiration to life.

After a grueling winter, a life steeped in dark and steely twilight, the first encounter with a wildflower is a joyful one. The beginning of May finds me surrounded by ruins, the country gray and desolate, the meadows unredeemed fields of blasted stems and seared leaves. I look closer, and seeing through the old skin into a new life, I find a blade of grass, a fern uncurling, a leaflet trembling. I happen on a flower blossom and am struck by its beauty, a beauty as simple as the space around it is momentarily sacred. The first wildflower might be a violet, a cluster of marsh violets in the streamside moss—tiny, five-petaled darlings!—or it might be a shooting star or an early salmonberry, a spray of magenta or a rosette of pink, it doesn't matter which: this is the warrant of life, the usher of the spring, and I'm a believer now, I welcome the advent of plenty.

Flowers are nature's mass indulgence, granted to all of us. If flowers were bells I'd never tire of ringing them. Here are enough shooting stars to win a war with. All the stained glass windows of all the churches of the earth lie shattered underfoot and fused to make this garden. Fresh corridors open, cool moist shades rich with the blended smells of elder and fern and loamy earth. The primrose blooms on the mountain, the creamy anemone over the sea. The cliffs brighten with purple lupine and yellow cinquefoil. Starflowers gleam in the forest glades. A sweet-as-candy mist hovers around the valerian. Fumes of photosynthesis leave me giddy. I nuzzle close and taste pink petals. Diminutive bells swing in the currents of my breath. Fragrances vie in the solstice air, pink distillates and green liquors, sun-gold juices and palate-drenching elixirs. Green, more green, from the silvery green of the willows to the dark impasto of the evergreens. Yellow paintbrush, purple-throated iris, wild rose and Jacob's ladder, immortal bog candle, shy maiden, blushing spirea, pink pyrola, nagoonberry, chocolate lily, saxifrage, rockcress, black-tipped groundsel, spring beauty, northern bedstraw, Sitka burnet, large leaf avens, fluorescent sweet pea and ooh and aah the rose purple orchid.

A blustery wind blows over this wild bazaar.

Get up! Come on! We'll wake in their lairs the wild snapdragons, we'll stir the grass of Parnassus, we'll fetch the gentian and the rhododendron, the harebell throbbing with its strange blue light, and, lethal and purple and velvety, the fabled monkshood. At the dome of the wild chive, at the tower of the goldenrod, at the spire of the fireweed we'll stop and raise our eyes. The engine of the sun sounds in our pulse, our wrists and throats and thighs, the plants mass around us, entwining ankles and calves and rubbing at hips, every square foot of earth hosting its cosmos of wildflowers.

May's flowers are long gone now. Petals lie like spent confetti in the moss. We've climbed the bloom pole and it's done. Seed heads blacken and rattle. Berries redden. Mushrooms populate the woods. Rusty stalks prophetically point skywards.

On the last day of September I find a yellow fleabane on the beach, and in the cottonwood grove three violet willow herbs. The yarrow soldiers on into October but can no further. They will be back. They'll all be back, blooming over their graves, and I'll be with them.

WIND

To live on an island in the Gulf of Alaska is to be played by winds from every compass point, soothed by sweet breezes and battered by gales. I had a taste of the wild Kodiak wind before I ever saw my homestead, a fifty-knot north wind that stranded me in town for several days. I asked my pilot, Jack Lechner, why we couldn't land on wheels instead of floats, and Jack sat me down and explained to me the peril of landing his Super Cub on a sloping beach in a gusting wind. He drew illuminating diagrams of an onshore wind pushing a plane into the cliffs and an offshore wind catching under the plane's wing and rolling it. Our only good choice was patience.

At night I wake and listen to the wind, to the cabin creaking and shuddering in the gusts. The invisible intruder shakes the latches and bangs the panes. The stove rumbles, the shadows leap on the walls. Through every crack in the weather side of the cabin, the cold air forces its way in, and in the drafts, objects move, a marble on the table, or a letter lying open at the foot of the bed. It's a good hour for ghost stories.

Small-craft advisories, storm warnings and gale warnings are common around the island. Cottonwood, on the north coast of Kodiak Island, stands exposed to the northerly windstream, but the windblast is moderated by Raspberry and Afognak Islands to the north. If we are at sea in the raft, a west wind or east wind blows us across Kupreanof Strait, and if trouble looms, we head for shore at once. In calm, a one-pound sinker anchors our raft, but a strong wind will drag us and our twenty-pound anchor toward the rocks or out between the capes toward Shelikof Strait, never a happy prospect in a windswept sea. If Homer's *Odyssey* taught me anything, it's that storm winds are anathema to seafarers.

A blowup in the wind tells first on the water surface. Advance breezes ruffle and darken the sea. Waves are raised, and soon the entire sea is driving. On a sunny day the wind can blow with a pure cutting ferocity, legions of whitecaps streaming in one direction like an army of angels at the end of time.

Living at the foot of a mountain we also have, in addition to the prevailing winds, the thermal winds that periodically blow uphill or cascade downhill, depending on the time of day and the barometric pressure. No wonder our weathercock trembles in place as if he can't make up his mind which way to turn.

The sawhorses blow over, the sandpaper swirls away, and bits of moss stick in the wet paint. A tarpaulin balloons and shrugs off a five-gallon bucket of paint like a demitasse. Earthly existence is dynamism. The wind ripping past our cabin at sixty miles an hour, I worry about catastrophe—the chimney pipe exploding or a spruce tree falling and sundering the cabin. The ocean waves are atomized before they hit the beach.

And this is merely wind. Add water for spectacle. Fog and rain blowing sideways. Windows buckling, tarpaulins shredding, loose boards breaking free. The spruce boughs rebound in thick, twisting masses; they spring and recoil, spewing drops of rainwater. The wind rails, the trees lash the sky, and the combers roll onto devastated beaches where the seaweeds lie windrowed in tortured shapes.

I love a wind-driven storm, a hair-raising howler—I love it when everybody is safe, sheltered inside after a drenching. As the wind subsides I hear subtler sounds. The leaves rub and vibrate in the mild air. All nature, all material nature, is the wind's harp. On a damp day the plants bristle and shiver and fret, and on a fair day they stream scent and color. In the fluttering of the cottonwood leaves—*ft-t-t-t-t-t-t*—a sunny breeze creates a dazzling pointillism of green lights and shades. The songbirds breast the wind, the butterflies tack up and down in it, the eagles soar, and the children stretch out their arms and catch the wind in the sails of their sleeves, shrieking with delight at the feeling of being blown before the wind, at the feeling of flight.

My companion in the waiting room of the air taxi, a petroleum engineer named Chip, is trying to get to Terror Bay on a mountain goat hunt. He has spent most of his vacation days waiting for the wind to let up. Chip's opinion of the wind is unforgiving. But if I am not in a hurry, the wind that plays havoc with the plans of travelers may thrill me. I love the drama of a blustery day when it's hats on and off to the weather. The spruce trees resemble scholars in conversation, bowing and gesticulating, demurring and attending to one another's words. They are discussing the nature of the wind, no doubt, and whether the wind is essentially vital or spiritual.

Energized by the wind, literally touched by it, I respond to the wind as to a living thing. The wind is behind me or the wind is ahead, but it's always near. It awakes in the north, it awakes in the south, it blows this way and that as my moods do. The wind has as many sides as a circle. It will have breath to spare when I am long out of mine.

So much of the day-to-day eventfulness of life at Cottonwood, so much that is beneficent and life-affirming, is thanks to the wind. I know two homesteaders who generate power from the wind. The municipality of Kodiak has raised its own giant wind turbines on Pillar Mountain above town. The wind frees the pollen, it lifts the spores, it carries the seeds of the trees and flowers, and downwind of today it plants the gardens of tomorrow.

XANADU

aughter and self-reliance go hand in hand. If you can laugh at yourself, you won't need anyone else to do it. If you find yourself chipping ice or melting snow in a bucket because the creek is frozen and your water barrel is empty and you're thirsty, you clearly have a lot to think about and you aren't going to get anywhere by cursing and lamenting. In Alaska's bush a sense of humor is a survival skill.

During a long stretch of isolation I lost track of the calendar and I didn't know what day it was. It seemed important to know the day, so I put the proverbial gun to my head and decided it was Tuesday. A minute later I heard somebody on the VHF radio wish somebody else a happy Ash Wednesday. I was as morbid as if I had lost a round of Russian roulette. But my only mistake, I realized, was in thinking that the day mattered. To a homesteader the day of the week is immaterial. Putting a gun to my head about it, proverbial or not, was off-the-charts absurd.

A hazard of lingering too long in Xanadu is that you start believing your hallucinations. You forget to elbow yourself or to shake yourself by the sleeve. Not having an alternate perspective can be deadly. An Alaskan acquaintance improved his health and his overall "vibe" by giving himself life-enhancing electric shocks, a therapy he swore by. He did this for many years and was ultimately found dead in his cabin, still hooked up to the apparatus. I'm afraid he just kept turning the dial higher and higher for longer and longer whereas a discerning companion would have unplugged the electrodes and told him to go outside and chop some wood.

A sense of perspective is desirable in itself and doubly desirable in your companions. Remember, your companions have companions, too, and you're one of them. I promised Martina that if she homesteaded on Kodiak Island with me she could count on a hot bath as often as once a week. I intended to spoil her silly. Our bath preparations—pumping water from the creek, heating it outside on a wood fire, scooping the hot water into a livestock tub—these admittedly weren't the pinnacle of modern convenience, and in bad weather it was sometimes necessary to delay our bath for upwards of a week. This wasn't satisfactory even for a male of the species. Our foul-weather solution was to heat the water indoors on the cookstove and to bathe in a plastic tote the size of an oil change pan. One way or another I made good on my courtly promises, and Martina was flexible enough not to resent the makeshift arrangements.

Be careful who you move into the bush with, that's all I'm saying. This should be obvious, but you'd be surprised. When word got out that Cathy "Catnip" Morris had moved to Deadfall Island with the charmer nicknamed the Wolf, people shook their heads knowingly. It was assumed the pair had embarked on an epic bender. We soon heard rumors of "disturbances." Catnip Morris radioed the cannery watchman, who radioed her father on Afognak Island, who radioed the Alaska State Troopers, who radioed Deadfall Island and talked the lovebirds down from their quarrel. My contact at the State Troopers, a dispatcher, confirmed that there had been a fight, but she assured me that Catnip had given as good as she got. Even so, what a companion to take into the bush with you! Where does a woman run from the Wolf on Deadfall Island?

A few years ago, after a medical emergency at Cottonwood, Martina and I vowed never to return to the homestead without renting a satellite telephone. Fortunately we only had to rely on the satphone once. We were fishing from the raft when our nine-year-old son cast a hook and caught his mother's eye with it. It sounds Freudian, I know. Martina happened to have a fish on her line and she refused to give it up. What's a hook in the eye when you have a halibut on the line? Her behavior—she clutched the bobbing rod in her hands while I tried to extract the hook from her eye—proves her passion for fishing, not the unseriousness of her situation. The rusty barb was caught deep in her eyelid. The point of the hook was a hairsbreadth from her eyeball. When I tugged on the hook with the pliers, her eye came toward me. I couldn't back the hook out.

"To hell with this," I said. "You're going to town."

I reeled in her stupid fish, which turned out to be not a halibut but the divine practical joke known as a bullhead, the biggest bullhead we've ever caught, a lantern-jawed monster. The children waited for us on the beach while I led their mother to the cabin. She looked like a pagan chieftain with the ornate fishing lure dangling from her face. I snipped the lure with wire cutters to lessen its weight and I called Andrew Airways on the satphone.

The weather was fine and Dean Andrew promptly arrived in the floatplane. And this is how my family enjoyed an unexpected trip to Kodiak town. At Providence Medical Center the doctors cut my wife loose and gave her a tetanus shot. Another fraction of an inch and she would have lost the eye, they said. We all learned a lesson that day about the hazards of casting for fish in tight quarters.

Although Kodiak is a small town, to us this was the glittering metropolis, and we made the most of being here. We flushed the toilets for fun and ate junk food. Martina, enjoying her eyesight at the supermarket, bought all kinds of things she didn't need. When we left the children in the hotel room that evening, they were leaping bed to bed and watching television.

Governor Frank Murkowski happened to be holding a reception in town, and Martina and I put our best raincoats on and went to see what a sitting governor and former US senator looked like in real life. He was standing in a greet-and-meet line, mostly a greet line, since I had no sooner met him than he was greeting the third person on. The Governor had a corroded oil pipeline and other important matters to worry about, and I was grateful that he troubled to meet me at all. His lovely wife, Nancy, chatted us up, and I looked around for the wine. When you are just in from the bush, twenty people in a room feels crowded, and there were twice as many hands as there were people in the room, all gesticulating and passing germs around. Everybody insisted on using the punch ladle when it would have been easier just to dip their cups in the bowl without a fuss.

As I stared at people's hands, I could have sworn I saw an envelope being transferred from the inside pocket of one jacket to the inside pocket of the Governor's jacket. Governor Murkowski had greeted his way through the line so fast that he came around to my wife again. He looked at Martina with a glimmer of recognition and I assumed that he remembered having met her eight minutes ago. But as they shook hands he reminisced fondly about a women's fashion show he had recently attended in the city of Anchorage.

What was he thinking! Martina had some choice words to say about him afterwards. I assured her that the Governor had only been trying to flatter her, and I kissed her punctured eyelid and smiled. "I'd say he found you rather eye-catching," I said.

With that she took my arm, and we walked down to St. Paul Harbor to look at the fishing boats, always a romantic thing to do in Kodiak town.

Y2K + 9/11

There's enough history on Kodiak Island to make even a dug-in survivalist reconsider the thesis that Kodiak offers an escape from the Coming Collapse. A foolproof hideout from doom is hard to find. The plaque by the downtown fire station shows how far inland the destructive tsunami of 1964 swept. Whole villages were destroyed and downtown Kodiak wiped out by the high waters generated in the 9.2 magnitude Good Friday earthquake, said to be the biggest ever recorded in North America. The catastrophic quake happened just fifty-two years after the eruption of Mount Novarupta on the Alaska mainland, a volcano that put the ashy taste of Pompeii in the mouths of Kodiakans. The town was buried in a foot and a half of ash and pebbles. Survivors left hair-raising accounts. Today when we dig at Cottonwood we find the ash layer from this eruption, and we mulch our garden with volcanic pumice that we gather from the beaches.

North America's biggest recorded earthquake and the twentieth century's biggest volcanic eruption—not a bad record, if you like drama on an epic geological scale. You came to Kodiak to get away from it all? Islands aren't shielded from history's tidal waves. In the age of bombers and ballistic missiles, Kodiak's strategic location makes it a target. A lot of good it does me to hole up on Kodiak if the crackpot dictator of the latest nuclear state decides to send Washington a message by nuking an island. During the Second World War the Japanese bombed and invaded the Aleutian Islands, and there was reason to think they had Kodiak in their sights, too. Our defensive fortifications proved unnecessary, but if things had ended differently, we might have been eating our salmon raw on Kodiak Island.

Sound farfetched? It always sounds farfetched until it happens. Have a look at the Alutiiq Museum and the Baranov Museum in town. The Kodiak Archipelago is the ancestral home of the Alutiiq people, who arrived here thousands of years ago and who live here today. They lost sovereignty of their lands during the Russian conquest of the 1700s. The Russians, wallowing in sea otter pelts and colonial degradation, built Kodiak into the prosperous capital of Russian America. In only a century, they were so miserable that they quit Kodiak and sold the whole of Alaska to Uncle Sam for $7.2 million. Any old luxury yacht plying Kodiak's waters in recent years—the *Turmoil*, the *Boadicea*, the *Clipper Odyssey*—is worth more than the pittance the Russians got for Alaska. These outcomes would have sounded farfetched to the Alutiiq in their heyday and to the Russians in theirs.

The tsunami of crude oil that blackened Kodiak's beaches and temporarily scuttled the fishing industry after the 1989 *Exxon Valdez* oil spill is the kind of event that in the long view of history plays into an arc of decay and collapse. We will never know. What is certain is that our machines and technology compete with us for control of our destiny. In the old days, when a civilization fell apart another one burgeoned elsewhere on the planet, but in our globalized world we have lost this insurance, this protective redundancy. Or maybe not. Here's a character in Edna Ferber's *Ice Palace* speculating about the aftermath of a nuclear war:

"'Eskimos don't need civilization. Your kind, I mean. We've had a kind of built-in civilization for hundreds and hundreds of years. We'd just go back ... to homemade skin boats and stone weapons and hunting implements, and fur-and-skin clothing—the stuff we've used for a couple of thousand years.'"

It always sounds farfetched until it happens.

A recent symbol of civilizational fragility was the Y2K bug, also known as the Millennium bug. Y2K signified a crash in the digital infrastructure of our information-age society caused by a failure of computer programs to accurately read the new calendar year as 2000, not 1900. It sounds foolish. As soon as 1999 was ushered in—at Cottonwood Homestead we listened on the radio to the New Year's countdown in Times Square—people started worrying about two things: a global champagne shortage and the looming calendrical snafu of Y2K.

The coincidence of Y2K with the end of the millennium frightened people. Governments at the highest levels sounded the alarm. There was talk of civil unrest. In Kodiak town, my friends the Pattersons took no chances. They watched a church-produced Y2K video and practiced Y2K readiness by putting up extra fish, buying a new four-wheeler, installing a woodstove, laying up ammo, stocking up on grains and dry milk, and adding chickens to their flock. "Right now I could sell a laying hen for twenty bucks," Shaw Patterson told me. "The price will go up. Be ready. Have trading wealth. Have contingency plans. It's not Armageddon, but people are in denial." I respected Shaw, who served in the Coast Guard, and it reassured me that he felt situated in Kodiak to ride out a cataclysm.

Y2K was boom times for enterprising survivalists empowered by the World Wide Web. Ironically, the internet, implicated in the whole doomed confabulation of civil society, made it easier than ever to find off-grid accessories and to link up with like-minded end-timers. When a technical glitch in San Francisco sparked a city-wide power outage that brought the urban body to its knees, a large-scale cyber-comeuppance like Y2K seemed less farfetched. I bought some gold coins and filled a few jugs with gasoline, but basically I agreed with my Kodiak neighbor Ed Flerchinger, who saw Y2K as a scam of profiteering fearmongers and who looked to pick up a cheap generator or two afterwards.

It's best to be practical about something like the end of the world. Don't court paranoia by watching for something you'll never see. A recluse in Viekoda Bay, across the peninsula from us, became so disillusioned waiting decades for doomsday that he finally sold his spread and moved. The couple who bought his place found the windows covered with tinfoil and caches of military meals buried on the property. At last word, the fellow was watching for the Big One from the window of his retirement home in Phoenix.

Y2K was a pivot point in the history of the human self-image. The talk of a "bug" causing universal havoc was a vindication for Luddites. The risk to civilization from its overreliance on technology mirrored the risk to every one of us for our overreliance on civilization. Y2K was, in the event, a nonevent, but the anxiety and mistrust it generated, followed so soon by the Dotcom Bust and the horrors of 9/11, lingered well into the new century.

If my friends in Manhattan couldn't get upstate in the chaos of 9/11, how hard would it be during a social meltdown to get from California—we had just moved there—to our Kodiak Island homestead? It's hard enough getting to Cottonwood in peacetime. When nine-year-old Miranda and I headed to Alaska in the summer after 9/11, the Transportation Security Administration was in its infancy and the only screening officer at our airport was one who sniffed people's shoes at the gate. What with the post-9/11 economic recession, Kodiak's flying services were hurting for lack of business, and Miranda and I got an inexpensive seaplane charter to our homestead. At Cottonwood we felt a long way from everywhere, safe from civilization and its discontents, and I could have tended our strawberries and rhubarb and blocked the world from my thoughts, but the national trauma had a hold on me and colored my dreams. In one dream, I was a smuggler. The new security and surveillance apparatus was making it hard to move my contraband. The parking structure where my package was hidden was being watched. Suddenly, people were screaming and running from the building. Hadn't I heard? Bombs were going off everywhere.

This spectacle of people running every which way in terror seemed to be the latest emblem of the human race. But was it new? People running from explosions, from napalm, from machine gunners in airports, from urban rioters, from the cops—running—running from one another: these were images I had seen all of my life. Hell, no, it wasn't new.

I watched Miranda occupying herself with crafts, with construction paper and scissors and adhesive tape. I had just walked her into her fourth-grade class at Cielo Vista in Palm Springs when one of the mothers took me aside and told me what was happening at the World Trade Center in New York. Since then, everybody liked to say that the country had totally changed, but had it? Or were we just being self-centered, as usual? I was glad for our Kodiak Island refuge, but I was sad to have to admit that there is no refuge, not really, not here or anywhere, and that my children's world in its hazards and demoralizing realities was going to be much the same as my world.

Miranda and I waved sparklers around for Independence Day. At the top of the hour, wondering what the world was doing with itself, we put batteries in the radio and tuned it to AM 560, the only radio station available to us. The latest suicide bombings and terror threats. "The Las Vegas threat." "The July Fourth threat." Terrorists might commandeer fuel tankers and ram crowds with them. People "of Middle Eastern descent" had tried to buy ambulances with cash. A decision had been made not to inoculate the American populace with smallpox vaccine. And, in case you thought Alaska was safely under the radar, Fort Greely and Kodiak Island were going to become "rivets" in the Missile Defense Shield. The Shield's purpose was to protect us from rogue aggressors like North Korea and Iran. The stock market, by the way, had closed near its low for the year.

Miranda and I listened to this recap as we dressed to go for a hike.

"Sounds like the world's going to hell in a handbasket," I muttered. "Don't worry, sweetheart."

"Don't worry about what?" she said.

"If you listen to the news these days you'd think the world was falling apart."

"Look, I'm a Viking," she said with a laugh, and she held up on her head the bright yellow helmet she had fashioned out of construction paper.

ZODIAC

It was springtime in the northern hemisphere, the last spring of the twentieth century, the last spring of the millennium, and the world was making war. Pessimists predicted a blowup in the Balkans, possibly a Third World War. Coincidentally the planet Mars, namesake of the Roman war god, dominated the night sky. It's been a long time since people read moral significance into the stars and planets, but the astronomer-prophets of the ancient Babylonians, Egyptians, Greeks, Chinese, Persians, Arabs, Mayans and so on would have found in the Mars ascendance a cause for speculation and even for war. The red planet, coming closer to Earth than it had in a decade, took a high path in the sky, allowing us to see it over the mountain behind our homestead cabin. On clear midnights in May, Mars hovered over the mountain ridge. In Alaska the days are already long in May, a discouragement to northern stargazers, but the planet Mars, then in the vicinity of the constellation Virgo, was molten orange and unmistakable.

As our hemisphere tilts toward the sun and the days lengthen, the quality of the darkness changes, too. Light is always immanent in the night, so that only at two and three o'clock in the morning is the northland darkness dark. The midsummer moon, seldom noticed, peeps along its arc, the great close moon, a lantern for lovers and outcasts and wayfarers. A full moon rises in the southeast while the summer sun shines on the northwest seas, and if my arms were long enough, I would reach and touch the sun and moon at once.

The stars and planets regain their relative brightness in late summer. In August I am treated to views of Saturn, Jupiter, the aurora borealis and the Perseids all in a night's watch. The aurora appears as a ribbon of rayed green light over Raspberry Island to the north of us. The green light silhouettes the island and crowns it with a vibrant radiance. The aurora hovers low and sinuous, or it leaps into the sky and the green streamers lap the stars and curl in an undulant wave over the cabin.

Black, starry nights return in September, and as the darkness reasserts itself, the Big Dipper reasserts its prominence in the northern sky. I have to remind myself that the Big Dipper is subsidiary to the Great Bear. To see the whole of the Bear I rise early in the morning, when all of the stars of the Bear's legs become visible. From night until morning the Big Dipper wheels in the sky, and the bowl rotates up and over as if during the night it had dipped into the ocean and tossed out its contents.

Miranda, identifying with the "littleness" of the Little Bear, declared it to be her favorite constellation. She was familiar with the biblical story of the Exodus, the journey of the Israelites out of Egypt, and she and I wondered, our faces raised to the starry October sky, how similar the view would have been for a family of Israelites sojourning in the desert thirty-some hundred years ago. For me it was easy to see the scattered firelight and a father and daughter or an Israelite family raising their faces to the stars to orient themselves or to wish and to wonder. Miranda was interested to learn that the tail star of the Little Dipper, the star we call the North Star or polestar, was not the North Star for the Israelites, Egyptians, Amelikites and the other ancient peoples we had read about. The earth's oscillation, different from its daily rotation and its annual revolution around the sun, causes the identity of the polestar, the indicator of the celestial pole, to change over long periods of time. The constellation Draco the Dragon, sprawling not far, in our eyes, from her beloved Little Bear, contains the star Thuban, which formerly was the North Star, and the Egyptians, when they built the Great Pyramids, oriented themselves by *that* North Star, not ours. Miranda and I pinpointed, in the nearby constellation Lyra, the bright star Vega, which many years from now will be the new North Star, and she was reassured to learn that in the far-off future the honor of being the North Star will revert to our familiar Polaris. In this way, keying on the North Star, she and I navigated millenniums of human history. To have this visibility beyond the endpoints of our lives is humbling, but it gives a sense of pattern, too, of meaningful connection. I have lived in great cities where I never saw or missed the stars, and in truth I did not experience the alienation as a loss. There was so much to see in the street, I seldom bothered to look up. But here on this island in the Gulf of Alaska, an acquaintance with the stars is more than a pleasure, it's a spiritual gain. A bath of starlight draws out the soul.

Getting to know the stars became a regular feature of our lives at Cottonwood. It kept us close to humanity even as we lived apart. A huge expanse of sky opens over the homestead, north and east and west and up into the Milky Way, allowing us to monitor, with the progress of the seasons, our progress through the zodiac.

It's a natural impulse on a fair night to gaze up at Cepheus the King or at Cassiopeia or to look twice at a curiously tinted or flickering star. I had seldom considered how busy the night is, busy with elusive flashes and mysterious lights, the blip of an orbiting satellite, a meteor's flaming out or the glow of a remote apocalypse. Martina wove for me a wicker chair of willow and alder sticks, a deep chair with an angled back, and this became my star-watching chair. Our only equipment, aside from the eyes we were born with, was an inexpensive make of 10x50 binoculars—better than nothing for bringing forward a fuzzy object like a nebula. With these unsophisticated means, we got to know the celestial neighborhood. Aquila the Eagle, Aries the Ram, Delphinus the Dolphin and Cygnus the Swan—they all shone above us, a menagerie sharing in the brilliant genius of creation.

"But I don't want to see Cancer, Dad, because then I might get it."

"Alright, sweetheart, we won't look at Cancer, only Leo. See the spruce tree? Look up from the spruce tree. See the stars that make a backwards question mark? That's Leo's head."

Miranda and I were admiring the star cluster Praesepe within the constellation Cancer, so she was unknowingly looking at Cancer the Crab, but I didn't burden her with the knowledge. What I should have done, in a gambit Miranda would have appreciated, was to reflect Cancer in a mirror, in this way imitating the hero Perseus, who looks at Medusa in his shield.

There is no end to the stories the stars tell us, stories condensed from racial experience and enshrined in the heavens, stories from Asia, America, Africa, from Islam and Christendom, from Greek and Roman antiquity. For Miranda, whose homeschool curriculum included a unit on the Classics, it was rewarding to learn of Pegasus, Hercules, Andromeda, Perseus, Medusa and the Pleiades and then to step outside and see them illustrated in the stars. In the Kodiak night the stars can shine with such surreal clarity that the details—of Orion's jeweled dagger, of the hunting dogs of Boötes—project in three or four vivid dimensions. I say four dimensions because, if you recline for long enough under the stars, you will glimpse, through the lifting veil of your breath, time itself, a gently shocking intuition of the passing light years.

Weeks and months go by. The constellations ascend and decline. The moon rises, sets, waxes and wanes. The planets traverse the ecliptic, orbiting our common sun. We see the planets at moonrise or at sunset, alone or in pairs or trios, Saturn with a crescent moon, or Venus by twilight with Jupiter and Mercury. In the long night, what stands out, what pulses and radiates warmth, is whatever opposes the darkness, not only the starlight but also the glimmer of the planets, the liquid splendor of a shooting star, the bright and generous moon reflecting in a pool of rainwater, the lamp of a fishing boat at sea, and the glow of light in the cabin window.

AFTERWORD

I n October 2001 I received from the State of Alaska a gold-sealed patent conveying to me 15.17 acres of land located on Kodiak Island's north coast. For me, this was a culmination of years of effort and more years of dreaming. In homesteading I had reprised my years in Alaska and enshrined my affection for the place. The gold seal didn't change any of that. Having lived at Cottonwood with my family, I was intimately attached to the place. I had known much solitude here, too, and in the exploring of my inner wild, in the building of who I am, the experience was vital. I sat down at the foot of nature to learn all I could, and I didn't come away disappointed.

It turned out that we were among Alaska's last homesteaders. I don't say this definitively. It is my understanding that Alaska's Homestead Act is still on the books. Shortly after I received the title to Cottonwood, the head of land disposal at the Department of Natural Resources in Anchorage told me in a phone conversation that Alaska's homestead program had ground to a halt. The program was too costly to administer, she said, and too many homesteaders had flunked out of the program to justify it. At the time of writing, I have confirmed with a natural resource specialist at DNR that Cottonwood was among the last homesteads granted by Alaska, and no entry permits were issued after the mid-1990s.

Alaska continues to honor, through auctions and over-the-counter offerings, its policy, articulated in the state constitution, of returning land to the people, but these lands must be purchased. The prove-up option, the opportunity to earn the land through a steadfast commitment of time and effort, is gone for now. Alaskans may someday bring it back. In the popular imagination, homesteading, the promise of it, remains a bright beacon. Frederick Jackson Turner, the historian who identified the development of American democracy with the homestead principle, with "the demand for land and the love of wilderness freedom," was not talking about Alaska when he famously declared the frontier to be closed. It is worth remembering that homesteading was never an uncontroversial program. The idea of returning the people's land to the people goes back to Jefferson, but it was not until working-class radicals, Western agrarians and antislavery legislators united behind homesteading that it made it into Abraham Lincoln's political platform and became law during the Civil War. Policymakers believed that in times of distress, homesteading worked as a social relief valve. Times have changed, certainly, and the realities of homesteading often fell short of the ideals, but nobody will persuade me that the hunger for space and self-determination is less today.

What is the difference between paying cash for a piece of land and getting ownership by homesteading it? Maybe not a lot. Anyone who champs at the bit to feel the freedom of the country underfoot would do better to heed the inspiration than to fret whether they are "homesteading" or not. "People found it was no cheaper to homestead than to buy the land at market value and to build and live there when they wanted," the head of land disposal told me. But surely this is beside the point. Homesteading was never meant to pay as a weekend diversion. Homesteading ends when the spirit of it ends, when people are seeking not salvation in the land but recreation. Besides, it cannot be true that building on "free" land costs as much as purchasing the same land and building on it. That defies common sense. Tell that to the unemployed handyman or the veteran of Iraq or Afghanistan or the young couple who have the time and will and resourcefulness to provide for themselves in the bush but not the lump of cash to buy the land with.

That said, homestead land may not be the choicest land. Too many homesteaders have jumped off for the wilderness thinking they were going to cut a fat hog, only to find there wasn't a hog to cut. Homesteaders take the land they get, but a buyer can be choosier, and if you can buy into good access, good dirt, good water, good game and a good amount of sunlight, you might be a good deal happier living off the grid.

However you come by the land, if you go out there and live on it for a season or a lifetime, go a little wild, grow something green and befriend the plants and animals, then you're a homesteader, living out your exile and claiming your promised land.

ACKNOWLEDGMENTS

You'll get dirtier homesteading in Alaska than writing a book about it, but you can get pretty filthy writing a book, too, and I'm glad it's done. The help of the following individuals in reviewing sections of the manuscript or otherwise advising me was invaluable: Jay Barrett (KMXT), Erik Berggren, Dan Beutel (Alaska Department of Natural Resources), Douglas Campbell (US Fish & Wildlife Service), Bud and Cherie Carter, Dan and Kim Dorman, Michael Engelhard, Willy Fulton, Bea Hagen, Dana Patterson, Richard Pederson and Laurel Peterson, Chris Provost, Amy Steffian (Alutiiq Museum), Toby Sullivan (Kodiak Maritime Museum), Mark Thomas, Thom Wischer, and Bree Witteveen (Alaska Sea Grant Marine Advisory Program).

Where I have used people's names in this book, it is usually with the approval of the named. In a few cases I have used pseudonyms to protect the privacy of those concerned. Many Kodiak Islanders did me good turns over the years, and my thanks go to all of them. I am deeply grateful to my family as well for their considerable input and support.

Certain chapters of this book were originally published in magazines: "Fox," "Outhouse," "Salmonberry," "Tidepool" and "Hippy Rig" in *Cirque*; "Bird & Birdsong" and "Cottonwood" in *NatureWriting*; "Cannery" ("Decline & Fall of a Great Alaskan Cannery") in *trampset*; "Wildflowers" in *Chaleur Magazine*; "Sea Lion" in *West Texas Literary Review*; "Eagle," "Otter" and "Rabbit" ("Our Homestead Neighbors") in *The RavensPerch*; and "Brown Bear" ("The Kodiak Brown Bear") in *Gold Man Review*. Many thanks to the editors of these journals.

In the face of the COVID-19 pandemic, Myles Lamont, Doreen Martens and the other wonderful people at Hancock House stood by this title, and I appreciate it. Without their commitment, the project could not have been completed.

Works that I cite in this book or that I consulted while writing it include:

Addiss, Stephen, Akira Yamamoto, and Fumiko Yamamoto. *A Haiku Menagerie: Living Creatures in Poems and Prints*. New York: Weatherhill, 1992.

Anderson, Warren, trans. *Theophrastus: The Character Sketches*. Kent, OH: Kent State University Press, 1970.

Armstrong, Robert H. *Guide to the Birds of Alaska*. Seattle: Alaska Northwest Books, 1990.

Bakeless, John, ed. *The Journals of Lewis and Clark*. New York: Penguin Books, 1964.

Bloom, Harold. *Poetry & Repression*. New Haven: Yale University Press, 1976.

Emerson, Ralph Waldo. *Essays*. Boston: Houghton Mifflin Company, 1883.

Ferber, Edna. *Ice Palace*. Garden City, NY: Doubleday & Company, 1958.

Gide, André. *Fruits of the Earth*. London: Penguin Books, 1982.

Holzworth, John M. *The Wild Grizzlies of Alaska*. New York: G. P. Putnam's Sons, 1930.

Hudson, John, and Robert H. Armstrong. *Dragonflies of Alaska*. 2nd ed. Juneau: Nature Alaska Images, 2010.

Murie, Adolph. *A Naturalist in Alaska*. New York: The Devin-Adair Company, 1961.

Nash, Roderick. *Wilderness and the American Mind*. New Haven: Yale University Press, 1967.

Pratt, Verna E. *Field Guide to Alaskan Wildflowers*. Anchorage: Alaska-krafts, 1989.

Roosevelt, Theodore. *The Rough Riders, An Autobiography*. New York: The Library of America, 2004.

Smith, Henry Nash. *Virgin Land*. New York: Random House, 1950.

St. John de Crèvecoeur, J. Hector. *Letters from an American Farmer*. Edited by Warren Barton Blake. London: J.M. Dent & Sons, 1926.

Thoreau. *Walden*.

Turner, Frederick Jackson. *The Frontier in American History*. Franklin Center, PA: The Franklin Library, 1977.

Waley, Arthur. *The Way and Its Power: A Study of the Tao Tê Ching and Its Place in Chinese Thought.* New York: Grove Press, 1982.

White, Helen A., ed. *The Alaska-Yukon Wild Flowers Guide.* Edmonds, WA: Alaska Northwest Publishing Company, 1986.

Zim, Herbert S., and Robert H. Baker. *Stars: A Guide to the Constellations, Sun, Moon, Planets, and Other Features of the Heavens.* New York: Golden Press, 1975.

RELATED TITLES

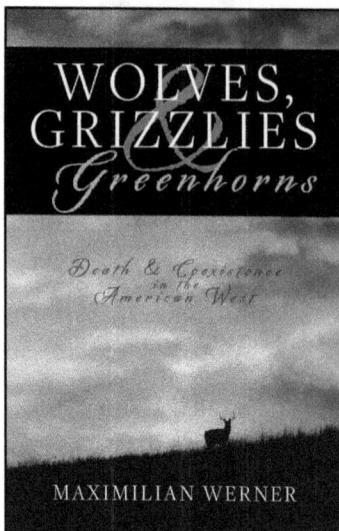

Death & Coexistence in the American West

Werner recounts the two-and-a-half years he spent tracking down and looking after a wolf pack that was rumored to have settled in the Centennial Valley of southwest Montana. Along the way he encounters and reflects on the lives of other animals, including deer, elk, fox, coyote, skunks, and grizzly bears. But he also encounters other humans too—ranchers, hunters, land and wildlife managers, cowboys—who offer their own, often conflicting perspectives about the natural world, other animals, and how both ought to be treated.

Wolves, Grizzlies & Greenhorns

Werner, Maximilian

978-0-88839-537-5 [paperback]
978-0-88839-578-8 [epub]

5½ x 8½, sc, 352pp

$26.95

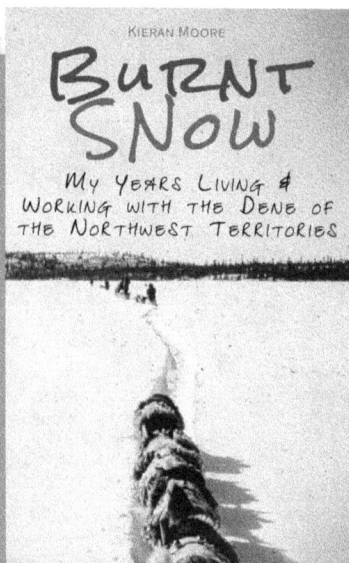

Burnt Snow

Moore, Kieran

978-0-88839-100-1 [paperback]
978-0-88839-356-2 [hardcover]
978-0-88839-265-7 [epub]
6 x 9, sc, 272pp

$24.95

My years living & working with the Dene of the Northwest Territories

The reflections of the authors encounters with some of the leading figures of the North are quite humorous and consequential in the later development of the North. He describes the Indigenous Elders who would influence him in countless ways, and how their teachings are later, the source of northern survival in otherwise seemingly impossible situations. This book reflects the people of that time, and their lifestyle of living off the land in total independence and their incredible life-skills of survival.

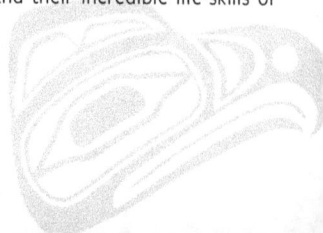

27 Years Off-grid in a Wilderness Valley

The Power of Dreams tells the story of a couple, already in their 40's, who uprooted themselves from urban life to follow their dream of living in the wilderness. They settled in a remote mountain valley called Precipice Valley, part of the ancient trade route linking B.C.'s Chilcotin plateau to the Pacific Coast.

Surrounded by mountain vastness they lived there for nearly three decades, much of it in near-total isolation. Their dreams sustained them while they carved out a lifestyle that was both rewarding and challenging.

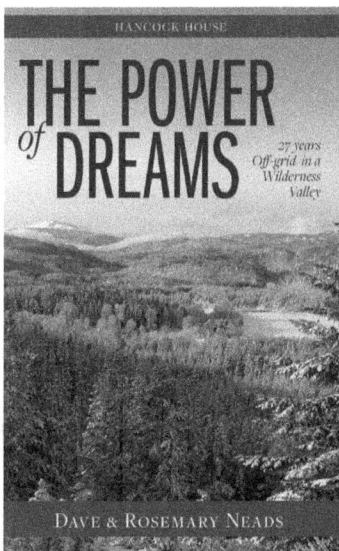

The Power of Dreams

Dave & Rosemary Neads

978-0-88839-718-8 [paperback]
978-0-88839-742-3 [epub]
5½ x 8½, sc, 246pp

$24.95

A trilogy of stories by the Edwards family about their fascinating life in the Bella Coola area.

Often called "The Crusoe of Lonesome Lake," because of a best-selling book written by the American journalist Leland Stowe, Edwards has gone on to live at least one more life and reveals himself to be a pioneer of a breed that no longer exists. Best known for his almost single-handed rescue of the trumpeter swans from extinction in North America, Edwards now related in his own words other aspects of his long, varied life, including experience with his missionary parents in India, as a telegraph operator under fire in World War I and his eventual return to Lonesome Lake.

Ralph Edwards of Lonesome Lake

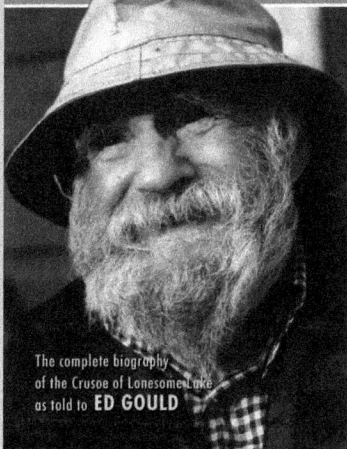

Gould, Ed & Ralph Edwards

978-0-88839-100-1 [paperback]
5½ x 8½, sc, 296pp

$19.95

Hancock House Publishers
19313 Zero Ave, Surrey, BC V3Z 9R9
www.hancockhouse.com
info@hancockhouse.com
1-800-938-1114

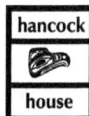